WINTER HILL ANGLEZARKE SCRAPBOOK.

Dave Lane

Compiled by Dave Lane, Derek Cartwright & Garry Rhodes

Photo shows aerial view of Rivington Pike with the surrounding tracks. Picture taken by one of the authors from a Mainair Blade microlight. This photo was taken long before the new "staircase" to the top was constructed

First Published – Internet edition	Oct 2003
1st Revision	Feb 2004
2nd Revision	Oct 2004
3rd Revision	Jan 2005
4th Revision	Nov 2005
5th Revision	July 2006
6th Revision	Dec 2006
7th Revision	Jun 2007
1st Paperback Edition A4	Aug 2007
2nd Paperback Edition 9 x 6 in	July 2008
3rd Edition **(now including Anglezarke)**	Dec 2019

Published & Distributed by Lulu.com
www.lulu.com

©Dave Lane, Garry Rhodes & Derek Cartwright 2019

dave@daveweb.co.uk   derek.cartwright@outlook.com

The right of Dave Lane, Garry Rhodes & Derek Cartwright to be identified as the authors of this work has been asserted in accordance with the UK Copyright, Design & Patents Act 1988

ISBN   978-0-244-83996-3

Introduction.

For what seems like most of our lives, We've wandered all over Winter Hill and Anglezarke in all seasons and in all weathers. There are many others like us! This bleak and lonely area somehow pulls us back there time and time again.

For those who cannot understand our love and affection for the place, Winter Hill and the surrounding moors must seem an appalling sort of environment except for on the nicest of summer days!

This book is aimed at the "aficionado" but we hope that even the casual reader will be able to get something out of it, if only to see why some of us find the place so fascinating.

This is not a book written entirely by us. It is a collection of articles, photos, and information about the Winter Hill and Anglezarke area that is gleaned from all over the place and all put together as a scrapbook.

We have gathered this small collection to satisfy both ourselves and others who are interested both in Winter Hill/ Anglezarke and the general area.

This scrapbook has been produced mainly for our own interest.
A copy of it (with colour illustrations!) will be placed on the Internet for free download – we've no idea yet where you'll find it but it WILL be there … somewhere …. eventually! This is a community project. Google it to find the free edition (in full colour)!

A printed back and white edition of the book will be made available due to requests from many who have requested such an edition.

Although much of this book has been written by the compilers, some of the material are merely extracts from the work of others.
Credits and acknowledgements to the writers are listed in Appendix 1. Our thanks to everyone involved.

Although Dave Lane is the person who put the final book together and published it, it would never have been completed without the help and encouragement of Derek Cartwright and Garry Rhodes.

At the present time, much of the moorland is bare and desolate. In bygone times this was not the case, so in this publication, older maps (usually from the 1849 edition) have been sometimes used to illustrate what the area was like one and a half centuries ago.
No attempt has been made to describe in any great detail the buildings or farms on the lower flanks of the hill as these are all more than catered for in other publications and web sites – listed in the Appendix at the end. Even Leverhulme's Terraced Gardens will receive only limited mention for the same reason.

This IS a "scrapbook". We just add things to the book if and when we feel like it! There's no rhyme nor reason …. we just do it … we've produced it because we just want to!

The compilers of this book receive no royalties whatsoever. Any profits if any will be given to Horwich Heritage Centre.

Dave Lane, Garry Rhodes & Derek Cartwright ……… December 2019

This is what the room at the top of the Pigeon Tower at Rivington looks like. The circular design above the fireplace contains the letters W.H.E.E.L which refers to William Hesketh and Elizabeth Ellen Lever. Lord Leverhulme's Motto underneath reads "MUTARE VEL TIMERE SPERNO" = To Change Or Fear I Spurn.
(from the Facebook pages of Hidden History of Horwich and the surrounding area)

Where and what?

Winter Hill is an unremarkable, fairly small hill, situated in the North West UK, located near to the towns of Bolton, Horwich, Chorley, and Darwen, on a Western spur of the Pennine range of hills. In this book, the term "Winter Hill & Anglzarke" has been deliberately left vague in order to include any adjacent areas of interest!

Winter Hill is marked on Ordnance Survey maps as being a mere 456 meters above sea level - or for those of us who are somewhat older – about 1,498 feet! Local pilots are only too aware of the height of Winter Hill, as the height of the top of the mast at about 2,500 feet tells them that they have only another 500 feet to play with before they are in the airlanes used by the big jets. Now you know why the microlight's fly fairly low over Winter Hill and Rivington Pike!

On a clear day, the view from the top of Winter Hill is quite an eye opener for those who have never seen the view before. Looking South, the whole of the Cheshire plain is clearly in view with Mow Cop in Staffordshire as the limit. The Welsh mountains are clearly visible to the South West with Snowdon sticking up right in the middle. Anglesey and the Great Orme at Llandudno can clearly be seen. Liverpool Bay, with the Seaforth cranes at Liverpool (along with the offshore gas rigs) are in view as are Southport (with its distinctive water tower), Blackpool Tower and we can see North as far as Black Combe in Cumbria. If you have a pair of binoculars handy then take a look at Lytham on the Ribble estuary and even the windmill on the sea front can be seen along with the Aerodrome at Warton.

There have always been rumours that on a really clear day (and **really** clear days are very rare) it is possible to see the top of Snaefell on the Isle of Man, around 100 miles away from Winter Hill. Although I have been on Winter Hill in what I would class as the most perfect "seeing" conditions I have never seen the Isle of Man from the Hill. I do have poor eyesight! No doubt someone will now contact me to say that they **have** seen the Isle of Man – and if they contact me I'll add that fact to this chapter! *(Since writing this, many HAVE written to say they HAVE seen the IOM!)*

Winter Hill is obviously a relatively "modern" name, as on Speed's map of 1610 and Molls's map of 1724 the given name is "Egberden Hill". As suggested by D A Owen in his booklet "Rivington & District before 1066 AD" the name Egberden Hill is "supposed to have arisen from one of the early kings who hunted in the surrounding forest. The most likely candidate is – Egbert, king of Wessex 800 to 836 AD who by 828 AD had included Northumbria, and therefore Lancashire, in his kingdom". Earlier documents from the 13th century indicate it was called Wintyrhold and Wintyrheld.

The highest point of Winter Hill is marked by the Ordnance Survey Trig point at the edge of the northern escarpment. From time to time this point has been used as the site of a bonfire beacon built and lit at some particular royal occasion – from memory I think the last commemoration beacon was lit in the 1981 to commemorate the wedding of Prince Charles and Lady Diana. Previous to that it was the 25th anniversary of Queen Elizabeth's reign in 1977. Other commemorative beacons have been constructed and fired in the Rivington Pike area in more recent years not to be confused with the Winter Hill beacons.

The upper parts of Winter Hill are fairly barren, with poor soil, poor vegetation and with the only visitors being walkers, mountain bike riders, cross country runners, model plane flyers, hang and paraglider pilots, cross country skiers …… and the engineers at the TV station on the summit. A private road does go to the radio mast and in "theory" other traffic is prohibited.

After reading this book, we trust that others may be enticed onto the hill.

++

The Geology of Winter Hill

Winter Hill was not always as it appears today. Once it was not even a hill, nor was it even in the earth's temperate region as it is today. As a result of tectonic plate movements, cataclysmic bending and flexing of the earth's surface and dramatic changes in climate, slowly but surely what we now see today has emerged. Without going into too great detail (unless someone would like to provide me with this detail for inclusion in a later version of this book) a brief description of the Winter Hill geological history follows.

When our planet earth was first formed some 4.6 billion years ago, the earth was in a molten state but slowly started to solidify accompanied by volcanic activity and surrounded by an atmosphere that does not resemble the atmosphere of today. Over billions of years, the earth began to stabilise and life somehow began on our planet. In the Winter Hill area no deep borings have been taken so we have no real record of exactly what lies under our feet at great depth. Closer to the surface however, we do know something about our more "recent" history over the last few hundred million years by studying the geology in mining shafts, shallow borings, quarries etc.

The "upper" portion of Winter Hill consists of a series of layers or seams of sandstones, shales and coal - often referred to as the

Millstone Grit, Lower, Middle and Upper Coal Measures. The layers include an endless variety of sediments, coal seams (along with their associated underlying bands of fireclay or ganister) and are approximately 8000 feet in thickness.

This area was once part of the great "Upper Carboniferous" delta of the North of England, a version of some of the more famous world deltas that we have today such as the Nile, Mississippi and Amazon. Somewhere to the north of Winter Hill was a huge land mass with a large river entering the sea (to the South) via a delta. At that stage in the earth's evolution, the surface of the "land" was continuously rising and sinking so the areas near the delta were continuously being raised above sea level, then dropped beneath that level in a succession of flooding's and periods when plant growth was possible. Over periods of time, the sandbanks and the muds were overlain with swamps and vegetation only to be inundated over and over again with the either the river or the nearby seas. Thus, over a period of time, the rocks (formed as a result of pressure) have formed in a seemingly endless cycle of marine shales, sandstones, mudstones and vegetative coal layers.

At some stage in the earth's history, the ground underwent tremendous pressures, and parts of our region were bent and twisted due to great internal tensions and this in turn was accompanied by dramatic earth movements where one part of the surface was lifted whilst a neighbouring portion sunk, thus forming "faults". There are a number of faults under Winter Hill. What we now see as the top of Winter Hill was once at sea level covered in lush tropical forests.

For anyone who wants proof of these earth movements I can tell you that it is possible to find fossil remains of those tropical forests (leaves, tree bark and roots, seeds etc) on the very top of Winter Hill ….. they can be found at various points in shale bands on the sides of the road running up to the television mast. Honest! ….. but you'll have to find the sites yourself …. I don't want to be held to blame for new "holes" appearing on the hill top!

There are two main seams of coal under Winter Hill and both have been exploited in the past. In fact, almost the entire section of one part of the south facing flanks of Winter Hill are to all intents and purposes hollow, due to centuries of coal mining, with only pillars of coal being left "in situ" to support the surface as we know it today.

The layers of rock forming Winter Hill are not horizontal but dip towards the south at a dip of 1 in 12. Due to the shape of the hill and the dip of the layers, the upper coal seam is at a fairly constant depth below the surface of the ground despite the fact that the hill is not level!

Apart from Winter Hill providing local people with coal in the past, it also provided stones and rocks for building houses and walls, fireclays and other clays for producing bricks and tiles. Hopefully, this book will provide you with details of all these industries of Winter Hill.

Tigers Clough.

Tigers Clough, or Shaw's Clough as it is usually marked on Ordnance Survey Maps is the wooded valley of the River Douglas which lies a few hundred yards to the north-east of Rivington School. Although today the clough is an oasis of peace, it was not quite so peaceful in

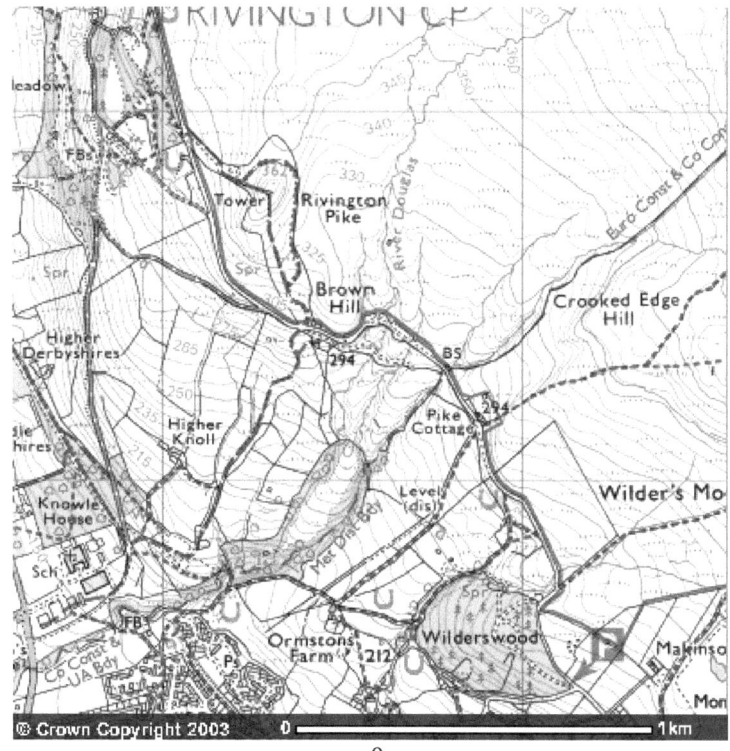

the eighteenth and nineteenth century. The clough at that time housed a bleachworks, a drinking establishment and with a brick and pipe works nearby along with a coal mine just higher up the hill. The clough can be best accessed by going up the road to the east of the school to the road junction. Take the concrete road going uphill and opposite the quarry go down the path to the river.

The bleach works mentioned above, was known as Knoll Bleach works and lay on both sides of the river, where some of the remains can still be seen. It was owned by a Thomas Kay and documents indicate that it was used for "rag bleaching". I have no idea what it means, but the works once contained one of the country's first "callenders" which I'm told is some sort of machine that was used to finish off the cloth by putting a glaze onto its surface.

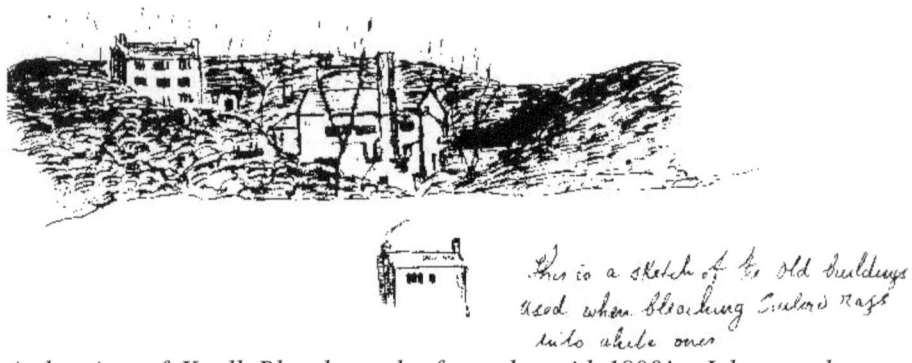

A drawing of Knoll Bleach works from the mid 1800's. I have only a photocopy of this drawing but I am informed that it was drawn in 1849 by a J Whitaker. Source of drawing unknown.

There are conflicting stories about the demise of the bleachworks. One tale tells of a large storm in 1850 which increased the river water levels to such a height that the water wheel and part of the dam were washed away. Another source says that at some time after 1868 Liverpool Corporation had the works demolished as it lay within their catchment area. Both tales may in fact be true with perhaps the works being severely damaged in 1850 and then finally demolished in the late 1860's.

One rather sad story about the bleach works is that in 1798 a local man, John Eccles, was caught breaking into and stealing calico from the works, and in August of that year, he appeared before the Lancaster Assizes and was sentenced to death and executed in September.

Near to the bleach works (believed to have been just downstream from it below the footbridge) and owned by the works owner, there was an alehouse managed at one time by a Mr Brindle. This seems to have been no ordinary alehouse for it was not only unlicensed but sold mainly illegally brewed alcoholic drinks (it was known locally as a "hush shop").

Mr Brindle was obviously not afraid of offending the authorities, for he commissioned a local artist to paint a sign for the drinking establishment and this sign was decorated with the heads of two tigers. This is believed to be why the clough is locally referred to as Tigers clough and not by its "official" name of Shaw's clough!

On the south-western side of Tigers Clough was located the large pipe works owned by the Crankshaws (also known as "Klondyke") which used the locally mined fireclay in the manufacture of some of it's products.

A tramway ran in the fields to the east of Tigers Clough bringing the fireclay direct from the mine level (located in the fields below Sportsman's cottage, later known as Pike Cottage) straight into the pipe works. A photo of the mine entrance can be found in one of the mining articles in this scrapbook.

Crankshaw's pipe works, Horwich.

Mankind has always seemed to be attracted to Tigers Clough! In the 1940's a local man was out walking when he spotted an unusual piece of stone in the river. When he retrieved it, he found that it was a six inch long axe head which had been highly polished. At a later date the axe was found to be made of a type of stone found in Scandinavia and was dated to the Neolithic period around 2,500 BC.

A walk up the clough is a delight at any time of year, each season bringing its own sights. The wild flowers, the trees, the ferns and mosses along with the birds and animals make it a pleasure to visit.

A trip up the stream from Rivington School to the Pike area, makes an ideal introduction to the geology of Winter Hill and a separate article is included in this scrapbook on a geological trip up the Clough which explains all that can be seen.

Just above the remains of the bleachworks, are two attractive waterfalls, best observed after heavy rain. Just above the waterfalls on the right hand bank, is a very odd shaped rock.

The rock has been hand carved with a pick or chisel (the marks are clearly visible) in the shape of a bowl, basin or bath but the purpose of it quite defeats me!

One assumes it may be something to do with the bleachworks but the size of the basin makes this somewhat unlikely. Anyone any ideas?

Although it IS possible to walk almost the whole length of the clough in the river bed, unless you are wearing wellingtons or prepared to get wet, this is not recommended, especially as the rocks are extremely slippery in some areas.

Tigers Clough is well worth a visit at ANY season of the year.

Later on in this Scrapbook is reprinted a geological walk which was written some time ago in a booklet published by Wigan Geological Society. It details a walk from Rivington School right up to the Pike via Tigers Clough explaining the geological things of interest to see on the route.

■■'

The unusual shaped "bowl" just above the waterfall in Tigers Clough

The Distant Past on Winter Hill.

People have been visiting Winter Hill for over 4,500 years. Although today, the hill is bare and fairly desolate, apart from the lower slopes, things were not always like this. From the techniques of "pollen analysis" and "pollen dating", it is possible to build up a fairly complete picture of what Winter Hill must have been like over the past few millennia. At some stage I am hoping to obtain detailed information about pollen analysis in the area, and this will be included in the scrapbook.

What is known, is that the top of the hill was not always as bare as it is today. It was once covered in woodland and there is no reason to suppose that perhaps people even lived up here amongst the woodlands thousands of years ago. There is ample evidence on and around the hill to prove that people lived in the area, even though no remains have been found of a true settlement on the top of the hill. The people of the area did however leave remains and artefacts which tell us a little about their existence.

We know for example that men worked on Winter Hill, owing to the finding of a stone axe in Tigers Clough, and the many flint chipping sites which have been discovered on the top of the hill. Flint does not naturally occur in this area, and the early inhabitants of the area (between about 2,000 BC and 1,000 BC) obviously traded with people in other parts of the country in order to obtain the natural flint.

Flint was used for many purposes. We know it was used to fashion arrow heads for hunting, axes for cutting, "scrapers" for dealing with animal hides, knives, and many other articles. We think that the trade in flint comprised of the "purchase" (probably by way of barter) of nodules or lumps of the material, and that the implements were made locally. This theory is backed up by the finding of several small areas of flint "chippings" or "flakes" on the hill, where men would have obviously spent some considerable time "working" on the raw flint, turning it into usable implements.

Probably the "earliest" find in the Winter Hill area is the stone axe that was discovered lying in the bed of the river Douglas in Tigers Clough by a Mr Southworth of Anderton, The axe was about six inches in length and was highly polished and after expert advice had been obtained, it was found that the stone probably originated in Scandinavia and was from the period around 2,500 BC. To my knowledge this is the earliest item ever found on Winter Hill.

The only other early remains found on the hill are the two "burial mounds" discovered near the peak of the hill, both thought to date from around the Bronze Age, and indicative that somewhere in the area was a settlement (or settlements) dating from this era.

The first burial mound to be found was the one now known as the Winter Hill Tumulus or Barrow which was discovered purely by chance when John Rawlinson and Tom Creear were walking on the moors in 1957. On the 24th March they spotted what appeared to be a "curved line of stones" sticking out from the peat. The stones were part of a "wall" some two feet in height, which surrounded a round area with a raised small mound in the middle of it.

In July of 1958 a group from Manchester University excavated the central mound but soon discovered that the site had been previously excavated (probably about 250 years earlier). A positive pollen dating showed that the site originated in the Middle Bronze Age round about 1,500 BC. Post the 2018 major fire little evidence is seen of the cairn other than a scattering of the stones.

Higher up the hill and on the southern heading edge, lies Noon Hill, upon which is the Noon Hill Saucer Tumulus. Although this had been known to exist for some time it was not until August 1958 that it was excavated. This was undertaken by the Bolton & District Archaeological Society and when the topsoil of part of the site was removed, it revealed two rings of stones one inside the other, the outer ring being about 52 feet in diameter and the inner one 32 feet. The outer wall consisted of "large stones" each about two foot six inches long, a foot wide and eight inches high. The inner circle of small stones were said to have been "strengthened with buttresses".

Inside the inner circle, were two piles of human remains, and nearby was found what is thought to be a cremation urn. I have been unable to find out if there was anything found inside the urn. Also discovered in the tumulus were two barbed flint arrowheads along with a flint knife. All discoveries are housed in Bolton Museum and have been on public view from time to time. So far as I am aware, no pollen dating took place on the Noon Hill Site, but examination of the items found, indicates a date of around 1100 BC for the burial mound.

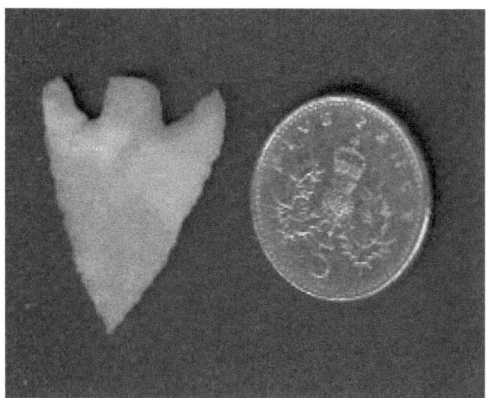

Various flints "chippings", "flakes" and flint implements have also been found on the moors but I have unfortunately never managed to find the exact locations. I remember seeing a map showing the sites of all the flint "finds" on the Hill it was pinned to the wall of the Head Rangers office in Middle Derbyshires Farm around 1977-82 but I have never managed to trace a copy of the map since that time. If anyone has a copy of the map PLEASE get in touch with me and if I can get permission, I'll put a copy in this scrapbook!

I find it particularly galling and frustrating, for although I have tramped and searched on Winter Hill for almost 30 years, I have never even found so much as a single flake of flint on Winter Hill and Anglezarke - even though other individuals have found dozens! (Garry Rhodes found a flint piece in early 2019 – see later in the book). The only flint I have **ever** found in the locality, was a superb barbed arrowhead (minus shaft) – shown above - found some 20 yards due north of the peak of Black Hill on Anglezarke Moor and is illustrated on the previous page.

So what's this upright stone on Anglezarke Moor?

Photo shows the standing stone discovered 27th March 2019 at **SD 62847 18385**, 290m ASL. There are no markings on it. Could it be an ancient standing stone, a boundary stone, how much of it is buried underneath the peat . Looks a bit odd to be "natural" … and if it was put there by man, when?..... Without a proper archaeological investigation, digging, pollen analysis and dating etc we'll probably never ever know the facts about this stone …. And how many more are there like that on the moors yet to find.

Pool on Winter Hill – Unknown history, age or function

This pool sits just to the Belmont side of Dean Ditch at SD 6706 1422. There is no evidence of any mining waste but could be a blocked ventilation shaft but its felt that is unlikely. The pool is surrounded by large stones and the pool appears to be on some generally raised ground. There are also some interestingly shaped stones in the vicinity. Let us know if you have any ideas as to its past.

Note the saddle shaped stone top right. December 2018.

A good place for a bite to eat *(Garry Rhodes MBE)*. The pool with less water in the spring of 2019. Note the Cotton Grass and the general recovery taking place after the 2018 fires between the two photos.

Pets Grave, The Street, Rivington

This is to be found opposite "The Street" building on The Street (road) in Rivington. The road runs along the western bank of the Upper Rivington Reservoir. SD 6200 1532. It is believed other marked pets graves are in the area but this is the only one clearly visible (Photo 2018)

Some pre-historic objects found in the area
(all held in the Bolton Museum)

Noon Hill Urn  *Two Lads Melon Bead*

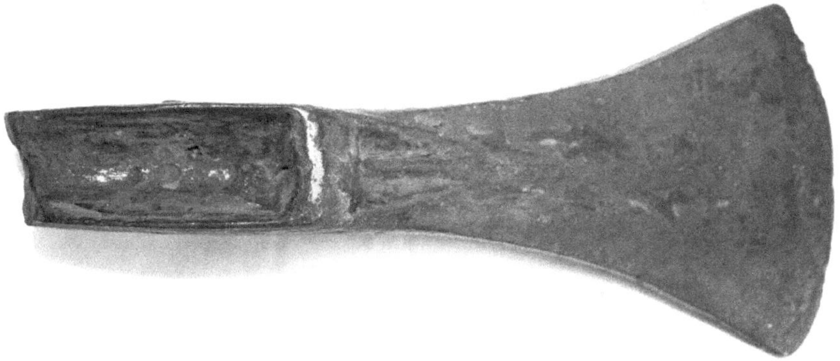

Charters moss, Turton Axe

Winter Hill Arrowhead *Noon Hill Arrowhead*

Delph Reservoir Axe

Lostock Axe

Belmont Spearhead

Clay Pipe finds

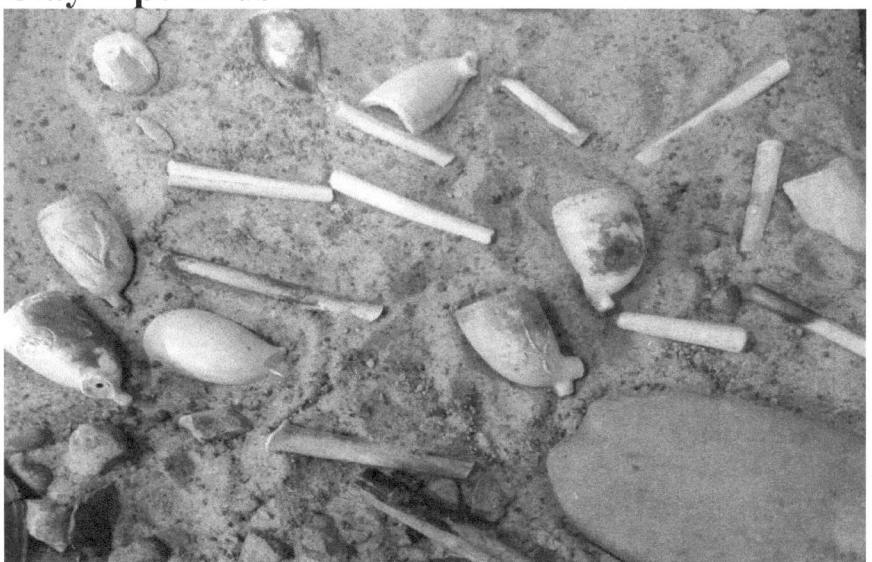

Clay pipes found on the eastern bank of the Yarrow Reservoir at low water during the early 1980's. Thought to be dropped by the men building the reservoir in the 1860's. Note the harp and other markings suggesting Irish origin. (Garry Rhodes MBE and Ian Harper). Horwich Heritage Exhibition July 2019. Other clay pipe fragments (stems and broken bowls) have been found at numerous locations across the moors by the authors particularly post moorland fires 2018.

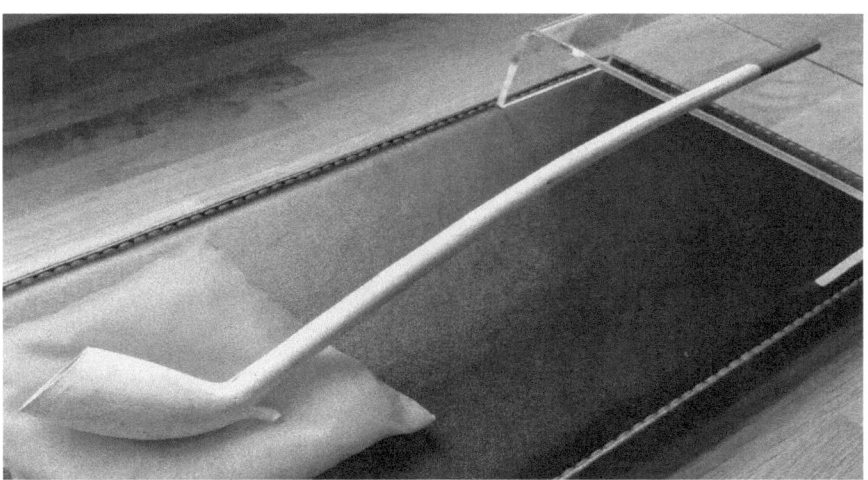

A modern day complete clay pipe donated by Ian Harper to Horwich Heritage for exhibition July 2019. The stem is approximately 200 mm in length

The Winter Hill Mass Trespass of 1896.

It is not widely known that a mass trespass took place on Winter Hill in 1896 nearly 50 years before the more famous mass trespass on Kinder Scout in 1932. It was the response of the people of Bolton to the closure of footpaths and roads over Winter Hill by the landowner Colonel R H Ainsworth JP of Smithill's Hall, in order to protect his grouse shooting.

The demonstration followed much controversy and demands for an enquiry, which were resisted by Col. Ainsworth. The organisers called on the people of Bolton to join them in a walk from Smithill's Hall, along the disputed Coal Pit Road track to Winter Hill on Sunday 6th September 1896. Over 8,000 turned up!

They were addressed by several speakers and the organisers asked the walkers to keep to the path and not trespass on the surrounding land.

Upon reaching the disputed track, the walkers were confronted by a fastened gate plus a group of police and men who were employed by Col Ainsworth.

The walkers jumped over the gate that blocked their path, eventually knocking it down and they uprooted the "Trespassers Will Be Prosecuted" notice, throwing it into the ditch to loud cheers. They also knocked over a police inspector.

After passing through Col. Ainsworth's land the route passed onto land leased by Mr Deakin of Belmont Bleach works, who since 1893 had been trying to close the Belmont to Rivington road over the moors.

When viewed from the summit of Winter Hill it was reckoned that the procession was over 1.5 miles in length.

The following Sunday, the 13th Sept another walk was organised and this time it was estimated that 12,000 people took part. They met at the junction of Blackburn and Halliwell roads and marched to Smithill's Hall then up and over the moors again.

This time the 60 police present who were positioned where the gate had been were more conciliatory and the gates no longer blocked the path.

The demonstrators were aware that they ran the risk of being prosecuted for trespassing, which would be very serious for ordinary working people would be unable to pay the fines which may have been levied and they might well lose their jobs if found guilty of an offence in court.

Col. Ainsworth did in fact pursue the question of access in the courts, seeking an injunction to restrain over 30 people and through them, the general public, from passing over his land. He also claimed damages.

When his case came to court in Manchester in March 1897, judgement was given in his favour with costs being awarded against the defendants.

(this article appeared as an information panel at the Rivington Visitor Centre).

The major local hill summits within the Winter Hill & Anglezarke area.

Hill	Metres	Feet
Adam Hill		
Brown Hill	325m	1066 feet
Brown Lowe	325m	1066 feet
Burnt Edge	325m	1066 feet
Counting Hill	433m	1421 feet
Crooked Edge Hill	375m	1230 feet
Egg Hillock	328m	1076 feet
Great Hill	381m	1250 feet
Noon Hill	380m	1247 feet
Rivington Pike	362m	1188 feet
Two Lads	389m	1276 feet
Whimberry Hill	340m	1115 feet
White Brow	358m	1175 feet
Winter Hill	456m	1496 feet

Round Loaf Neolithic Burial Mound from 2,000 feet!

The Geology of the Anglezarke area – with a brief tour of the Dean Brook area at White Coppice.

A great deal of information in this section has been gleaned from a publication called "Anglezarke Moor, a geographical description and field guide", by E K Isaac and published by the Ribblesdale Branch of the Geographical Association Nr 1 1972. Parts are also taken from notes of a field trip in 2006 led by Alan Diggles of the Open University Geological Society.

We start off this article with the subject of geology for one important reason. Virtually everything you can see, the rocks, the type of plants growing and many of the old industries present in the area are there purely as a result of the past geology of the area. Without some understanding of the geology, it is not possible to fully interpret what one is looking at today on the moors, in the quarries and in the streams. Knowledge of the past geology is the key to understanding the present.

Hundreds of millions of years ago, Anglezarke would not look like it does at present. It would not even be located on the globe where it is today. The earth is formed of a number of "tectonic plates" which move very slowly every year, the movement is akin to the speed that a fingernail grows.

Although this seems to be only a tiny bit of movement, over hundreds of millions of years, this has led to the British Isles being it's present shape and being moved from the equator (where it lay, around 420 million years ago) to its current location about 52 degrees north of the equator.

All the rocks we can find in the Winter Hill/Anglezarke area are fairly "modern" and were laid down from around 350 to 250 million years ago (the age of the earth is around 4,600 million years).

Different "periods" of geological time have been given different names, and our rocks of this area belong to the Carboniferous period. Many different "periods" followed the Carboniferous period and new layers of rocks would have been formed during these times.

However, over millions of years, these newer rocks have all been eroded away in this area, due to weathering, glaciations and general erosion and so we have a geological "gap" of over 200 million years about which we know nothing.

Let's look at the period we do know about. In Carboniferous times (363 to 290 million years ago) Winter Hill and Anglezarke lay on or just north of the equator. This period, is split into three divisions, Carboniferous limestone, Millstone Grit and the Coal Measures. In the area we are considering, rocks from the limestone period, lie far too deep underground so we will not consider them apart from commenting that this was a time that the area would be covered in a shallow warm tropical sea, with flourishing sea life including corals.

At a later time, the sea levels fell slightly and our area of the Pennines became a vast river delta with water coming from high mountains in adjacent areas to the North and North West. The rivers and their associated deltas would have been gigantic in size, with the rivers originating in Scotland and perhaps even as far away as Norway, and Northern Germany. Large amounts of sediments and silt were carried by these rivers and deposited in our area, forming the rocks of the Millstone Grit Series.

Eventually (still in the Carboniferous period) the climate warmed still further becoming humid, the land raised slightly, such that it began to support swamps and tropical forests. Due to the ever-changing pattern of the deltas, this meant that at times the forests and swamps would be above sea level and sometimes below it. Sometimes the vegetation was above water, sometimes it was covered in yet more layers of sediment. Stagnant pools of fresh water would often form.

This was a warm, lush environment for plant life to flourish. In the deltas and swamps, grew trees and plants which are long since extinct and are only known through the fossils which we find today. Exotic trees such as the *Lepidodendron, Calamite, Cordaites* and *Sigillaria* grew along with various types of ferns and tree ferns. When the waters invaded, fish, *Goniatites* (a forerunner of the ammonite), *bivalves* and *gastropods* flourished in the warm waters.

Eventually tectonic plate movements caused massive faulting over the area (this is known as the "Variscan Orogeny") and the ground was later covered up by many different layers of sediments which formed in entirely different climates.

The vast amount of rocks formed after the carboniferous period (perhaps almost a kilometre in depth) were later eroded away over hundreds of millions of years by wind, water, ice and glaciers and so once again, the carboniferous period rocks have arrived at the surface ….. although most of the area does have a "capping" of relatively "recent" glacial deposits.

These glacial deposits arrived less than 20,000 years ago – we'll try to get round to writing an article on this subject and include it in a later edition of this Scrap Book - along with other geological information which explains why this area looks like it does!

This then is Anglezarke, situated on the Western boundary of what is geologically known as the Rossendale Anticline. An area of rock formed over 300 million years ago when our earth was a very different place. It consists mainly of Carboniferous rocks of the Millstone Grit group. These sandstones were deposited towards the end of the Namurian period when the filling of the Craven Basin, by southerly flowing rivers, was almost complete. Later, rocks of the Westphalian (Coal Measures) were deposited.

The rocks are virtually horizontal, with a dip generally, of no more than 10 degrees and consist of fairly massive, course to medium grained, cross stratified sandstones.

The sandstones are separated by shales, mudstones and siltstones which are little exposed, except at stream sections and usually, just above the sandstone, can be found fossiliferous marine bands containing goniatites and bivalves.

Examples of all the above can be seen when walking from White Coppice cricket ground, up through the quarry and following the riverside track as far as Drinkwaters Farm.

This path follows the route of the east trending Great Hill Fault (this fault displaced the rocks on the downthrow side by 230m) which lies underneath your feet.

There is another major Fault in the area, running North to South generally following the escarpment of Anglezarke Moor running from White Coppice to Alance Bridge . This is the Brinscall Fault separating the rocks of Anglezarke Moor from the heavily faulted area to the west.

This results in exposure of Helmshore and Fletcher Bank Grits on the high moorlands to the east and on the western downthrow side of the fault, the younger, softer rocks of Upper Haslingden Flags and Rough Rock.

The area was mineralised after faulting, resulting in veins yielding galena, barite and witherite. Mining areas include White Coppice quarry, the Dean Black Brook area, Stronstrey Bank (Manor House area) and Lead Mines Clough.

In White Coppice quarry you can see the Great Hill fault with its 2.7 m wide vein of highly weatherised fault breccia containing calcite, barite and witherite. At the base of the quarry is a sealed up trial adit. The adit was sealed by the Water Authority during the 1990's

The quarry consists of Fletcher Bank sandstones which show fining up and contain sub-rounded thumb-nail sized quartz pebbles.

On the quarry face are slickensides *(a slickenside is a smoothly polished surface caused by frictional movement between rocks along the two sides of a fault – one is also seen at the mine waterfall in Lead Mines Clough)* and high up on the underside of an overhang is a fossilised tree bark.

The sealed up entrance to the adit. This trial tunnel is horizontal and extends into the hillside approximately 30 meters.

A little further up Dean Black Brook on its south side there is another fault with two spoil heaps containing traces of barites, calcite and galena with the remains of bell pits tracing the line of the fault. Here the Brook turns at two places through 120 degrees and back again exploiting the joints and faults in the rock

Yet further up the stream, again on the north side of the stream is a partially sealed up adit (see below) to the left of which is a fine example of slickensides and deposits of limonite deposited by mine drainage. To the right of the adit a fault is marked by a shallow inclined trough with differently eroded breccia.

Partially sealed adit, Dean Black Brook, October 17th 2019.

Go on just a little further and you'll arrive at one of this writers favourite geological spots in the area. The valley widens and there is a bluff on the northern bank.

There are exposures of Fletcher Bank Grit and overlying this are Helmshore Grits, between which are shales and siltstones with ironstone bands.

To me the best part of this spot is the overlying 5m or so of glacial till. This contains erratics which have been carried to this spot by the glaciers.

They include limestones from the Yorkshire Dales, Granites from Shap, Borrowdale volcanics from the Lake District etc ….. **just love this spot!**

These erratics are found in the bed of the stream so no scrambling is involved! You'll know you're at the right spot with all the rocks near the stream smashed open by geologists!!!!

Dean Black Brook running through the remains of White Coppice Quarry. Photo taken on 26th June 2015 by Steve Glover . Photo from Flikr

Early Humans on West Pennine Moors

The last Ice Age ended around 12000-10000 BC with the first post ice age humans inhabiting the British isles at around 8000 BC, the land mass becoming an island around 6000-5000 BC. Its possible that hunting parties from these early settlers moved across what we now call the West Pennine Moors but the evidence is limited.

More evidence exists from the later nomadic groups and the eventual settlers and farmers. The area became forested following the end of the ice age which Neolithic and Bronze age settlers began to clear, this clearance continued through the dark ages and medieval period by the Anglo-Saxons and Vikings.

Many features from the Neolithic and Bronze age (4000-800 BC) are visible, some which have been listed as a scheduled ancient monuments others where the actual status of the feature has yet to be academically determined.

Cheetham Close on Turton Moor is the site of Bronze Age stone circle and is a scheduled ancient monument.

Around Anglezarke Moor and Winter Hill there are a number of prehistoric sites with the same status, Pikestones which would be contemporary to Stonehenge (3400-2400 BC) and Roundloaf (yet to be excavated and confirmed), the latter being a landmark clearly visible from many routes and viewpoints from around our moors and the wider country side

A burial mound and cairn c1500 BC was identified in 1958 on Winter Hill around 0.5 km west of the summit. This site was badly damaged during the 2018 moorland fires as previously discussed.

Around the same time another site further to the west, at Noon Hill was found to be a burial site consisting of two concentric stonewalls which had two sets of burnt human bones, a broken urn containing more bones, two flint arrow heads and flint sacrificial knife in the centre. The site has been dated to around 1100 BC. Both of these sites are considered Scheduled Ancient Monuments

Winter Hill Cairn, post the moorland fires of 2018, photo 2019.

Noon Hill Cairn 2019. Winter Hill in the background

Noon Hill Urn. Horwich Heritage Centre Exhibition July 2019. The exhibit notation describes the location as Anglezarke its actually Rivington Moor

Chambered Cairn, Black Coppice Anglezarke

The exposed chambered cairn above can be seen at Black Coppice and other cairns exist at various sites around Anglezarke and the wider

Winter Hill Moors. An example being the double kerbed cairn (below) in the vicinity of Hurst Hill and Rushy Brow, Anglezarke which is thought to be of a similar age to the Winter Hill burial mound and cairn.

Double kerbed Cairn, Rushy Brow Anglezarke circa 1500 BC. SD 63025 17418

Un-named Cairn near Rushy Brow/Hurst Hill Anglezarke photo 2019.

Many modern day cairns (last one/two hundred years) are due to walkers and others taking a stone to add to a pile which eventually stands tall. Some of these sites however could well have been the site of pre-historic cairns, a sample are shown below.

Modern day walkers cairn on the top of Roundloaf, Anglezarke.

Modern Day walkers cairn, Hurst Hill, Anglezarke

Two Lads, January 2019

Two lads (image from http://winterhilllancashire.blogspot.com/)

The Origin and Development of the Moorland.

(Sections of this article are taken from one of the information panels in the Rivington Visitor Centre and are reproduced with their permission)

Winter Hill – and the surrounding upland areas – have not always been as bare and empty as they now appear. At one time they were forested and contained many different types of trees and bushes as has been proved by pollen analysis and pollen dating tests done on the moorland. So what happened to change things?

The process of deforestation started as soon as human settlements began in the area. The natural resources provided by the forest provided building materials, fuel and to a lesser extend food for the settlements. Early inhabitants may have cleared extensive areas of forest around their settlements for simple agriculture.

Demands for more basic materials and increased areas for agriculture would have led to a joining up of clearings to create large open tracts of moorland. One pollen analysis investigation of Winter Hill showed a clearly defined woodland clearance of the area in the Norse period, followed by considerable woodland regeneration thought to be through the Middle Ages.

It is possible that the original clearance could have been earlier, perhaps even Roman, but I have as yet not managed to get hold of the carbon datings that were carried out at Harwell for this investigation. Pollen analysis was also carried out in the 1980's at Round Loaf Tumulus, Black Brook and Pikestones as well as on Winter Hill. The Winter Hill measurements were taken at SD 627 172 at a profile depth of 1m 46cms.

Grazing.

Probably the single most important factor in the development of these man made moorlands was the introduction of grazing livestock, particularly sheep. Sheep will nibble almost any vegetation down to ground level thus preventing the generation of tree species. Continual grazing by sheep alone will, in time, convert a woodland into a moorland. The practice of running large flocks of sheep on the moorland has not only contributed to the deforestation but has maintained a virtually treeless landscape.

Fire.

Fire would have played a part in the reduction tree cover. Fire can occur naturally in a forest due to lightning strikes and it can devastate large areas. In the years following a forest fire there is usually an increase in the seedling growth of "pioneer" species such as the fast growing birch, willow and rowan.

These in turn provide shelter for the slower growing and less numerous species such as oak, ash and pine. Over a long period of time the character of the forest would be restored. Should fires occur on a frequent basis or grazing of livestock be established then the pioneer species would be prevented from regenerating ultimately causing the death of the forest and the creation of moorland.

Today, periodic burning is part of moorland management. The intention is to burn off the mass of dead vegetation from previous years and encourage early growth of grasses for the grazing livestock. Given the right conditions, controlled burning will remove the dead vegetation without damaging the plant roots and the resulting ash will return much needed minerals back into the soil.

However uncontrolled fires due to accident or vandalism can over a period of years have a detrimental effect on the mix of moorland vegetation, leading to a loss of habitat for insects, birds and mammals and it reduces the value of grazing moorland for livestock. In severe cases it can also result in the burning of the underlying peat (sometimes to a great depth) leading to the complete loss of all vegetative cover.

The soil or peat.

As if mankind has not done enough damage to the moor, nature has not helped either in latter times. The rocks of the area tend to be Millstone Grit, a rather rough form of Sandstone. Soil is usually formed both by the weathering of rocks and the rapid breakdown of vegetation which in theory should provide good soil along with the nutrients necessary for plant and tree growth over a period of time.

Unfortunately Millstone Grit breaks down mainly into rather rocky sand with little nutrient content and the high rainfall on the moorlands washes out most of the other nutrients. These factors combine and peat begins to form which in turn makes the land acidic in which many plants just will not grow. Thus we have Winter Hill as we have it today!

Moorland Plants of Winter Hill.

Not being a botanist and I had rather hoped I'd be able to persuade someone else to write this section (any offers?) so for present you're stuck with my rather simplistic explanations as to what grows on Winter Hill!

There are two major types of grasses, purple moor grass *(Molinia Caerulea)* and wavy hair grass *(Deschampsia flexuosa)*. Purple moor grass is very common throughout the UK and is often the dominant grass on damp moors, heaths and fens around the country. It's perennial and forms tufts or tussocks with the flowerhead usually dark purple (but occasionally pinkish, yellowish or green). In height it varies from 15 to 100cm and flowers between July and September.

This is the "ankle breaker" on parts of Winter Hill forming large tussocks, which are partially obscured by the long flowering stems in summer – and this period they are a curse for the hayfever sufferer.

The other variety of grass common on the hill is the wavy hair grass but this forms smaller tussocks and flowers in June and July forming delicate heads appearing like a pink mist on the ground. This is the commonest grass on the moorland in the area. The only other major type of grass found on the hill is mat grass *(Nardus Stricta)*, a hard & fibrous grass growing between 10 and 40 cm in height forming dense tufts. This is unpalatable to sheep.

One type of grass seen in many of the damper areas of Winter Hill is cotton grass *(either Eriophorum vaginatum or Eriophorum angustifolium.* This is instantly recognised by everyone with its white tufty cotton like flowers between April and June and it grows only on wet ground.

There are also a number of sedges and rushes on the hill (you can tell the difference between grass and sedge easily enough, in cross section grasses are round and hollow whilst sedges are triangular). I haven't got a clue about the names of the sedges on Winter Hill so if there are any knowledgeable botanical readers out there then please get in touch – or write a full article for inclusion in the next update.

Rampant on parts of the moor is bracken *(Pteridium aquilinum)*, and probably the best known fern, unfortunately it is also one with the most nuisance value as a weed. It can be poisonous to livestock if eaten in quantity but is normally avoided by cattle, sheep or rabbits and so it spreads in their grazing areas fairly rapidly thus reducing the value of the land for grazing purposes.

The far reaching underground rhizomes makes eradication difficult. This plant dies away every winter and what might have been a pleasant place to walk at that time of year can become a nightmare in mid summer – especially when it's wet! Bracken only thrives on dryish ground.

Also found on Winter Hill is heather and a similar plant called crowberry. Bilberry *(Vaccinium myrtillus)* is also rampant in some areas and makes delicious pies if you have considerable time to spare, collecting the fairly small berries. A good area for bilberry is to the west of Wilderswood and around the Wilton quarries at the northern end of Scout Road.

I'm not going to disclose the exact location, but on the top of Winter Hill is a fairly large patch of cranberry.

In many areas on the hill sphagnum moss grows in profusion both in small patches and in raised bog areas. Sphagnum is unique in that it can hold vast quantities of water even in dry seasons, some varieties holding more than others.

Also on the moor are quantities of mosses, lichens and ferns. One day I really must get around to learning what they are all called.

A Victorian local painting of the main reservoir system (Anglezarke and Rivington) roughly from the current Anglezarke view point

A cold afternoon mid winter over Winter Hill and the Pike from around 1,500 feet

THE ANGLEZARKE LEAD MINES.

Some of the information that follows was originally published in various publications – mainly from "The Anglezarke Lead Mines" by Iain A Williamson MSc in the Mining Magazine Vol 108 Jan-June 1963 and also from a further article in the Mining Magazine dated May 1946).

History.

The lead mines at Anglezarke are well publicised in booklets and visitor information boards in the area, yet little appears on the Internet, or in freely available literature, about the finer details of the place. Over the years I've heard a number of people saying "one day I'm going to do a full write up about Anglezarke lead mines" but after 40 years of waiting nobody seems to have written anything about it! There have been a number of articles in various professional journals which have given more details but nothing substantial has appeared for the general reader.

The Anglezarke lead mines are ancient! The first references we find of it were to do with a lawsuit (in the late 17th century) between a Lady Margaret Standish of Duxbury, near Chorley and a group of local landowners led by Peter Shaw of Rivington. It was Peter Shore and one George Smyth who first discovered the lead veins and they formed a mining partnership (along with a Yorkshire lead miner John Jowle from Arncliffe, West Riding, who acted as advisor) with the landlord of the area, Sir Richard Standish. It was agreed that any profits from the mining venture would be split as follows:

Sir Richard Standish – One tenth of the profit would be paid as "royalty" plus a further two fifths as a "partner" in the venture.
John Jowle – One tenth of the profit.
Messers Shaw and Smyth = two fifths of the profit

Extracts from the Chancery Court proceedings of the Court case in 1694 mentioned above say the following:-

"The works were accordingly made and carried on at a very great expense to the partners and much against the will of Dame Margaret Standish, then wife of the said Sir Richard Standish, she believing the same would prove successless and thereby her husband, already much indebted, be harmed and damaged in his estate, …… For a long time they had no success but at length a very hopeful vein or mine of lead was discovered in Anglezarke ….. They continued working until the death of Sir Richard in November 1693, when Dame Margaret, his widow went on in his place for four months during which time complainants spent much time on the same ….. The work in the four months after the death of Sir Richard's death was so good and the quantity of ore so great that complainants and Dame Margaret obtained to the value of £20 or £25 a day, clear of expenses, and were likely to have increase of the same, but Dame Margaret being desirous to have all advantage for herself on May 1st. last past, with violence turned complainants, set doors on the said works and bolted them, so that they and their workers were

prevented from working there ..... When the Sheriff gave order on complainant's behalf she cut up the engines, tools etc and turned a river into the mines and gives out she would rather the whole mines and veins were lost than that complainants should have their share therein, and insists Sir Richard was only tenant for life and had no power to make the indenture with the complainants". (Extract from the Chancery Court proceedings, 1694, quoted in Shaw's "The Records of a Lancashire Family" published in 1940).

Although Lady Margaret lost the court case, she then took the matter further and petitioned the House of Lords but again lost her case. The mines remained flooded and sealed off and the next we hear about them was on the 9th of March 1721 when Sir Richard Standish, the son of Sir Thomas Standish, took out a lease with Sir Henry Houghton of Houghton Tower, near Blackburn. According to records in the Lancashire Record Office (DX 931) Sir Henry agreed to take *"a parcel of Common or Waste Ground in Anglezargh, near to the Black and White Coppys ..... with all Mines and Veins of Lead Ore Riders Strings and Cross Veins" (Lancashire Records Office DX931)*

The lease was for the usual period of 21 years and included the rights to build a smelting mill at a place called "Wharf in Anglezarke" – this location probably being Warth or the present hamlet of White Coppice. That mining progressed with some results is indicated by the purchase of royalty ores by the London Leas Company in 1731 and 1732 from "Anglezarke in Lancashire" (Raistrick, 1934, p 140). A slightly later development between 1753 and 1766 is suggested by the purchase of Anglezarke ore by the ill-fated Clitheroe Mining Company (Kerr 1875, p8)

Probably the most active period of mining was between 1781 and 1790 when Sir Frank Standish worked the mines, during which time the locality became famous for the discovery of witherite.

Numerous shafts were sunk , one, the New Engine Shaft, to a depth of 126 feet and a drainage adit, the South Level was constructed.

Between 1781 and 1787 the recorded production averaged about four tons of lead per year, although the last two years of mining a total of 73 tons was produced (Watt, 1790A, pp 605ff). Apparently some copper was also produced, since Conybeare and Phillips (1822, p 390) refer to the "copper mine of Anglezarke", unfortunately no further information is given.

The number of workers employed in the enterprise varied between 10 and 16 although the surface layout was fairly considerable. When the chemist Parkes(1815) visited the then abandoned mine in 1810 – having first found it necessary to engage a guide "to so obscure a part of the country! (op. cit p.203) he noted the former sites of a large water wheel, a warehouse and a smithy.

As with many a contemporary mining venture financed by a wealthy amateur there were considerable labour problems engendered by the relative ignorance of Sir Frank Standish in mining methods.

He engaged successively and dismissed successively several different teams of miners "who all conspired to defraud him of their time, and endeavoured to impress his mind with the idea of the small quantity of Ores that could be procured….. to induce him to lease the mine to them (op cit p205-206). Not surprisingly, therefore, about 1790 and after costing several thousands of pounds the project was again discontinued. By 1802 the mines were derelict, despite the proprietor offering "liberal terms to adventurers" (Mawe, 1802, p131)

The latest records of mining consist of a series of papers held in the Lancashire Records Office and appertaining to the period between 1824 and 1843 (DX 949-987c).

In July 1824, a lease covering the Lead Mines Clough area was granted by Frank Hall Standish to John Thompson, iron merchant of Wallgate, Wigan. The 21 year old lease (DX949) permitted Thompson to work "all manner of Mines, Veins, Pits, Grove, Rakes and beds of lead Ore Booze, Smythorne, Calk Calamine, Black Jack and Metallick Matters whatsoever (except coal and Cannel)". The royalties payable were £1.5s per ton of lead minerals, 15/- shillings per ton of Calk and Calamine and other matters to make brass of (except Black Jack) and 7/6d per ton of Black Jack. One eighth value of any other mineral.

1 = Rough Ore; 2 = Powdered Ore; 3 = Witherite; 4=Zinc Blende

Adequate plans and sections were to be drawn, shafts protected and never less than eight miners to be employed full time "so as to make a full and complete trial" (op.cit).

In November 1837, however, Thompson relinquished his lease, having some time previously ceased active prospecting at Anglezarke during which time several shafts between 70 and 80 yards deep had been sunk. Clearly his efforts were unsuccessful for he spent "some thousands in search of lead ore and never found a bound weight (DX/968)

Although Standish considered advertising the mines after Thompson's failure any further hopes he had as to the mineral potential of Anglezarke were finally dispelled by the adverse report of a Bakewell mining engineer, William Wager saying *"I regret to say that in my opinion is that the uncertainty of success which is greater in the case of these than of the generality of mines, renders rather questionable the prudence of incurring the great expenses of erecting and carrying on the work which would be absolutely necessary to make the Experiment"* (DX/982)

Discovery and Early Interest in Witherite.

The first published chemical and mineralogical description of barium carbonate, described them as "Terra ponderosa" was by the late 18th century Birmingham physician, botanist and mineralogist Dr Withering.

In the account it was stated that the specimen "was got out of a lead mine at Alston Moor in Cumberland" (Withering, 1784 p293). Soon after publication however Withering informed James Watt junior that his specimen had in fact been collected from Anglezarke)Watt 1790, p599) which was afterwards quoted by most authorities as the original locality. De Rance (1873m p66) stated the exact locality to e the Stronstrey Vein north of Lead Mines Clough, but omitted to state the source of his information.

Subsequent to Witherings original description the mineral was renamed Witherite by Werner.

As early as 1700 the Anglezarke Witherite had attracted attention, for Dr Leigh, a celebrated 18th Century naturalist noted the occurrence of a certain "spar" which upon analysis was reputed to contain arsenic.

The medicinal effects of the mineral were well known to the local inhabitants *"who take a Scruple at least of this in "Fits of the Stone", in which it vomits, purges and works violently by Urine: There are some who have been so daring as to venture to take a Dram of this particularly one James Barn's wife and child, but alas! To their woeful experience they found the sad effects of it: for in about 9 hours afterwards they both expired (Leigh, 1700, p70-71)."*

The same lethal effects of Witherite from Anglezarke were recorded by Watt some 90 years later in a series of gruesome experiments with dogs (Watt, 1790B, pp 609-618).

Even in recent years local poultry breeders have collected witherite at Lead Mines Clough and used it as the principal ingredient in home-made rat poison. Although Leigh recorded arsenic as being present, recent analysis by Mr W Beesley show this element to be totally absent in the three samples he examined.

In the middle parts of the 18th Century Josiah Wedgewood, the celebrated ceramist and potter, was experimenting with "cawk" (witherite) as a body material for the production of his Jasper ware, perfected about 1776. In his personal laboratory notebook Wedgewood refers to "Cawk aerated from near Chorley, Lancashire".

Unfortunately there are no records as to the amount purchased by Wedgewood, but in a series of letters to his early associate Bentley, there are numerous references to the secrecy with which it was conveyed to Etruria, in the crushed state to disguise it's nature (Farrer, 1903).

Despite such secrecy, however, "certain German porcelain maufacturers (Mateyard, 1866 p10) were obviously acquainted with the Anglezarke mines. In the 1780's two Frenchmen visited the abandoned mine dumps and collected witherite which had been left by the early miners as valueless (Parkes, 1815 p209).

After this visit a local farmer, James Smithels, until apprehended by the owner of the mines "on certain moonlight nights" collected witherite from the mine dumps and despatched it to Germany for which he was paid £5 per ton (op cit) (pp211-216).

His nefarious activities are the only record of any profit being made from the Anglezarke witherite!

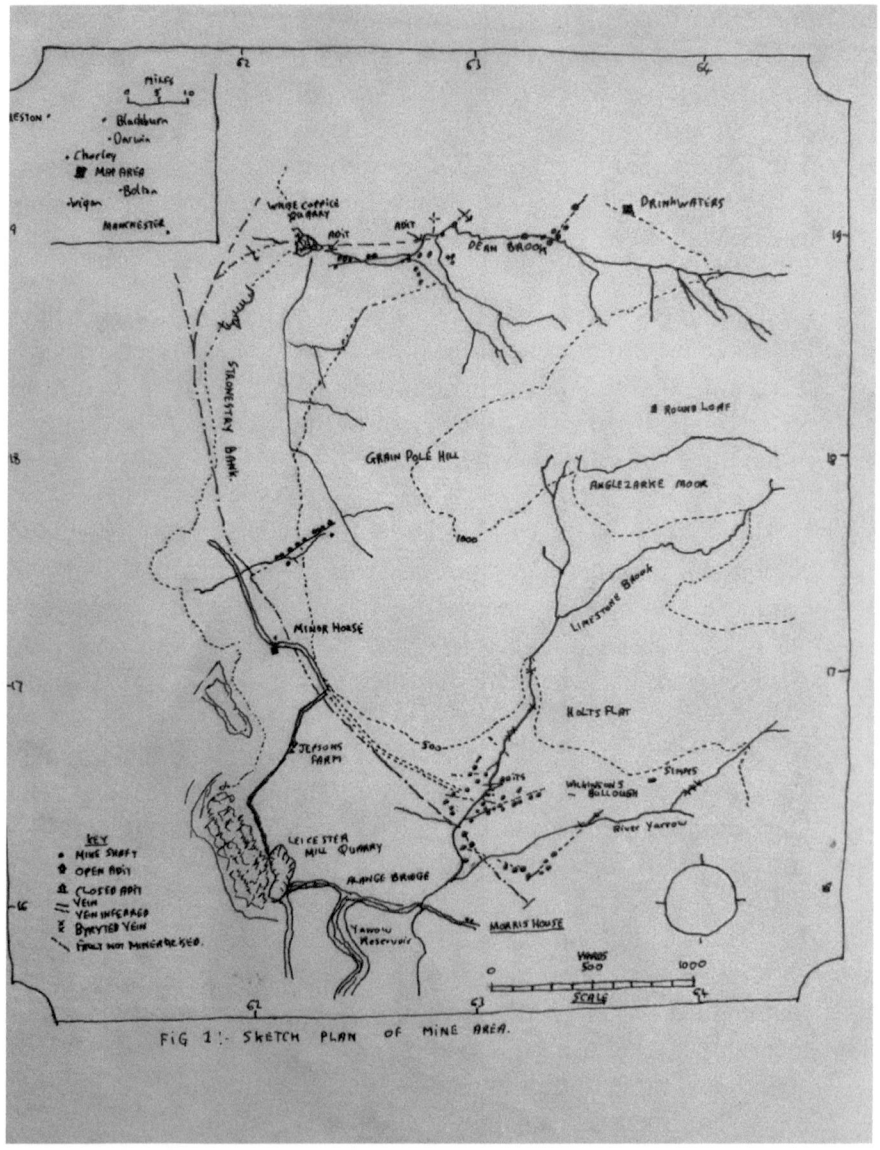

FIG 1:- SKETCH PLAN OF MINE AREA.

The drainage sough at the side of the stream in Lead Mines Clough

The delicious cold water spring hidden in the grasses near to the Water Wheel chamber in Lead Mines Clough. Just search around in the undergrowth – or just listen for the sound of it ..... and you'll find it! Mind you ... the water does come from the vicinity of a lead mine .... So is it safe to drink? Well ..... I'm still alive over 50 years since I first drank from it!

The Visit of James Watt junior, to the Anglezarke Lead Mines circa 1780's.

On the 30th November 1789, a paper by James Watt junior was read at the Manchester Literary and Philosophical Society. The original paper can be seen in Volume 3 of that Societies Memoirs pages 598 to 609. The first page is illustrated below.

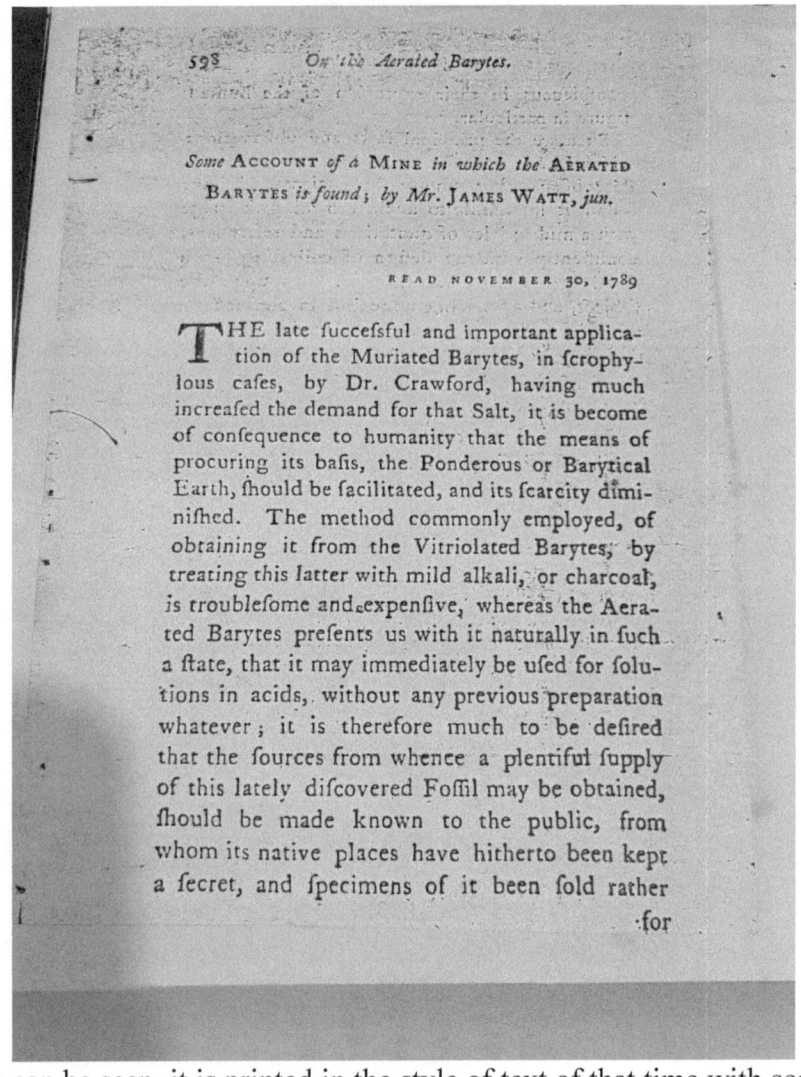

As can be seen, it is printed in the style of text of that time with some of the letters not looking like they do nowadays. To make it easier to read, a "more modern version" is given below.

On the Aerated Barytes
by James Watt Jnr

The late successful and important application zff of the Muriated Barytes, in scrophylous cases, by Dr Crawford, having such increased the demand for that Salt, it is becoming of consequence to humanity that the means of procuring the basis, the Ponderous and Barytical Earth should be facilitated, and its scarcity diminished.

The method commonly employed, of obtaining it from the Vitriolated Barytes, by treating this latter with mild alkali, or charcoal, is troublesome and expensive, whereas the Aerated Barytes presents us with it naturally in such a state, that it may immediately be used for solutions in acids, without any previous preparation whatsoever, it is therefore, much to be desired that the sources from whence a plentiful supply of this lately discovered fossil may be obtained, should be made known to the public, from whom its native places have hitherto been kept a secret, and specimens of it been sold rather for curiosity, that for use.

I have undertaken to lay before the Society an account of the only mine in England in which according to the best of my information, any Aerated Barytes has been discovered. At the same time I will submit the few observations which two short visits have enabled me to make upon the natural history of a fossil, concerning which the curiosity of mineralogists has been excited but never gratified.

The first intimation of the Aerated Barytes existing naturally, was given by Dr Withering, who published an excellent analysis of it in the Philosophical Transactions, for the year 1784, wherein he has left us of little to desire respecting its chemical properties. However he was misinformed as to the place from whence his specimen came, which he supposed to be Alston Moor, where I have good authority for advancing that none has been found. He has since informed me that he believes it came from the same mine of Anglezarke, which forms the subject of the present paper.

The mine of Anglezarke lies within a district of the same name, situated on the property of Sir Frank Standish, Bart – about three miles to the east of Chorley, in this county. The country is hilly and of a stratified or secondary nature, consisting of alternate strata of Sandstone and Argillaceous Shistus, interlaid here and there with thin beds of coal. The Valley, which is traversed by the principal veins, runs in an Easterly direction, hills on both sides of it are low, though steep of ascent. I found the strata on the south side of it in the shaft called the New Engine Shaft, to follow one upon another in the following order of thickness.

Loose stones and Sand	*0.5 yards*
Sandstone	*7.5 yards*
Argillaceous schistus and coal	*0.5 yards*
Argillacious schistus	*1.0 yards*
Sandstone	*16 yards*
Argillaceous schistus	*16.5 yards*
(Recorded in Staple Shaft) Shales and sandstone	*11 yards*

In the last stratum, in another part of the mine, an Underground Shaft has been sunk eleven yards deeper, in working which they cut through two or three small beds, about one foot in thickness, of an exceeding hard bluish Sand-stone.

The Sand-stone which forms the second and fifth strata, consists of small angular particles of Quartz, intersperced with others of Mica, and agglutinated by an argillaceous cement, so as to form a very hard aggregate of a reddish grey colour.

The Argillaceous Shistus, which is called Shiver by the miners, The differs little from that which is in general found incumbent upon Coal. It appeared to contain no marine exuviae, but abundance of thin laminae of Martial Pyrites between its plates; at least this was the case with those pieces which were found near the vein.

The Strata dip from East to West, with a general declivity of about five inches in two yards. Those on the North side of the veins, or towards the valley lie six yards deeper than the corresponding ones on the South.

The mine consists of several veins intersecting these strata, nearly perpendicularly and running in various directions, as represented in the annexed plan. Most of the veins appear to have their beginnings*

(* A quantity of stagnant water lying in the Chorley Road Vein prevented me from examining wether these veins were continued to the West of it, but the overlooker assured me they were totally cut off by it, which is no uncommon case) in the Chorley Road Vein which crosses the valley at its entrance, from whence they run eastwards into the slopes of the adjacent hills.

The Old or Sun Vein, which is the principal one, runs for the most part in degree twenty-one of the miners compass, which is a small deviation from due East. It is in general from six inches to three feet in thickness and does not fall quite perpendicular, but inclines and dips a very little to the North till it arrives at the bottom of the second stratum of Sand-stone, when its inclination becomes of a sudden much more considerable, in so much that in the sixteen and a half yards to the bottom of the shaft it is thrown five yards out of the perpendicular.

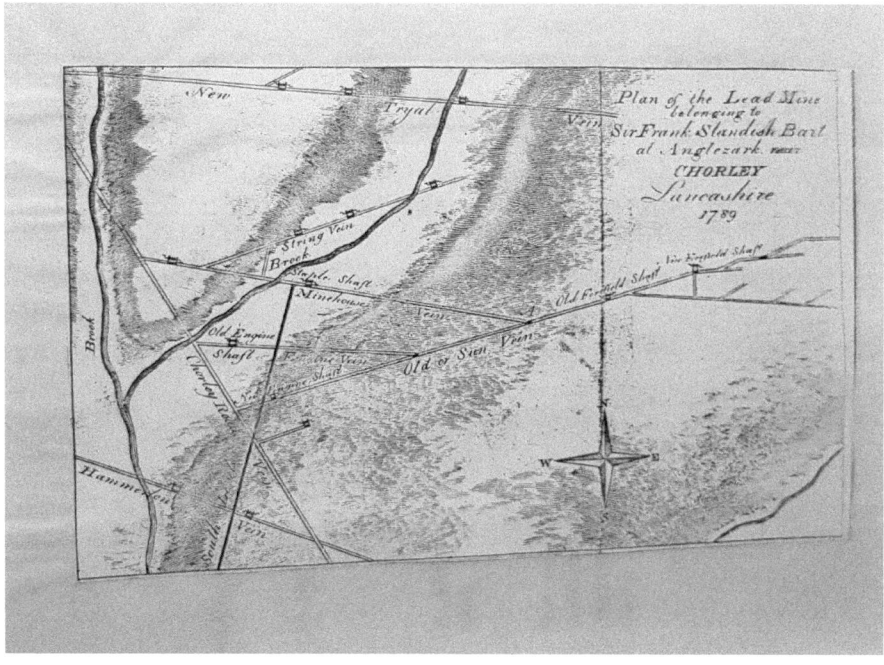

The same happens to the Engine and Mine-house Vein proceeds a small one called the String Vein, which runs parallel to the Sun Vein.

To the North of all these lies the New Trial Vein, which apparently has also its rise in the abovementioned Chorley Road Vein and runs in the direction shown in the plan, which seems to indicate that it likewise at some distance falls into the Sun Vein; it is nearly of the same dimensions as the others, but has not been hitherto much worked upon, owing to its lying low, and its being difficult to carry off the water.

The Matrix of the veins is Aerated and Vitriolated Barytes. The former is found in the greatest quantities next to the surface, where it is almost free from any mixture of the latter but becomes more and more contaminated with it in proportion as the depth increases, until in the lowermost strata it is scarcely to be met at all, the vitriolated have usurped its place.

There is an evident transition from the Aerated to the Vitriolated Barytes which may distinctly be observed through its different stages or graduations, in all parts of the mine. Small quantities of Calcareous Spar are also found in the lower part of the Sun Vein.

The ores are the common Galena or Blue Lead Ore, plentyfully attended with its usual satellites, Blende or Black Jack, and Martial Pyrites.

The Aerated Barytes near the surface does not contain much Lead ore, but when it is found in the second stratum of Sandstone, it forms the richest part of the mine. In the immediately following stratum of Shiver, it becomes more scarce, and indeed its presence there is not looked upon as a good omen, as it then contains large quantities of Blende and Pyrites but little Lead ore. But whatever the Matrix be, it is a general observation that the vein is richer in passing through the strata of Sandstone, than those of Shiver.

The ore is sometimes found in the form of a regular vein, but more commonly in irregular nodules or clusters, disseminated throughout the matrix.

Where the vein is very thick, the greatest part of it is usually filled up with detached pieces of Sand-stone and Shiver, which is more particularly the case where one vein runs into another. In sinking the Underground Shaft which I mentioned before, the quantity of ore decreased in proportion to the depth, until at the depth of ten yards they entirely lost it, the vein still continuing of the same thickness.

The Matrix was loose Vitriolated Barytes. They were endeavouring to regain the ore and had applied a small pump, worked by a water wheel in the valley above, to raise the water to the level, called "South Level" which carries off all those of the mine.

It appears from the best of my information that this mine was first worked about a century ago; it was then left standing during a period of sixty years until the year 1781, since which it has been regularly worked.

To give some idea of the small extent of it, it will only be necessary to mention that during the first five years of this latter period they did not raise above four tons of lead per annum, and that in the last three, they have raised in all only seventy three tons, which difference seems to have been occasioned by the driving of the South Level, at the depth of forty two yards from the top of the New Engine Shaft, for the purpose of clearing the mine of its water, which before was raised to the surface with much difficulty by a water wheel. The number of men employed now is from ten to fifteen.

As the greatest quantities of the Aerated Barytes lie near the surface, they were probably gained during the very first period of working the mine, it being usual here to take the uppermost part of the vein first, and clear all before them as they go deeper. But as that fossil was never supposed to be of any use or to possess any intrinsic value; in all probability it has never been removed from the spot and great quantities of it must be contained in the old heaps of stones and rubbish thrown out of the mine.

Much of it may also be had from the old works or what is called "the Old Man" in the interior of the mine, having been placed there with other stones and wood to prevent the sides from falling in after the vein had been worked out. Another source from which it will probably soon be obtained in large quantities is the New Trial Vein, which has hitherto been little worked upon,but where an essay is now intended to be made. The quantity of it gained in that part of the Sun Vein, where they are now at work is very inconsiderable.

I purposely avoid entering into a more minute detail of the various parts of the mine, of the method of working the Vein, or of such other circumstances as might appear neither peculiar nor interesting, and shall close this account with a description of the Exterm (?). Characters of the Aerated Bartytes; as well for the information of mineralogists, who have not had an opportunity of seeing it under so many different circumstances, as for the instruction of those whose business requires that they should have a sufficient knowledge of it, not to confound it with other fossils. The Aerated Barytes is in general of a pale greyish white colour, but it sometimes inclines to the milk white and at others has a slight yellowish tinge, which is a token of the presence of iron.

It is found in solid masses, sometimes filling the whole of the vein, at others interspersed amongst the Vitriolated Barytes; the masses are generally rounded on the outside, and affect something of a globular form. It is seldom found externally crystalized; I have, however, observed four varieties of it in that state.

The one in which a number of small Crystals radiated in the form of a star from a centre; these Crystals were about half an inch in length, very thin, and appeared to hexagonal columns rounded to point.

The other varieties were the six-sided column, pointed with a pyramid of the same number of faces; also the double six-sided, and the double four sided pyramid.
It has a strong Gloss or Lustre upon the recent fractures; its fracture, in one direction is striated or radiated, composed of small convergent fasciculi, when broken transversely it assumes a kind of glassy or chonchoidal fracture, like Quartz.

When extremely crystalized, its fracture does not appear radiated in any sense. It splits into irregular, rather longish fragments.

The large masses are frequently composed of globular concentrical pieces, several of them lying one on the outside of another, and having a roundish one in the centre, to which the radii or fasciculi of the rest are pointed. It is semi-transparent, or diaphanous, just soft enough to admit of being scraped by a knife.

Is brittle and heavy, but in a somewhat less degree than the Vitriolated Barytes. It's specific gravity has been found to be from 4.3000 to 4.338.

Perhaps to some, after the censure which that excellent chemist Mr Kirwan has lately passed on the utility of external descriptions of fossils, this delineation of those characters, by which, without having recourse to the more tedious chemical ones, the Aerated Barytes can invariably be distinguished from all other fossils may appear superfluous.

But many eminent mineralogists still differ in opinion from that gentleman, both with regard to the sufficiency, certainty and utility of these characters; and I hope soon to see the grounds of their dissent clearly stated and sufficiently established.

However, before such descriptions can be carried to that degree of perfection, to which the acute observations and accurate distinctions, of a "Werner" have raised them amongst the Germans, it will be necessary both to adopt new words into our language, and to fix more precisely and mineralogically the meaning of those we have already.

The Standish of Duxbury Family.

The Standish of Duxbury family are all decendents of the Standish family of Standish Hall.

In 1281 Jordan se Standish bequeathed some land to the three children of the then Rector, Robert de Haydocke and this leads one to think that their mother was a member of the Standish family.

The three are named in the title deed as Nicholas, Hugh and Matilda. Hugh, one of the children, acquired land in Duxbury and called himself Hugh de Standish of Duxbury. He left three sons at least , one of whom inherited the Duxbury Estate, and so the Standishes of Duxbury became established.

A conveyance of 1335 shows that Richard, son of Hugh, had been granted the lease of some land in Duxbury by his brother William. The different Standish families tended to use the same Christian names and it is often confusing to distinguish between them unless their domicile is included.

Extracts from an article in the Lancashire County Records Office Annual Report for 1969 and 1970 entitled "The Standish of Duxbury Muniments".

Some material on this has long been known among Lord Kenyons muniments "H.M.C Rept. 1894 (quoted by R C Shaw: "The Records of a Lancashire Family" pp136-8 and I A Williamson: "The Mining Magazine" March 1963 pp133-139). Also in this collection we have a detailed lead mining agreement dated 1692. The rate was 15/- a ton for ore mined and prepared for "smelting milne or merchant" Dame Margaret Standish was sued because, although she had opposed her late husband, Sir Richard, in his mining ventures, until a good vein was suddenly struck, after his death she sought to disallow the rights of his partners in business to royalties from the mines. She ruthlessly tried to influence all parties, including workmen.

After this fracas the mines were closed but were revived in 1721, when Sir Thomas Standish leased waste near "White and Black Coppys" and mining rights to Sir Henry Hoghton. Thenceforth till 1790 mining continued. The documents found with the county records (DX/930-987) shed some life on this period. They include the above lease and a long letter by John Swainson of Kendal, an amateur mineralogist, written in 1826, advising the re-opening of the mines, not only for lead but for "carbonate of barytes" which not only had been used by Wedgewood in producing jasper ware, but was also useful for the production of caustic soda from salt and so might well be even more profitable than the lead.

The letter contains an extensive quotation from the relevant essay of Parkes, the chemist, published in 1815, who visited the old mines. In volume III of the "memoirs of the Literary and Philosophical Society of Manchester 1789, Mr James Watt junior, gives a full account both of the mines in Anglezarke at that date and of the properties of carbonate of barytes, with a good map.

After the death intestate and without issue of Sir Frank Standish, numerous claimants to the estate appeared. The guardians of one Frank Hall, who later took the name of Standish, anticipated the others in taking possession immediately. Because the heirs connection with the last baronet was somewhat complex, many bearers of the name

Standish felt they might have a better claim. The most famous of these was "Tom" Standish alias Standly, a Blackrod weaver, who blocked himself in the Hall in 1813 and was only to be ejected by the military. Having served sentence for riot, he took to litigation and by 1820 was back in Lancaster goal for debt! On appealing for release, his scheduled debts equalled £2,563.11s 6d. His assets, apart from "excepted goods" were only his "title" to the Duxbury Estates, said to be worth £15,000 a year.

In 1832 Frank Hall Standish wrote of being prepared for a siege at Tom Standish's hands. An anonymous letter from a loyal tenant in 1833 tells us that Tom was rallying the local aged to his side and that a Wigan butcher was providing money for a full genealogical research programme on his behalf, hoping to receive £30,000 if the case succeeded. A Peter, a James and a John Standish also pressed their claim.

Duxbury Hall in Duxbury Park, Duxbury Woods near Chorley in 1840.

In a delightful specimen of semi-literary an unknown person wrote to the Steward of the Duxbury Estates informing him of the rights of Peter.

Clearly some people were out to make their fortune by sponsoring numerous unknown heirs, since a letter of 1841 written by one of the amateur record searchers in such a persons pay to the solicitors of Frank Hall Standish revealed that the same Wigan butcher was backing Peter Standish too!

In DX/1036 is enclosed a printed notice to Duxbury tenants, signed by James Standish, advising them not to pay their rents. Such notices were presumably paid for by the butcher and his friends.

Frank Hall Standish was an enigmatic character. A cripple and a bachelor, piqued, it is reputed, by Parliaments refusal to revive the baronetey in him, he entrusted his estate to solicitors, Messrs Gorsts and Birchall (Deputy Clerks to the Peace) and lived mostly at Seville, where he wrote and collected works of art. Resentment over the baronetey may have caused him to bequeath his art collection to the French king "in token of my great esteem for a generous and polite nation", though his lawyers denied this.

The accounts of the lawyers from 1828 to 1844 give a very good idea of the state of his affairs, including industrial developments on his estates.

The Anglezarke lead mines were again worked from 1824 for a time but in 1838 an expert reported that the risks of loss were too great to render it worthwhile.

In 1840 Frank Hall Standish died in Cadiz and the Hall passed to his second cousin, William Standish Carr - who changed his surname to Carr-Standish.

He served as High Sheriff of Lancashire in 1846 and died in 1856. He left the hall to his son William who died in 1878 and it then passed to William's three sisters, whose trustees sold it to the Mayhew family in 1891 and the Hall and the lands passed out of the family.

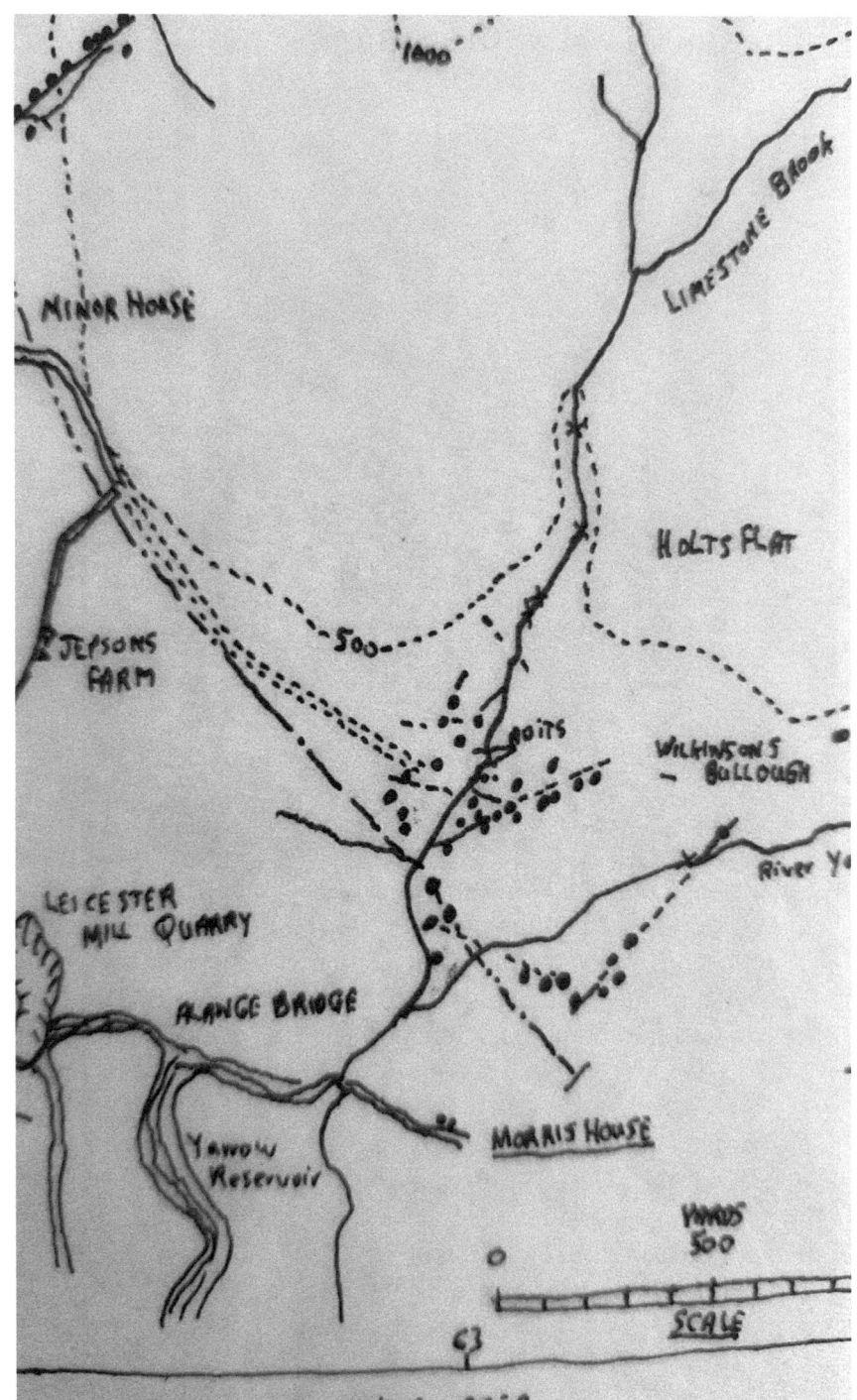

Close up of the main Shaft area on the Lead Mines Clough diagram.

The story behind the Stump.

Scotsman's Stump is the name given to a gaunt iron pillar on the top of Winter Hill located directly in front of the TV station. The "stump" is topped with a plaque, which states "In Memory of George Henderson, traveller, native of Annan, Dumfrieshire who was barbarously murdered on Rivington Moor at noonday November 9th 1838 in the 20th year of his age".

One of the best descriptions of what happened that November day can be found in M D Smiths excellent book "About Horwich" (I understand that another excellent description can be found in the booklet "Murder in the Heather" by David Holding – published in 1991 by the Friends of Smithills Hall). I'll try to give a potted resume but I have to admit that most of my facts came from Mr Smith's book

Poor George Henderson was a young man of 20 who earned his living as a travelling packman or salesman, who sold goods in the area for his Blackburn based employer. He obviously travelled the same route with great regularity, for every other Friday he would meet another packman and the two would meet at Five Houses beer house on the moor and then travel together back to Blackburn.

On this occasion George Henderson never turned up for the usual meeting.

His body was found on the hilltop, having suffered severe gunshot wounds. There were a number of people on the moor that day, some of whom reported the presence of a man carrying a shotgun in the area where Mr Hendersons body was found. The man seen was said to be James Whittle, a 22 year old collier who by coincidence lived in one of the "Five Houses" on the moor.

Whittle was arrested and stood for trial at Lancashire Assize courts but was found not guilty by the jury and was therefore discharged.

The exact site of the murder was at the side of the road opposite the main entrance to the television station located at the top of Winter Hill, and originally a tree was planted at the spot as a memorial to George Henderson. In 1912, the tree was removed and replaced by an iron post and plaque.

Around 2018 Horwich Heritage arranged the repainting and general renovation of the stump.

The Mines of Winter Hill

Winter Hill, especially on the southern side, was once extensively mined for coal. The coal mining activities were so great that that the higher slopes on the Horwich side of the hill are virtually "hollow" except for pillars of coal that were left "in situ" in the mines to stop total roof collapse.

Mines on the Hill included, Montcliffe Colliery, Mountain Mine, Wilderswood and Wildersmoor Collieries, Burnt Edge Colliery, Winter Hill Mine and many other smaller enterprises. The coal seams outcropped at various places on the hill and initially local people would dig away at these points to hew easily obtainable fuel, both for personal use and for sale. Many of these enterprises may have been only one man digging on his own, but others may have been groups of men or a family working on the outcrop. Many of these mines were probably only of small size and would soon be abandoned because of air problems, flooding, roof collapse or other reasons. Because of the small nature of these workings, there is little obvious evidence of this type of working left on the moor.

Once the location of the coal seams were known, small shafts would have been dug to intercept the coal under the surface. These diggings were in the form of "bell pits", so called because the shaft would be dug to the seam then the coal extracted at each side of the shaft forming a bell shaped hole. Once the coal was extracted, another shaft would be dug nearby and in some areas around Horwich whole groups of these pits can be found. There are the remains of some bell pits to the east of Rivington Pike.

Apart from the outcrop workings, the bell pits, and the major commercial undertakings, there were also a number of "trial" workings on Winter Hill, some of which produced small quantities of coal and others which were soon abandoned. The workings to the west of Rivington Pike fall into this category - and one of these shafts is described in this article.

Some of these mines and coal workings will be described below, but readers will have to excuse the lack of exact or precise details of some of the mines due to the dangers inherent in any coal mines. Take my word for it, roof collapses are **not** uncommon, some coal mines **do** contain gases, they **can** be **very** dangerous places. Don't even **think** of going inside old coal mines. All of the underground photographs in this article, were taken by experienced people fully equipped with all the latest safety equipment and mining safety technology. The mines under Winter Hill are particularly dangerous because "pillar and stall" working was practiced in the whole area and the underground workings are rather like a maze on a massive scale, with square miles of passages entered via only one entrance/exit. One's chances of getting lost are pretty high, and apart from going into the "entry" points and pottering near those entrances, the writer has NOT explored the mines even though I was with fully equipped groups.

1. Mining remains near Rivington Pike.

The area around the Pike contains a number of mining remains, shafts, adits and spoil heaps but very little remains today except surface markings. The shafts and adits have long since been sealed.

Very little documentation exists about these mines and what little does exist, is not very explanatory or informative.

The only entrance open in recent times has been a shaft which first opened up in the early 1980's following severe storms on the moorland.

This was located on the moor behind the pigeon tower, on the banks of the stream just above the water tank. Due to the dangerous nature of this shaft (and one on the opposite bank) they were quickly filled in by the Coal Authority. No records were made of the shafts, no photo's were taken nor were any measurements made.

Some years later one of the shafts re-appeared and was quickly explored. The shaft was very unusual in that it contained a short series of steps carved into the side near its entrance, it being the only known example of this in the area. A very poor quality photo is shown below with the steps visible on the right hand side.

The map below shows the drift entrance. The quarry behind the Pigeon Tower is in the bottom left hand corner of the map.

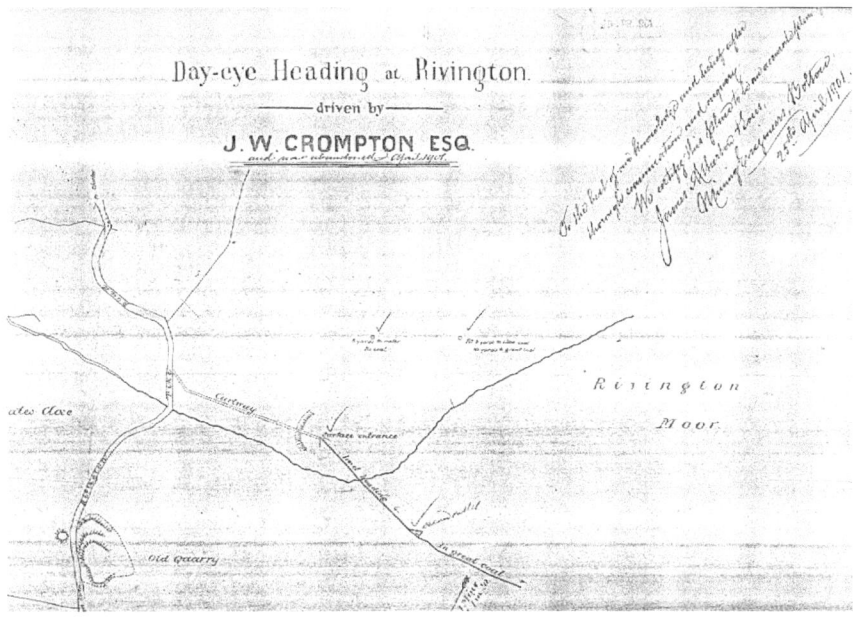

Other photo's were taken within the shaft but it was very wet and muddy, and the extreme condensation on the camera made the pictures unusable. At the bottom of the steps, the tunnel continued for only a very short distance before being blocked by glutinous mud. Two plans exist of mining remains in this immediate area and they indicate that the tunnel went only a short distance. The shaft was soon filled in by the authorities before proper measurements could be taken.

My memory has it that this shaft was much deeper than the earlier mentioned one and had a ladder sloping deeply down on one side of it. If anyone else has memories of this shaft, further details would be appreciated.

Further down the hill heading towards the moorland road is a small pile of mining spoil. This marks the entrance to the drift mine which led into the coal workings. The drift has long since vanished but its location is clearly shown on old maps. A trackway led from the tunnel entrance down to the road.

2. Montcliffe Colliery, Horwich.

The colliery was located on the north side of Georges Lane above the Mill at Wallsuches and lay behind the row of houses at the hamlet of Moncliffe.

There were two shafts at the mine, numbers 1 & 2. The number 1 shaft later became the main hauling shaft with number 2 being used as an air shaft, following the use of the mine for water extraction purposes - providing drinking water for the town of Horwich (there is a separate article on this subject elsewhere in this publication). Number 1 shaft is 381.25 in depth and number 2 is 429.02 feet

Few photographs exist of the mine but those I have managed to find are produced on this and the next few pages. The first photo shows the number 1 shaft behind the houses. The air or vent shaft is off the photo just to the right of the right hand chimney on the white cottage. The man is believed to be Mr Reg Brownlow.

Number 1 shaft taken around 1960

The number 1 shaft, photo taken around 1966.

The number 1 winding engine at Montcliffe.

So what's it like today underground?

The bulk of the Montcliffe workings were accessible only via the now filled in shafts and so there is no access to these parts of the mine. There is however an adit entrance leading to near the base of one of the shafts and a brief exploration of this part of the mine was made by an industrial history mining group some years ago. This section of the Colliery was known as the Margery Mine.

After an initial trip and due to the dangerous state of parts of the workings, only one further visit has been made (up till March 2005). This perhaps a shame as it would have been useful had maps been drawn of the tunnels purely for historical purposes. The tunnels explored do not appear on the main Montcliffe Colliery map I have in my possession.

The workings are entered via a long adit which is around 3 foot 6 inches in height. Movement is extremely uncomfortable due not only to the low height but also to the pipe which occupies part of the floor space and a sort of crouching crab like shuffle is the only way to progress. The adit is perhaps several hundred yards long (it was not measured - but it felt like several hundred yards from my recollections). The tunnel is cut through gritstone. A rockfall is

encountered which almost blocks the passage but can be negotiated by a crawl underneath some "hanging death" types of rock.

Once through the rockfall, the coal measures are encountered along with an entrance to one of the main shafts (now fully filled in). I have no recollection of seeing any fire clay either above or below the coal seam at this point and the coal lies directly beneath the sandstone bedding plane. The coal seam is around 3 foot in thickness.

The condition of the passages within the coal seam are generally good, although in some areas the sandstone has shaled off the roof.

Photo showing a miners helmet left underground after the mine closed. The helmet and other items spotted underground have all been left as they were found.

There are a lot of unknowns about this part of Montcliffe Mine. Why was it called Margery Mine? Why does very little coal seem to have been extracted? Why is there a tunnel which just doubles back on itself? All very odd.

I will admit that although I've only been in this mine once, I wasn't too keen on it at all and I left whilst others in the party explored further!

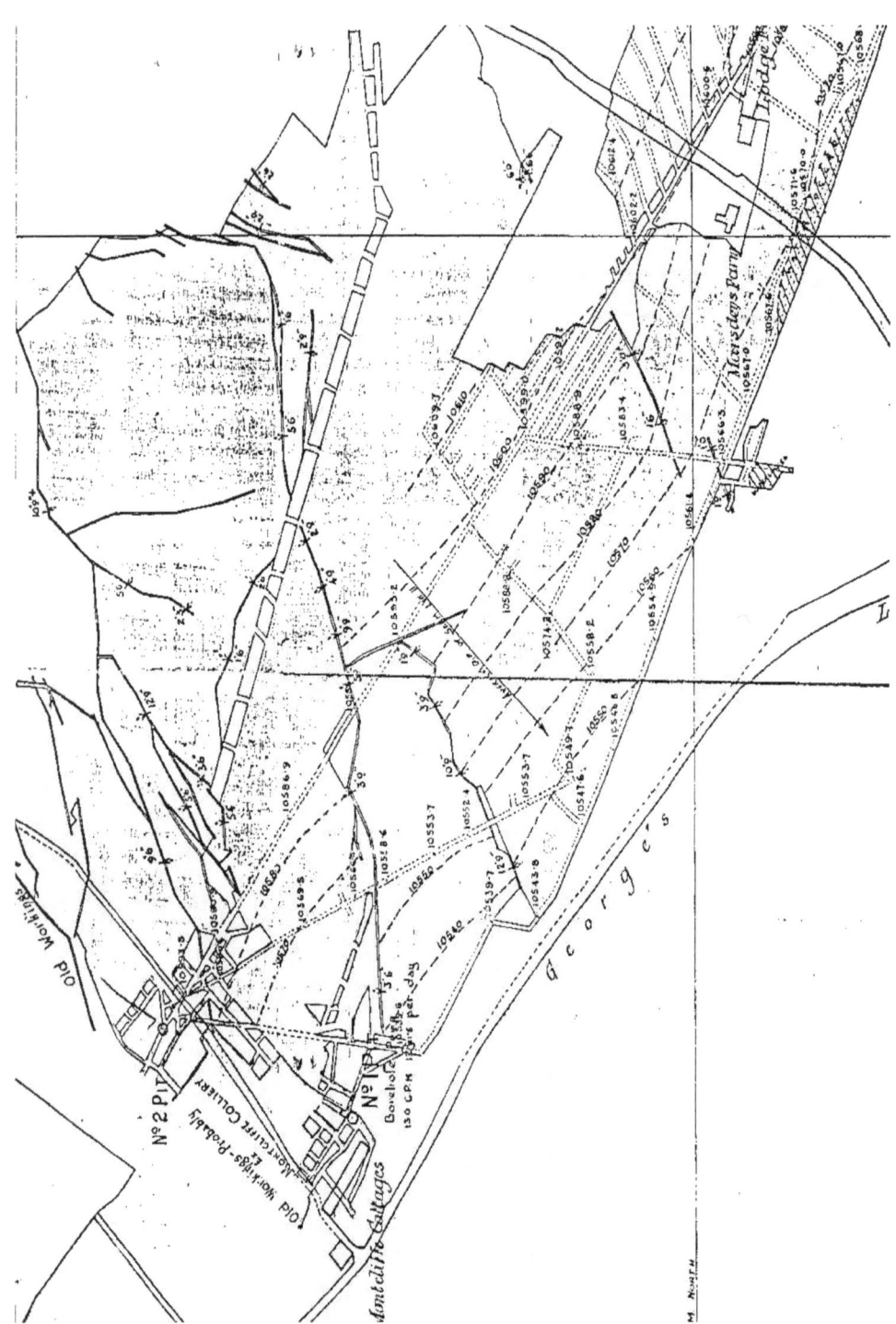

Copy of mine abandonment plan for Montcliffe Colliery dated 1968

3. The Wilderswood & Wildersmoor Collieries.

These mines cover a vast area with a very complex tunnel system in which it would be very easy to get lost. The mines operated on two levels, each working a different seam of coal. The seams are the Little Mine and the Great Mine, with Little Mine being some 25 feet above the Great Mine.

The Wilderswood Drift Mine was privately owned and extracted both coal and fireclay via it's main drift entrance in the fields just below Sportsmans Cottage (later known as Pike Cottage) on George's Lane. The mine ceased operation in 1961 and the drift entrance is now securely blocked.

The main drift entrance, now filled in.

The main rock of the area is sandstone/gritstone and the Little Mine coal seam is only around 10 inches thick but it is underlain with several feet of fireclay which was also extracted for use in Horwich. The average extraction of material was about 5 feet and the lower levels of fireclay was often left in situ as can be seen in the next photograph.

There were a number of entrances into Little Mine along with some underground links into Great Mine. The entrances were a mixture of adits and shafts but as the coal seams lay only just underneath the surface the shafts were only shallow. All the shafts and adits have been filled in and sealed.

The photo's in this article were obtained only when collapses occurred underground and new temporary entrances appeared on the surface (often widened and shored by the explorers!). It must be stressed that during recent explorations in this mine NO sealed original entrances have been breached whatsoever and entrance has only been gained through new holes appearing on the surface.

There is of course great controversy about the exploration of these mines. The "authorities" do not like people who explore old coal mines and they – quite rightly – have to consider public safety especially in this age of endless compensation claims! Unfortunately in their zeal for public safety, the authorities seem determined to wipe out all evidence and all practical signs of the areas mining history. Indeed in over the years they have spent tens of thousands of pounds obliterating all signs of mining activity on the top of Winter Hill. Fenced shafts (totally blocked already!) have been bulldozed. Any signs of mining activities have been filled in as quickly as possible. So far as I am aware, no historical records (ie photographs, measurements etc) are being made of the sites prior to their total destruction. Most of this clearance work was undertaken in the late 1970's and early 1980's. Similar clearance work was carried out across the Darwen Moors as part of the same initiative.

Unfortunately – or fortunately – people other than the "authorities" think differently. They want to know more. They want to know the history of a place. They want to explore that history for themselves. Whilst wishing to abide by the law, they are at the same time, torn by the wish to learn more about the history and they want to explore further. This is not a new phenomenon as the photo below illustrates!

Photo taken in the late 1970's prior to an underground exploration of a small tunnel entrance into the Little Mine located in the valley below Two Lads. This had opened up following a period of heavy rain which to a gallery collapse. In the years after this this the entrance self-sealed following more collapses. No evidence can now be seen of this tunnel.

Whatever the rights or wrongs of the explorations of the tunnels of Winter Hill, I am grateful to those explorers who have let me have copies of their underground photo's so that we can all share in the history of Winter Hill.

Over the years (late 1990's), two further entrances to the Wilderswood and Wildersmoor complex have been discovered and explored.

One entrance was on the lower slopes of Winter Hill and one was near the top of the hill. The upper entrance (SD 65633 13842) was first spotted on a cold and frosty day when a walker saw steam coming from a small hole in the ground.

The steam was obviously warm air coming out of the mine and condensing on contact with the cold air outside. The "team" were alerted, and the small hole was enlarged until easy entrance to the mine tunnel beneath could be effected.

A metal lid was used to cover the hole and grass was placed on top. On a later date, the shaft was lined with wood for safety purposes, and a ladder installed, making it easy to enter the tunnels that lay about 8 feet below the surface.

The tunnels radiating from this entrance were explored over the next 12 months but only on a very intermittent basis due to the proximity of public footpaths and roads.

Eventually the entrance was discovered by the "authorities" – probably because most of the grass covering the entrance had died and on at least one occasion I found the entrance lid partially off.

Due to the presence of bats in the tunnels the entrance was sealed with a concrete surround, topped with an iron grill to enable the bats to enter and exit.

Within months, the grills were sawn through by unknown parties and the authorities had no option other than to fill in and completely seal the entrance.

There is now no sign of the entrance – nor of the nearby shakehole which some naughty people might have decided to excavate once the main entrance had been sealed! Both have now been totally filled and sealed.

Adjacent to this part of the tunnel system was an area where the coal was extracted in 1960/1 by opencast to recover the pillars of coal left by the earlier mining operations.

The tunnel entrances in between the pillars were sealed with large timbers and the entrances collapsed and filled with earth and stone. At times in the past, these entrances have been semi-exposed with the whole area finally being sealed and covered in the mid 1980's.

The entrance lower down the hill is "intact" but the mine is inspected and visited only about twice a year to protect the location and any further comments from me would be inappropriate! A few more underground photo's are illustrated below.

Exploring a timbered roadway in the vicinity of Sportsman's Cottage. The photo above shows a portion of the mine very near to Two Lads.

Roof collapses are evident and have occurred in relatively recent times.

An amazing find! The main winding wheel for hauling tubs up the incline from the drift entrance - still intact.

A brick lined section in the lower Wilderswood section ...... and yes ...before you ask ... that is the person you think it is on the right hand side of the photo ... Fred Dibnah is hard to recognise without his flat cap!

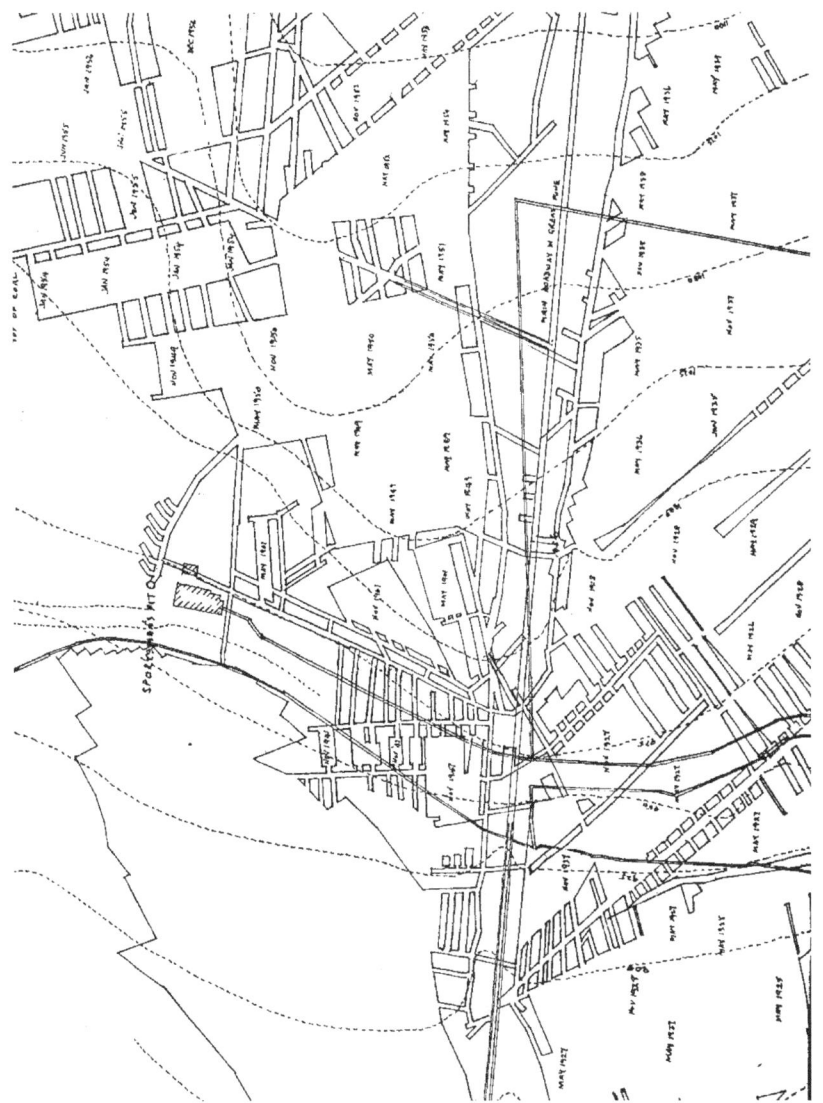

Part of the abandonment plans of a small portion of the mine. This shows the area to the north and south of Sportsman's cottage. The walls alongside George's Lane are indicated by the darker double lines. The straight tunnel passing through the centre of the map is the main haulage way leading from the drift entrance to the south of the cottage. This tunnel goes right up the hill and ends a few hundred yards south of the TV mast on the summit. The tunnel may in fact be linked to the Winter Hill Tunnel on the other side of the hill but no maps seem to exist of this area and so far, no underground links have been found.

MIDDLE WHEEL AND SMITHY

P. MOSS, R. ADAMSON & B. ARMSTRONG INSIDE THE MINE

4. Mountain Mine. Winter Hill.

The mine was operated by Messrs J Crankshaw & Co Ltd and opened in 1860, closing in October 1908. The mine was part of "Wildersmoor Colliery" but may have been a separate enterprise from what we **now** refer to as "Wildersmoor Colliery".

Mountain Mine was located mainly to the east side of the road leading to the TV masts on Winter Hill, although considerable workings also extended to the other side of the mast road. The earliest major mining enterprise on Winter Hill apart from small bell pits, outcrop workings and the small coal extraction mines would appear - according to old mining maps of the area - to be those workings entered via the **Winter Hill Tunnel** on the Belmont side of Winter Hill just beyond the masts. It is difficult to determine exactly where the Winter Hill Tunnel "mine" and Mountain Mine started and ended for plans of both mines show common areas of coal extraction. The earliest **recorded** date of coal extraction that I have so far found in the whole complex is 1833.

The total Wildersmoor complex included at least seven major adits or drifts, plus at least nine main shafts and various other air shafts, "pits" and many other smaller entrances (mainly adits) all linking into the system. Many of the coal and clay seams were worked to the surface outcrops. There are no known **open** entrances to the mine. The water authorities seem to have "commandeered" one drift entrance for water extraction purposes. The "Dip" (or angle of gradient) of the workings is 1 in 12 towards the south.

The surface of the moor in this area indicates a massive amount of coal working with bell pits, collapsed tunnels, possible mine entrances, mounds of excavated material etc all over the place. All entrances are completely filled in and sealed (and all have been examined from the surface). From time to time a collapse occurs underground leaving a hole on the surface, but the "authorities" soon fill these in, sometimes within days of them appearing.

I have been unable to locate any early photographs of the Mountain Mine either on the surface or underground. If anyone can help you can contact me at **dave@daveweb.co.uk**

Looking at all the plans of this area it would be safe to say that this whole portion of Winter Hill is hollow and massive amounts of coal and fire clay have been removed over a period of more than 150 years. Most walkers on Winter Hill have no idea of what is under their feet or the hard toil that was carried out in the Winter Hill mining enterprises.

On most Ordnance Survey maps - even the very latest edition of the Explorer West Pennine Moor chart - the Winter Hill Tunnel (SD 66329 14676) is marked just to the north west of the TV mast on the left hand side of the footpath running down to Belmont Road. All through my life I have wondered where this tunnel went to, but have never ever managed to find anyone who knew any details about it. The location of it is easy to spot and there were obviously two entrances next to each other. There is also a fairly obvious track leading from the mine to the present footpath so it is safe to assume that coal extracted from this entrance was taken down to Belmont rather than being hauled across to moor to Horwich.

Due to the recent discovery of an old mining map (or to be more honest a dawning realisation of the location of coal mines on a map I'd had for years) I can now tell all those folk who have long wondered about the Winter Hill Tunnel exactly where it goes. The tunnel is fairly straight and runs in a southerly direction for a distance of 300 yards passing through areas of coal which were removed by "William Garbutt and William Ailam Mason" probably around the 1850's. The end of this straight tunnel lies approximately directly opposite the main entrance to the TV station underneath the suspension cables. At the end of the tunnel is a maze of old workings with another major roadway heading southwards towards the Number 7 and 8 shafts which were about 700 yards from the Winter Hill Tunnel entrance near to the road up the hill to the TV mast. The number 7 & 8 shafts appear on both the Mountain Mine plan and that of the Winter Hill Tunnel.

If you walk down the footpath about 100 yards lies the remains of the "New Tunnel" entrance to the coal workings on the right hand side of the path. The location can be easily spotted due to the spoil heaps – and the millstone grit sidewall of the entrance can be easily found. Judging from the state of the surface above the line of the tunnel heading up the hill, it is safe to assume that that it has all collapsed since the mine was closed.

The ground surrounding the Winter Hill Tunnel entrances also shows signs of extensive underground collapses near to the entrance. I do not have any underground maps of this mine

++

Heather matters: *redressing the balance*

Clive Weake & Ian Harper

The West Pennine Moors, which cover ninety square miles of moorlands, valleys, farmland and reservoirs in south Lancashire, have seen a 50% loss in heather cover, mostly between 1963 and 1988. Clive Weake and Ian Harper describe the projects taking place to redress the balance.

The attraction of the landscape and all that it holds has made the moors a traditional recreational venue for many generations of local people from the surrounding towns of Bury and Bolton in the south and Accrington, Blackburn, Chorley and Preston to the north and west.

As this pressure has increased, management of the area has been co-ordinated through the West Pennine Moors Recreation and Conservation Plan. The work of the plan is taken forward by Lancashire County Council with support and funding from North West Water, Bury and Bolton Metropolitan Borough Councils and the Countryside Commission.

The management takes many forms including the provision of recreational facilities, access, information and interpretation, working with local communities, and also conserving wildlife and landscape. West Pennines has large open expanses of moorland, nearly all of which is used for rough grazing. Up to the late 1950s and early 1960s much of the moorland had a good cover of heather and bilberry, but since the disappearance of the gamekeepers who were employed by the previous Liverpool and Bolton Water Corporations, the moors have suffered from grazing and large uncontrolled fires. As a result, much of the moorland is now dominated by *Molinia*.

A recent survey commissioned by the West Pennine Moors Conservation Advisory Committee used three sets of aerial photographs dated 1946, 1963 and 1988 to chart the rate of decline of heather cover.

Figures showing the amount lost and the rate of decline were most disturbing, revealing a 50% loss in heather cover mostly between 1963 and 1988.

The Countryside Rangers have now started the daunting task of redressing the balance. The first project converted 4 ha of rough grazing on Anglezarke Moor just north of Belmont Village and part of Manor House Farm.

The second project will take in 15 ha of rough grazing at Higher Pasture House Farm to the east of Belmont, using funding from the Countryside Stewardship Scheme.
The following procedure was used on the 4 ha project following advice from John Phillips of the Joseph Nickerson Reconciliation Trust, whose staff have pioneered this work in Scotland:

March 1991. The previous winter's build-up of dead grass was burnt off. At the same time strips were burnt into existing heather stands on the north west slopes of Anglezarke Moor, to prepare for heather seed collection.

August 1991. The area was left until the resulting fresh growth of grass was flowering. Roundup herbicide was then applied to kill off the grass.

September 1991. The grass had completely died back, six weeks after the application. The area was then burnt again to get rid of the dead material.

November 1991. The remaining tussocks and top two inches of peat/soil were rotavated.

December 1991. The area was fenced out from the rest of the moor to protect the plot from sheep grazing.
The seed trash collected from Anglezarke Moor using a vacuum technique was applied. These seeds germinated and appeared as seedlings in July 1992. These are now very healthy plants.

February 1992. Some of the area was covered with trash from heather bales donated by the North York Moors National Park. Germination has taken longer but there is now a high density of young seedlings.

May 1992. More seed trash was collected from the burnt strips and put down in July 1992. These have now germinated and the young seedlings are easily seen. The remaining areas of the plot were seeded in April and July 1993 and should germinate in 1994.

Heather seed

Seed has been collected from the Moores Estate adjacent to Wycoller Country Park using a vacuum technique, and seed collected from North West Water's Longdendale Estate in the Peak District, using a harvester made available by the Joseph Nickerson Reconciliation Trust.

The heather seed trash was applied at a rate of 10 grams/square metre, i.e. less than a handful. We have estimated that there are approximately 320 seeds/10 grams and it is expected that 65% will germinate.

Now that seeds have germinated successfully, future trash will be mixed with sawdust in order to spread it further. Up until now the seed has been broadcast by hand. On the larger scheme it is intended to use mechanical seedling with a standard tractor-mounted spreader.

Herbicide

Roundup was applied at a rate of 6 litres/ha. A high concentration is required to kill off the *Molinia*. This herbicide has been approved as safe to use in catchment areas by North West Water.

Regrowth

Disturbance of the peat by rotavating has resulted in a fresh growth of rushes and rose-bay willow-herb.

The rushes have been spot treated with Roundup, while the willow-herb has been hand pulled. The grasses are now beginning to grow back. This does not present a problem as the heather seedlings are now established and should be able to compete.

Grazing

It is hoped that light summer grazing will be introduced in 1995 or 1996 to keep grasses down and encourage the heather to till out. The fence is unlikely to be removed as the plot will offer good grazing on the edge of a large unproductive moorland, so the sheep would over-concentrate on it.

Future work

The present plot is a very small proportion of Anglezarke Moor (0.3%). We would like to continue and extend the work but this is dependent on the farmer agreeing to give up more land. Constraints will be long fence lines and finding sufficient heather seed.

One option would be to restore large areas without fencing thus reducing the impact of grazing damage. The scheme is intended to start the ball rolling and encourage others to take on the initiative or at least become more involved.

Monitoring

Monitoring of progress on the first plot will start this November using quadrats and fixed point photography. We are discussing a system for monitoring both the extension of the work on to the wider area of moorland and the effect of changing sheep grazing regimes.

This will involve Lancashire County Council Planning Department. It is quite possible that changes in grazing will have positive effects and lead to overall improvement in heather cover.

Problems

The biggest difficulty with the project has been establishing a reliable source of heather seed, which is not commercially available at a realistic price:
- It is not possible to keep collecting from Anglezarke Moor as there are few heather stands suitable for strip burning.
- The heather bales from North Yorks Moors National Park were of great value, but this is not a realistic source for the much

bigger schemes we are now working on, for which a larger number of bales would have to be transported.
- The seed from the Moores Estate, Wycoller, was collected by contractor using a vacuum technique. We will continue to pursue this as a supply, but there are constraints of time and weather.
- The seed from Longdendale is a good source and we are currently looking into the possibilities of ensuring a regular supply of large quantities of seed.

Where we go from here on the large scale is a complex issue involving the tenant farmer, the landowner North West Water and possible shooting interests. To carry out large scale works would require a major cash input which means that the farmer and landowner would be looking for a return. The conservation budgets available through West Pennines are limited and intended to prime projects.

Clive Weake was Head Countryside Ranger, West Pennine Moors. Ian Harper was Access Area Countryside Ranger, West Pennine Moors.

The Whimberry Hill Area.

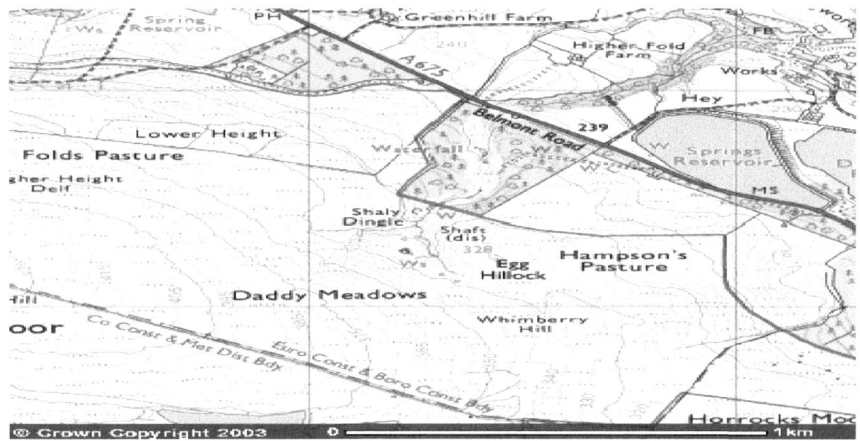

This is an area of Winter Hill which is much ignored by most people and on many days it is possible to walk all over the moorland from Scout Road to Belmont, without even **seeing** a living soul let alone meeting one - even in summer.

Although superficially it appears totally bleak and desolate with nothing of any real interest, for the searcher, there is much to be seen and many mysteries to be explained.

Perhaps one of the reasons for the lack of visitors, is the fact that there is no really easy access point to the area despite the main Belmont Road passing nearby. The nearest access points are from the Wilton Quarry area or from the San Marino Restaurant (Formerly the Wrights Arms Public House) Belmont Road.

On the Ordnance Survey maps, no footpaths are shown in this area except for the Wilton Arms to the TV mast footpath – but footpaths DO exist -although in places they get a bit "thin" and indistinct. Off the paths the going can be a little rough as much is that awful "hillock" grass which is just perfect for twisting ankles - and in summer some parts are covered in bracken.

There are patches of heather all over the place. The one form of vegetation which does NOT exist on or near Whimberry Hill, is whimberries! This is perhaps indicative of how, over a period of time, the whole character of an area can change. There is just no way that a hill can be named Whimberry Hill if they didn't actually grow there in earlier centuries.

The area is bordered by Scout Road to the East, Belmont Road to the North, Dean Ditch to the South and the Wright Arms footpath to the West.

The area contains numerous quarries, a large number of wells, some peculiar underground watercourses, geologically interesting small valleys, an old coal mine, a wood (private property with no access) which is full of pheasants/grouse and much more of interest.

We'll start with the quarries. By far the biggest ones are Horrocks Fold Quarries on either side of Scout Road (more commonly known as the Wilton Quarries., numbered 1,2,3 & 4) but on the moorland there are many others to be seen …. Spakes Delph, Martha Tree Dell, Sandstone Delph, and Higher Height Delph, Coal Road Delfs ……..all are – or were, the main ones. All produced sandstone/millstone grit. There is no evidence of any form of drilling in the early quarries so the rocks were probably removed with wedges and other implements.

To the Western side of the spur forming Whimberry Hill is a small valley which contains some rather odd things connected with water. Firstly there is a "well or shaft" …. Pictured below. This is near the termination of the northern end of one of the great ditches running from the top of Winter Hill.

On the 1849 Ordnance Survey maps it is marked as a shaft. The shaft is only a few feet deep and is filled with rubble.

Right next to this, is an underground watercourse, a tunnel about 2 feet in height with stone walls and stone slabs forming the roof with soil and vegetation on top.

Parts of this tunnel have collapsed and the structure can be clearly seen.

The culvert was obviously dug out and roofed ….. but for what reason?

The place forms a natural valley anyway and a stream would have flowed down it quite naturally.

Why was it covered? More to the point, where does it start and finish?

Is there a connection between the shaft and the watercourse for the two are right next to each other.

At various places along the course of the tunnel, the roof has collapsed but I have still not been able to trace either its exact course or it's start and finish point. Perhaps others may be luckier!

On the Ordnance Survey map of 1849 the wells and tunnels are shown, but again there is no hint to the exact purpose of them.

On the map, the course of the tunnel (or rather tunnels as there are apparently two of them although I've only managed to find one) is

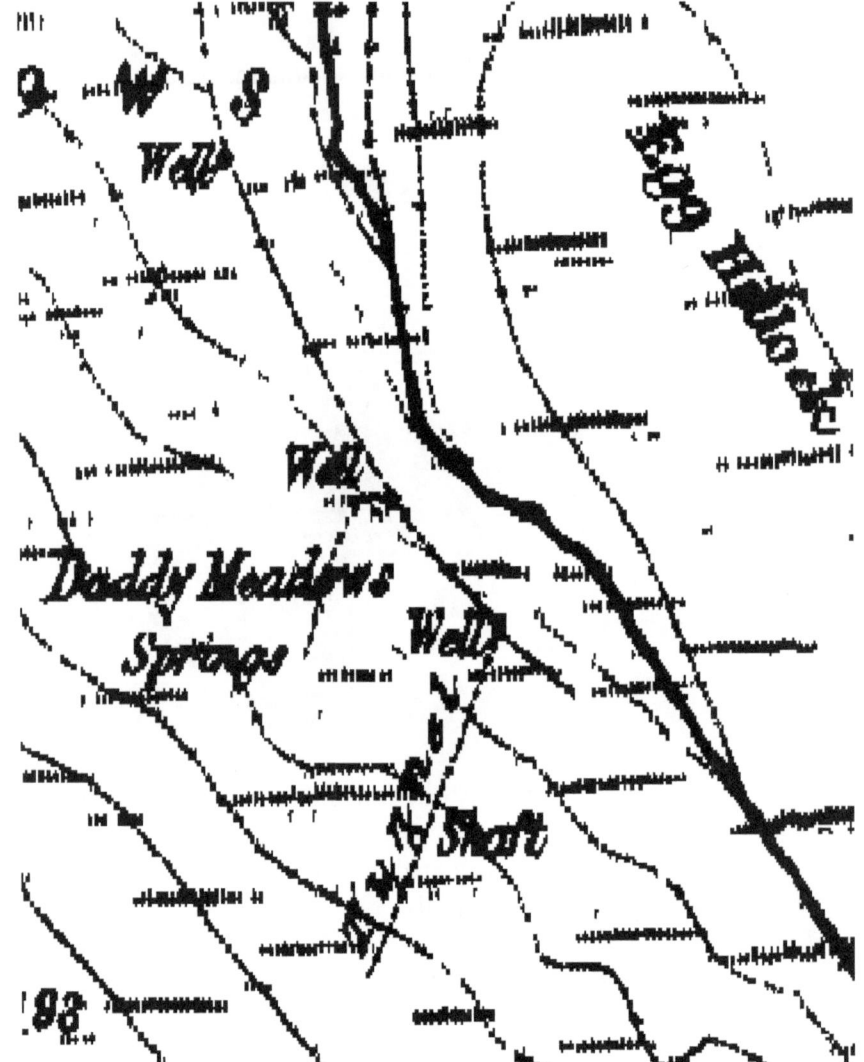

shown with the word "Well" at the "entrance" of it. All rather odd!

Moving Westwards we come to Shaly Dingle, an apt name for the place as various streams in the locality have cut through the surface boulder clay down to the bed rock exposing layers of shale on the sides. The beds of many of the streams are covered with pieces of this shale (some contain fossils).

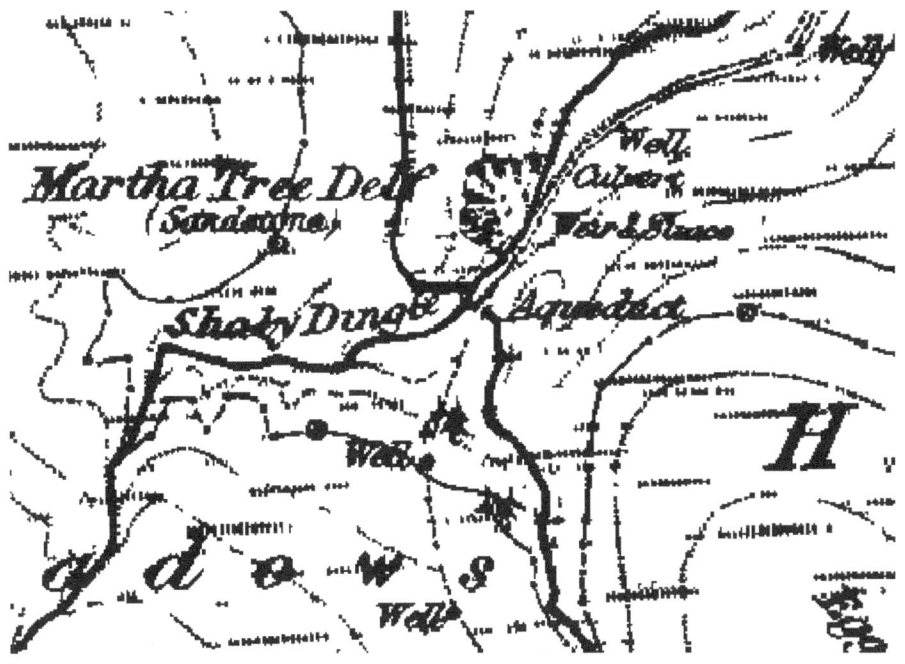

On the modern day maps there is little marked on the chart but on earlier maps.

Shaly Dingle lies at the confluence of three streams, the water being channelled into Springs Reservoir which lies on the other side of Belmont Road. In this small area, there are wells, an old coal mine and a quarry.

The coal mine can be seen in the south eastern tributary on the western bank, and it appears to be a standard NCB concrete capped shaft complete with the odd tapering square block on top. I can find no record of any details of this mine. Centuries ago people must have been aware of the coal in the area as the odd coal seam can be clearly seen in the banks of some streams nearby – complete with coniferous fossils.

On the hill in between the south eastern and south western tributaries lie a number of walled shafts. On old maps four of these are marked as "wells".

They all lie fairly near to springs where the water comes out of the ground. At present I can find no information about these wells or their purpose ….. were they for nearby homes, or perhaps for the local mine or were they connected in some way with the nearby reservoirs?

The wells are all fairly shallow, a deeper one is covered with a wire grill and all are filled with stone rubble, some have a small amount of water at the bottom and most are beautifully decorated in moss and ferns. Well worth a look!

In summer the grass and bracken surrounding them will be much

higher and it may be difficult to find some of them at that season.

Each of the tributaries are worth investigation if only for the geology visible in some of them. The northern heading tributary is perhaps the most interesting. The stream has cut through the boulder clay and near the surface it contains a large number of rounded stones formed by glacial action many years ago. Lower down, the stream has cut through the gritstone rock which is greatly faulted and the current bed of the stream is formed of the carboniferous period shales. Several coal

seams are visible in the sides of the stream along with the associated fireclays. Leaf and tree fossils can be found near the coal seams.

At one point I found in the bed of the stream, a block of sandstone clearly showing the ripple marks caused by the tides when this rock was sand lying on the bottom of a shallow sea. The rock showed various layers of ripples as each successive tide put down another layer of sand and then rippled that new layer as well. All this happened "on Winter Hill". Amazing!

Also visible in the walls and beds of the streams are small rocks whose composition clearly illustrates the moving power of early glacial action in the area.

Some lumps of granite were probably carried southwards from Cumbria or Scotland along with quartzite rocks from who knows where. Go take a look!

There is a fairly large and active spring in the eastern bank of the main stream (the middle one!) but all over the place are bits of fairly modern clay piping indicating that that perhaps in Victorian times attempts were made to "pipe" this water to some other place. Anyone got any ideas or information about this?

Just below the confluence of the three tributaries is an interesting display of brickwork. At one point, the pathway crosses over the south eastern stream with a brick embankment, the stream passing underneath through an attractive arched hole.

On old maps this is marked as "aqueduct" so one assumes pipes or something similar – surely not an open waterway – passed over this structure.

Lower downstream is a large brick embankment on the eastern side of the stream marked on the map as "weir and sluice" although I see no signs today of any weir or sluice!

On the opposite bank is the Martha Tree Delph Sandstone Quarry along with a rusted piece of rail, presumably used for tubbing the stone out of the quarry.

A pipe with flowing water sticks out into the stream from underneath the quarry but there is no clue as to where this water originates. Perhaps the quarry was considerably deeper than it is today (it was in

use in the early 1800's and perhaps even earlier) and the water is coming from the original floor of the quarry.

Downstream, the stream enters the private plantation of conifers but over the fence yet another well can be seen by the side of the track.

This woodland is one of the beauty spots of the whole area, and it is a great pity that it is closed to the public. In the middle of the wood is a magnificent waterfall in a majestic setting especially when the stream

is in full flow following heavy rain. Within the woodland there is an old tunnel that has been explored for a distance of about 150 feet - but it is almost completely silted up at that point and further progress is impossible. It is not known whether the tunnel was dug for coal or water purposes – there is however no sign of coal and as the tunnel heads in the general direction of further wells, it is assumed that the tunnel was at one time connected to the water supplies of the area.

The foundations of the TV mast.

(*This article appeared in "The Structural Engineer" January 1966 No 1 Vol 44*)

The anchor blocks are constructed of mass concrete to resist the uplift component from the stays and are normally designed with a safety factor of two. The blocks are also checked for passive pressure on the front face to resist horizontal movement. The mast base of a conventional pinned structure is designed to support the direct thrust and the shear.

The base for each of the 1265 ft masts consisted of a large reinforced concrete raft to carry the six columns of the superstructure. These rafts were 35 ft square and 5 ft 6 in thick. However, due to the presence of old mine workings under Winter Hill, an extensive soil investigation was necessary. A search through the records of the National Coal Board showed that these mines had been worked between 1861 and 1881 but the extent and size was not at all clear from the available maps.

One borehole was taken at the mast base to a depth of 120 ft and one at each of the outer anchor block positions down to 50 ft. Seismic soundings were also taken but owing to a heavy overlay of peat these were not considered reliable.

The boreholes showed the workings to occur between 44 and 47 feet below the ground. Although it was difficult to predict the degree of settlement, it was likely that differential movement would occur and this could not be tolerated with a fixed base design. In the circumstances it was decided to sink four 6 ft 6 in diameter shafts, one in each corner of the 28 ft square base.

The shafts were lined with precast tunnel sections for their full depth, the sections being added to the bottom as the work progressed. When nearing the mine workings special precautions had to be taken in case either gas or water was encountered with the breakthrough. Fortunately, however, neither was encountered.

When all four shafts had been sunk, the workings in the immediate vicinity of the mast base were compacted with a mixture of sand and weak concrete. The columns were constructed so they were free standing within the shafts to allow for a limited horizontal movement of the ground. The columns were founded about 5 ft below the workings on good quality rock (see diagram).

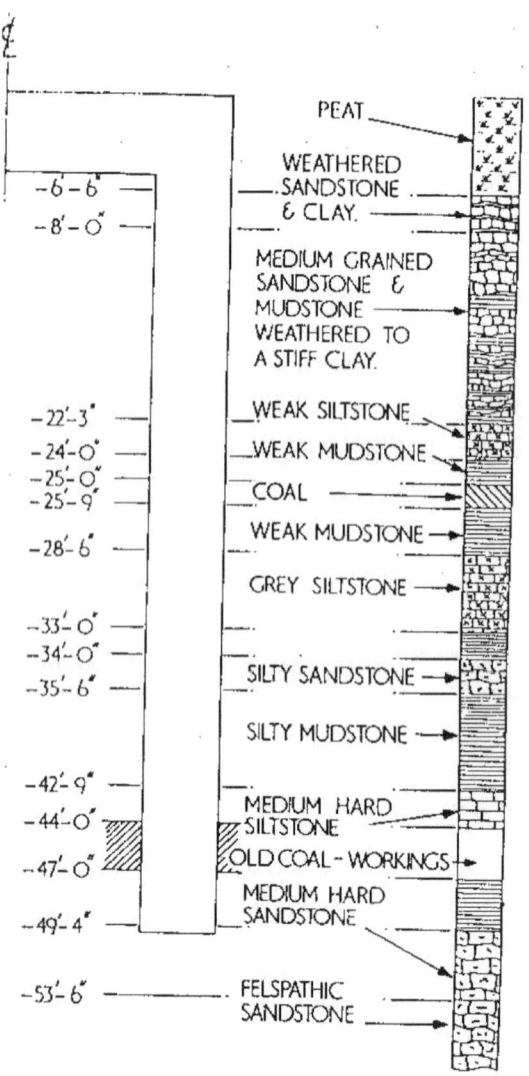

The anchor blocks were basically of traditional design, except that to provide the necessary passive resistance the fronts of the blocks were were extended down into the solid ground below the peat. This resulted in a variation in block design depending on the depth of peat at each location. At one or two positions small streams ran a few feet in front of the blocks and it was necessary to divert these as an additional precaution.

Earthing of masts is not normally a difficult problem. The structure is earthed at its base by means of aluminium or copper tape connected to earth plates or rods sunk into the ground. The stays are also earthed in a similar manner

TV Mast Construction Photo's
(Thanks to Bill Learmouth for the photo's)

WINTER HILL TV COVERAGE AREA. (Analogue TV only)

BBC 1 (North West)	ch 55
BBC 2	ch 62
ITV	ch 59
Channel 4	ch 65
Power (Max erp, vision)	100 kW
Polarisation	horizontal
Receiving aerial group	C/D
Mean ht. of aerial	294m agl, 732m aod
Transmitter site	near Horwich, Gtr. Manchester
National Grid Reference	SD 660144

Key: Service area
     Relay station ▲

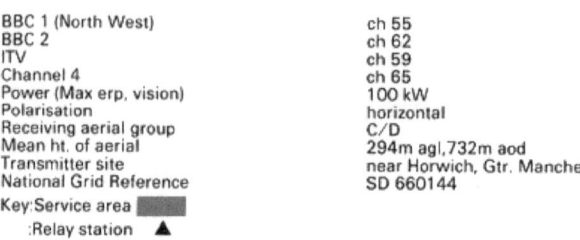

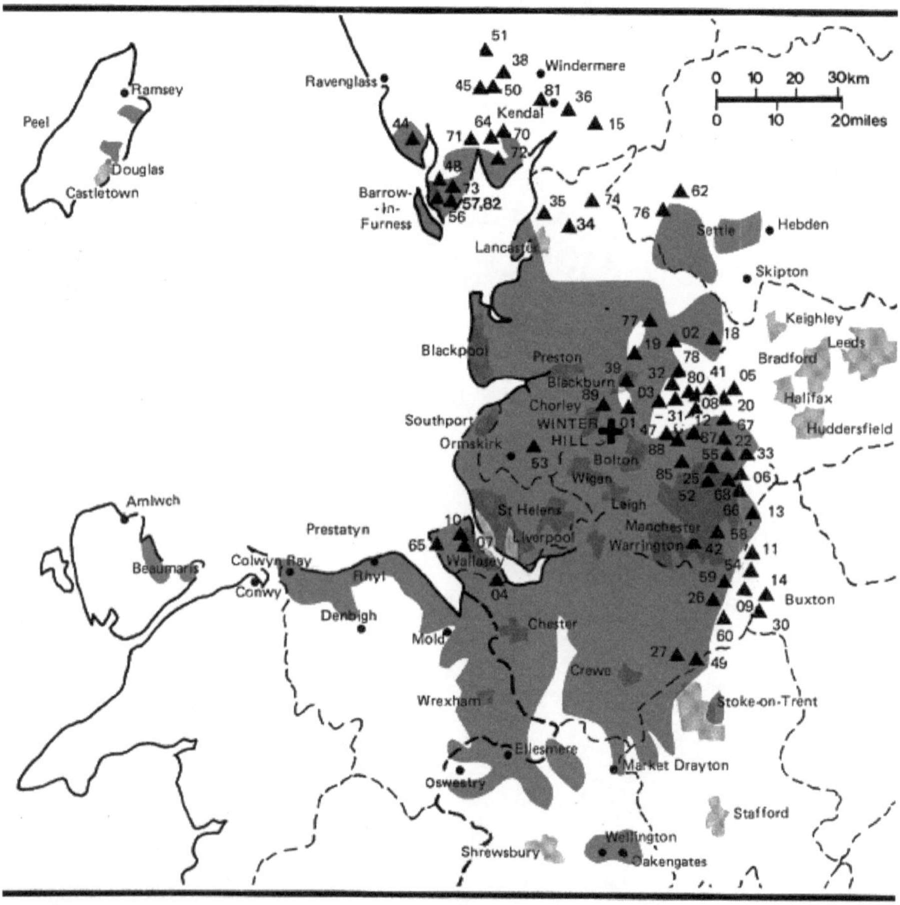

The service area is indicated by the coloured part of the map, but the boundary should not be interpreted as a rigid limit. As the quality of television reception can be very different at places only short distances apart, there are, inevitably, small pockets of poor reception which cannot be shown.
Details of relay stations are shown overleaf in numerical order.

The Making of the Mast ..... by William Kay of Adlington ...... *by William Kay*

The television station on Winter Hill in Lancashire was built for the Independent Television Authority, (later the Independent Broadcasting Authority), which had been set up by Parliament to broadcast and control the Commercial TV services then coming into being

The Winter Hill station was built during 1956 and '57 and broadcasting of Granada programmes commenced in Sept 1957, the transmitting aerials for the service being mounted at the top of a 450ft steel tower which resembled a large electricity pylon. The services at that time were in the 405 line VHS system, but with the proposed introduction of 625 line UHF system and a requirement that BBC1 & 2 should also transmit from Winter Hill, it became obvious that the 450 ft tower would be inadequate for the job. The ITA therefore decided to erect a new mast and to this end commissioned a 1000 ft one of novel design from British Insulated Callender Construction (BICC).

This mast was to be of cylindrical construction and to be held up by stay lines (thick guy wires). Work commenced on the new structure in 1964 with the digging of an enormous hole for the foundations, which were to consist of a large concrete raft with four corner legs, rather like a table. Interestingly, three of the four shafts, dug to accommodate these legs unexpectedly intercepted old coal mine shafts which had to be backfilled and strengthened before the foundations could be started. In the centre on top of the raft was built a reinforced concrete base to which the tubular mast was to be bolted. This was a break with the convention as guyed masts are usually supported on a single large ball bearing to accommodate all the swaying and twisting movements that occur in these structures.

The tubular mast body was then erected by the process of bolting half cylindrical sections of galvanised steel each 10 ft high and 9 ft diameter to each other, work thus progressing at the rate of 10 ft per 2 lifts of steel. The early lifts were accomplished by the use of a transportable crane. At this stage an ingenious device was brought into play consisting of a long steel tube with a jib crane head fixed to its end. This was mounted vertically inside the mast cylinder and used to lift the sections. As these were added, the jib crane was jacked up and relocated into the next section, and so was always in position for the next lift.

As the mast grew, temporary stay lines were attached to it to steady it until eventually the anchor points for the permanent stays were installed and those final stays fitted. The construction of the mast was completed in 1965. As much of the work took place in the depth of winter, one must admire the courage, fitness and tenacity of the rigging staff who carried out this work in often freeing conditions At this point it should be noted that the mast isn't quite what it seems, in fact the 9 ft steel cylinder only goes to 600 ft after which it changes into a lattice mast for the rest of its height. The transmission aerials for all the TV services are mounted in this section However this section is itself covered by a cylinder of about 11 ft diameter, this being made of fibreglass, which acts as a weather shield whilst allowing the transmission waves to pass through. The overall height of the mast is 1015 ft. For ease of access to aerials a passenger lift going to 600 ft was installed during the original construction.

Two further masts of this type were built, both 1250ft tall at Emley Moor near Huddersfield, and the other one in Lincolnshire, giving ITV and BBC services to those regions.

Then, Horror of Horrors, in March 1969, in the face of severe icing up and adverse weather conditions, the Emley Moor mast collapsed. Anxious eyes, (particularly my own, as I was on duty under the Winter Hill one at that time), were directed to the Winter Hill mast and its remaining sister in Lincolnshire, both of which were heavily iced up. Luckily they survived, but both of them were subjected to intense investigation and to a programme of modification and strengthening over the past ten years. Now it is probably true to say that they are as safe as any mast in Europe.

Over in Yorkshire, where the TV service was restored within four days, using temporary structures, the fallen mast had damaged some property and closed a road The Local District Council were reluctant to allow erection of another permanent mast, but eventually a compromise was reached and the present concrete tower was built to carry the broadcast services The above events make it unlikely that any further cylindrical masts of the Winter Hill type and height will ever be erected. Also, as terrestrial Digital TV and Satellite services progress, the need for these structure will recede. Footnote: When the 1000 ft mast came into operation, the original 450 ft tower at Winter Hill was dismantled and rebuilt in Scotland where it continues to give sterling service.

The Night the Welsh invaded Winter Hill! ..... *by William Kay*

It was 21.05 hours on a typical Winter Hill early March evening (the 4 March 1977 to be exact) when the assault was made. The night was clear and stars were shining, however a thin ground mist wreathed the road and moor land. I was the senior shift engineer on duty that night along with two other shift engineers, Mike Ingram and Peter Dennis.

Peter was manning the control desk, whilst I was in the test room repairing some piece of equipment. By a stroke of good fortune Mike was just heading for the kitchen via the entrance hail when the incident began. He rushed to the test room and informed me that we had intruders on the premises. I immediately followed him to the hall where I saw that the glass panel in the front door had been broken to gain access and I was just in time to see someone going away from me down the corridor leading via the garage to the UHF transmitter hall. I shouted to Peter to contact the Police and then, accompanied by Mike, followed the intruders into the UHF transmitter hall I switched on the lights as I went for the intruders were using torches.

On entering the transmitter hall I saw four people, two young men and two young women in the room. One of the women was operating the HT Isolator and earthing switches of the 'A' transmitter, (almost the quickest way of switching off).

I immediately challenged her but she continued to operate the switches. I went up to the transmitter and switched it back on again. In all there was a break in transmission of about 15 seconds. I subsequently found out the 'B' transmitter had also been switched of by the same method. The intruders made no effort to stop me re-powering the transmitters; they just stood back from me whilst I did it. As I stood there guarding the 'A' transmitter whilst Mike stood by the

'B' I noticed that one of the women was carrying a carpenter's hammer. I was glad I hadn't spotted that before.

When my panic subsided and I was in control of myself and of the situation, I questioned them about their motives They informed me they were members of the Welsh Language Society and that the intended disruption of the Winter Hill transmissions was part of their campaign for a 4th channel for Welsh speaking Wales. Winter Hill had been chosen because Granada programmes beamed from it not only covered NW England but also leaked over into north Wales, and this they objected to. I tried to explain that radio and tv signals are no respecters of geographical or political boundaries, and I tried to point out to them that inhabitants of N. Wales did not have to tune their sets to the Granada channel if they did not wish to receive it. But all this fell on deaf ears.

At about 20.25 hrs the Police arrived, first the Horwich police, then those from Chorley and lastly the PC from Adlington. As the Winter Hill station is actually on the Chorley side of the boundary, and in the Adlington section of the Chorley Police area, then the privilege or pain of arresting the culprits fell to the Adlington PC.

When the prisoners were searched, there was found in the handbag of one of the women, a quantity of 6 inch nails. The idea had been to disrupt the transmission and then to barricade themselves in the transmitter hall by nailing all the doors shut, thus preventing early re-powering of the transmitters. This part of the plan luckily was thwarted by our good luck and Mike's prompt actions. This was of course the reason the woman was carrying the hammer. The Police questioned me closely as to whether at any time they had threatened us with the hammer, but in all truth, I had to say that the group behaved impeccably after being challenged. In fact it seemed a major part of their policy was to get arrested and go to court to extract the maximum publicity for their cause.

As the Police were leaving they asked what would be the cost of replacing the glass door. Just off the top of my head I said '£100'. It was eventually replaced at a cost of £30 but the damages set by the court and paid by the miscreants was the sum of £100, so that night I made a profit of £70 for the IBA. The group pleaded guilty and were sentenced to some months in prison I believe.

The Welsh finally got their 4th channel but when 1 look at the programmes that appear on all channels in general, I often wonder if those four people still think it was worth their sacrifice.

William Kay
Ex ITA/IBA/NTL engineer, Winter Hill.
++

Horwich Water supplies from Montcliffe Colliery.

In the late 1800's, the rapidly expanding town of Horwich was desperately short of water. Despite being surrounded by water catchment areas and reservoirs, the town itself had great difficulty in providing clean water for its inhabitants as all the water supplies in the area were owned by other towns and cities. Things reached crisis point in the 1880's and something had to be done about the water shortage.

The following paper is taken from the memoirs of the Manchester Geological Society of 1891 which explains both the problem and the solution.

Water Supply at Horwich

By Mr Joseph Crankshaw.

A glance at the map of Horwich and district shows the surface of the ground studded over with reservoirs, some of them an extent as to be denominated lakes. On the North, the Belmont watershed is appropriated by the Bolton Corporation Waterworks, a series of bleachworks extending right away down to Bolton. On the East are the large reservoirs of the Halliwell Bleachworks, and Dean Mills. To the South-east the Bolton Corporation have been tunnelling for years in the Millstone Grit, and are now constructing a large reservoir for storage of the water found. On the West the Liverpool Waterworks appropriates the upland waters from Rivington Moor and a large share of Wildersmoor. In the township itself the staple industry, up to quite recently, was bleaching, for which a large quantity of good water is required. In 1876 the Blackrod Local Board obtained power to construct a reservoir which impounds a portion of the surface water from Wildersmoor, and also springs in Wilderswood and underground waters from old coal workings.

It will thus be seen that the district Is one in which there is plenty of water, and the water, whether in streams from the breezy uplands, or in springs which gush forth from the millstone grit, is of good quality.

Up to 1884 there was no town water supply. The place was sparsely populated, and each group of cottages had its spring or well, and although there were dry seasons when the wells and springs dried up, and the inhabitants had to carry water from considerable distances, still they never suffered anything like the same inconveniences from scarcity of water as other districts, or even as the neighbouring townships of Blackrod and Aspull. After the public spirit shown by Blackrod in constructing their large reservoir in Horwich, and appropriating the best available supply, the Horwich Local Board seemed to think that something should be done, and a considerable sum of money was dribbled away, in making half-hearted enquiries into various schemes which were afterwards abandoned, and ultimately an arrangement was made with the Blackrod Local Board for 50,000 gallons of water per day at 6d per 1,000 gallons. In 1885, the Lancashire and Yorkshire Railway Company decided to bring their Locomotive works to Horwich, and the place, after being at a standstill for years at once became a busy scene of activity, building being carried on in all directions, and a largely increased water supply being required. The dry season of 1887 completely exhausted the Blackrod storage, and the Horwich Local Board were informed that they would have to look elsewhere for their requirements for over 50,000 gallons per day. Under the circumstances the Blackrod supply could never be anything but partial, as the level of the reservoir was far too low to supply the higher parts of Horwich.

The Horwich Local Board found that they had allowed the whole of their watershed to be appropriated, and the only water supply available was from the Moncliffe Colliery belonging to Messrs H Mason & Son. Popular prejudice was very much against this water, as it was imagined that because it was pumped at a colliery it must of necessity be contaminated, but this had to some extent been overcome by the dry season, when temporary arrangements were made for pumping the water into the Blackrod reservoir, where it constituted practically the whole water supply.

The Local Board also found that it was a case of Hobson's Choice, one or none, this being the only feasible scheme available, so Messres Frank France and James Atherton, of Bolton, were authorised to inquire into this supply, and the following extract from their report fully explains the scheme, and may be of some interest to the members of this society :-

"In reporting on the question of the obtaining of a water supply for your Board's District from the shaft at Montcliffe, in addition to the 50,000 gallons per day now obtained from the Blackrod Local Board, we think it may be desirable to state, first the conditions under which the water is found, then to remark on its quality, the freedom from pollution or otherwise of its surroundings, and the mode in which it may be made to serve all the populated parts of the district.

Firstly, as to the conditions under which it is found:-

The water is found near to the bottom of a shaft which was sunk many years ago at Montcliffe, in the higher part of Horwich, for the purpose of winning a mine of coal and fireclay. The shaft is 130 yards deep, and is sunk through strata which consists mostly of sandstone and shale, the geological formation being that known as "Millstone Grit". No water appears in the mine on the higher side of the shaft, nor along the level proceeding from the bottom of the shaft, but at the inspection recently made by us we found the water made in some straight roadways which had been driven on the deep of the shaft, and only a short distance away therefrom. In these roadways the water poured in continuous streams from the roof, and as it had passed through beds of sandstone of so great a thickness, it seemed evident that it must be well filtered. In appearance the water was bright and clear, and the floor on which it continually gathered showed that it contained the merest trace of iron. This is not often the case in water associated with coal mines.

On arriving at the water we took a sample for analysis. A second sample was taken near the pump foot, to reach which it was necessary to walk partly through the water necessitating a slight disturbance. A third sample was taken on the surface at a point known as the "Tunnel Mouth" hereafter referred to. The three samples were sealed up on the spot and were afterwards forwarded to Dr Frankland, of London, for analysis, in order to ascertain the fitness of the water for domestic use.

We made a careful inspection underground with a view to ascertain if the water was likely in any way to be fouled by the workings of the colliery.

We found all the coal lying on the easterly side of a 26 yards fault, hereafter referred to, had been won with the exception of pillars left to support the roadway between the pumping and ventilating shafts, and a small area now being worked some 150 yards on the rise of the first-named shaft.

Throughout these workings the strata were entirely dry, and as a consequence not a drop of water finds its way from the parts where the workmen travel to the water which is the subject of this report. The present surroundings of the water may be considered absolutely free from, and liability to, polluting influences. This being so, we made inquiry if it was likely these conditions would remain.

The mine has been worked out to the beforementioned fault, which runs in a direction SW to NE, and at a distance of about 200 yards on the W side of the pumping shaft. And about 170 yards to the west of it, and the coal still remaining to be got under the present lease lies to the north and west of this fault, throwing the mine down 26 yards.

To win this coal (which has not hitherto been worked) the ventilating shaft (which is 170 yards on the west or rise of the pumping shaft) will have to be sunk 26 yards, and the coal raised there, instead of (as at present) at the pumping shaft. In this case this shaft would only be used for pumping. This would be a further guarantee against the possibility of pollution of the water. Whether any water might be found in the new workings, could only be ascertained by proving, and if there was, it would be at a lower level.

The hamlet of Montcliffe can be seen at the top centre of the picture. The water from the mine travelled along a pipe from the pumping shaft, this being located in a tunnel which emerged just to the north of the reservoir. The reservoir is now no longer used and is dry (not surprising as there is a huge gap in one of the retaining walls!)

We found the pumping shaft in very good condition, and the rams and pump stocks which were in the shaft in perfect order. The pumping engine is of a very good make (Messrs Hathorn, Davies and Co, Sun Foundary, Leeds) and of recent construction. To raise all the water made at present requires only 4.5 to 5 strokes per minute, equal to about 140,000 gallons per day of 24 hours, besides which 9,000 gallons are pumped to the surface for the supply of the houses at Montcliffe. This we consider (after the exceptionally long drought of the past summer) may be taken as the minimum yield. In winter the engine is said to run at about 6 strokes per minute, if it was run at 10 strokes 358,000 gallons would be delivered in the 24 hours. The pumps are in duplicate, there being two rams each of 10 inch diameter, and two sets of pump stocks. These are arranged so that either set can be worked in case of accident. The pumping arrangements are very good.

Quality of the water.

The result of Dr Franklands analysis is:- The water is excellent in quality for drinking and all dietic purposes". He states also – "that it contains the merest trace of organic matter" and "is entirely free from any evidence of contamination with sewage or other animal refuse matters".

These analyses prove the water to be of a very superior character for domestic purposes.

++

Winter Hill Summit and Dean Ditch Area.

This area of Winter Hill is a mixture of the ancient and modern, from the remains of bygone times to the technology of the future. The future is represented by the plethora of radio and TV masts which are scattered near the peak and have slowly grown in number over the last few decades.

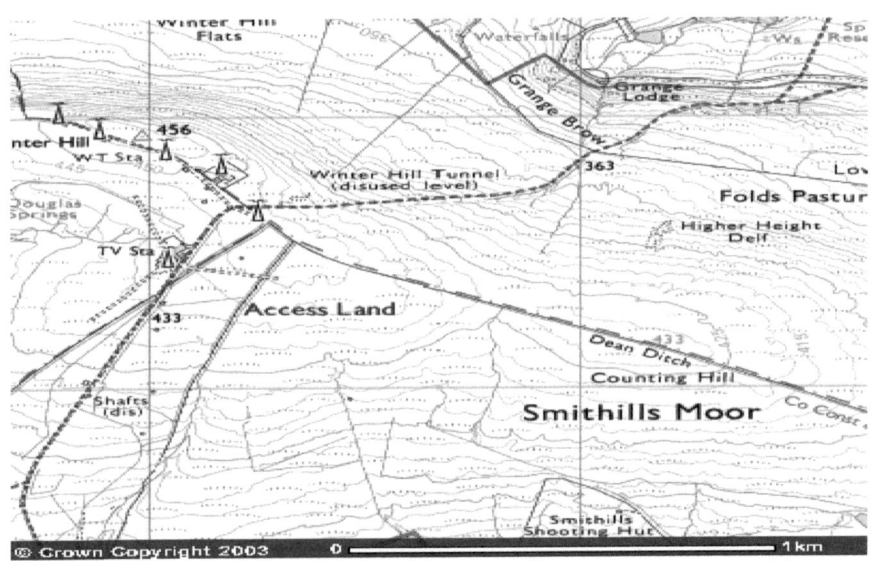

The first masts to be built were three small structures located to the east of the OS survey column that were erected in 1948 initially for Police, Fire and Ambulance communications.

The next mast to be built was the original IBA TV mast which arrived in 1955 but this was soon replaced by the present structure in the

1960's which is over 1,000 feet high (328 metres). The Post Office mast and its base building was built in 1955.

All the mast structures are constantly updated and developed to keep pace with modern communications technology.

The exact figures I have for the height is that it is 1,015 feet 4 in tall and the transmitters have a range of round about 50 miles covering the Manchester and Liverpool conurbation's and within its area it reaches over 7 million people. It's known as an "enclosed cylindrical mast" and it used to have a lift inside it – but now the engineers and riggers have to climb up a vertical ladder – or rig up a cradle to one of the cables on the outside. They have to climb up to maintain the aerials, paint the mast and to ensure that the red aircraft lights are working.

The transmitters do not have to be switched off for routine maintenance as all the systems are doubled up so the mast can continue broadcasting if something fails. If there is a really serious fault it can be run on reduced power until the engineers can sort out the problem. The station is run using only skeleton staff and is remotely controlled from another location.

All the masts at the top of the hill are used for a variety of communications purposes for local services, businesses and organisations.

The TV channels transmitting via the TV mast are BBC1, BBC2, ITV (Granada), Channel 4 and Channel 5 aong with the new Freeview digital channels. Radio channels transmitted from here include Radio's 1, 2, 3 and 4 along with Rock FM, Jazz FM, Century 105 and BBC Radio Lancashire.

In the early days when the current TV mast, it was thought that there may have been a risk to the resident engineers in times of inclement weather (possibly mast collapse). In view of this a building was erected part way down the moorland road where the staff used to be housed at those times. The Portacabin type structure was said to be at a greater distance from the mast than the mast height so in the event of a mast collapse (as in the Emley Mast incident) the staff would be safe. This building has since been removed but the metal fence that used to house it and concrete base remain. The cabin was apparently donated to a local venture Scout operation in the early 1980's.

The mast still presents dangers for the unwary in the winter months, when icicles can form on the support cables which crash to the ground if a sudden thaw occurs. You have been warned!

Their was once warning boards with orange flashing lights to alert walkers of the possibility of falling ice from the cables or mast itself. These were housed on either sides of the mast on the mast road. The boards have now been removed.

The familiar red aircraft warning lights mounted along height of the mast structure following construction were replaced by considerably brighter red lights to meet new legislation around the late 1990's.

Dean Ditch.

From the mast heading eastwards towards Horrocks Moor and Scout Road is the seemingly endless drystone wall which was built to mark the municipal boundaries. On modern maps this is marked as the County Constitutional and Metropolitan District/European Constitutional and Borough boundary. The wall is quite a feat of engineering and must have taken some considerable time to build. It seems to vary in height between six and seven feet for its whole length of almost 3 kilometres. There are few quaries near the hill top and although rocks can be found on the surface the bulk of the material to make the wall must have been carried up the hill. I have not spotted any gates or breaks in the original wall although parts of it are now in a fairly poor state.

The dry-stone wall follows the route of an ancient ditch which although today is known as Dean ditch, it was originally called Dane or Danes Ditch. A number of place names in this area indicate that the Danes once settled in this part of Lancashire (and don't forget the Scandinavian stone axe found in Tigers Clough dating from before

2,000BC) and from pollen analysis we know that much of the deforestation of the moor took place around this period so perhaps the name Danes Ditch may not be too wide of the mark. The ditch is not visible for the full length of the wall but even when it vanishes, its route can be traced through the slightly differing colour of the vegetation seen at certain times of the year.

A footpath runs along the full length of the wall and the panoramic views available on clear days makes this a good place to stretch the legs. The path starts at the stile at the side of the most south easterly of the antenna masts. Within a few yards of the stile a depression can be seen on the left hand side of the path heading towards Belmont. This marks the route of the collapsed underground tunnel, known as the "New Tunnel" which starts lower down the hill. Just over the wall on the Horwich side – and according to old maps (SD 66356 14536), there used to be an adit or drift entrance to this area of the coal workings but there is very little sign of it today. Near to the site of the adit entrance can be seen many areas of disturbed ground all caused either by surface coal workings or by collapsed workings beneath.

The path along the wall has few surprises except for several spots where rocks appear to be in fairly unnatural formations forming circles.

The above photo on the left is particularly interesting. The original surface of the ground one to two thousand years ago would have been several feet lower than it is today, before the build up of the peat. In those days, these rocks would have been on the lying on the surface and not sunk as at present. I'm not suggesting ancient stone circles ...... but it's an interesting thought!

Whilst I wander on moorlands where I know people once lived in ancient times, as well as looking for flints, I also keep my eyes open for any signs of prehistoric art. This artwork usually consists of either cups, rings or lines carved or cut in rocks. An example of a typical cup and ring boulder was found on the banks of the Lower Rivington Reservoir just a few years ago and can be seen today outside the Anderton Hall Conference Centre at Horwich.

After years of searching I have so far found no "art" on Winter Hill - or elsewhere in the area! However on the Horwich side of the Dean Ditch wall, I did spot a stone which I thought just "may" have once contained "cups" although with the extreme weathering the rocks have to contend with in this environment, it is doubtful whether any "art" whatsoever would not have been weathered away millennia ago.

Back to the top!

From the TV mast, major footpaths branch in all directions. There are clear paths to Rivington Pike, Noon Hill, Two Lads, Coal Pit Lane and Scout Road to name the main ones. The Scout Road path has already been described and it links into the paths and artefacts described in the Whimberry Hill article. The path to Rivington Pike starts near the cattle grid by the TV mast on the road to Montcliffe and the signposted track to Coal Pit Lane is on the opposite side of the road. You can't miss the Coal Pit track nowadays because of the "paved" footpath for the first few hundred yards of its length.

Rivington Terraced Gardens.

A guide to their history, vegetation and wildlife.

This article is an amended version of a publication of this name produced by the North West region of the British Trust for Conservation Volunteers in the 1970's. The contents have been amended slightly to protect the exact locations of some of the rarer plant species mentioned. My thanks to BTCV (NW) for allowing this information to be reprinted.

Introduction.

Rivington Terraced Gardens stand out on the hillside below Rivington Pike as an arm of fairly dense woodland, in contrast to the surrounding moorland. A tall tower, "the Dovecote" marks the northern boundary of the gardens which consist of 45 acres of mixed (deciduous and coniferous) woodland. Below the gardens lie Lever Park, north west of which is Rivington Village.

The Historical Development of the gardens.

The area covered by the gardens was was deciduous forest until the early 16th century when it was felled. With grazing and regular burning of the vegetation it became rough grazing moorland, with only a few trees left in the Lower Gardens below what is now Roynton Lane.

It remained so until 1900 when William Hesketh Lever bought the site, having enquired whether Liverpool Corporation, who owned the reservoirs in the valley below, were interested and found they were not. Lever was born in Bolton and became wealthy through manufacturing soap from vegetable oil and formed the Unilever Company at Port Sunlight in Cheshire. Landscape design and architecture were among his main interests.

The first building to be erected on the site of the gardens was **"Roynton Cottage"** in 1901. The cottage (or **"Bungalow"** as it is often called) faced west and was built of pine timber and glass. It was designed by Johnathon Simpson, a local architect.

He also designed three lodges to accompany the bungalow between 1901 and 1902 in similar "Victorian Bungalow" style but with thatched roofs. The outline foundations of **South** and **Belmont Lodges** can still be seen. **Bolton Lodge** is the site of the new toilet block. Roynton Lane which passes north through the middle of the gardens was also built at this time.

The Original Wooden Roynton Cottage circa 1908

In 1905 Lever commissioned **T H Mawson**, a well known landscape architect and former horticulturist, to design the gardens. Thus in the following year the two lawns were laid out – a square one adjacent to the bungalow and an elongated serpentine shaped lawn (the **Great Lawn**) below this. Two garden houses were built overlooking the latter.

These can still be seen and are similar in style to the other three garden houses built later. All have unusual circular pillars built of small stones, mullioned windows, and a "terrace" on top with a facade of large stone cross pieces. (Some of the mullions and cross pieces are now missing however.

A **Roman style footbridge** was designed by Lever himself and its large central arch supported six smaller arches can be seen spanning Roynton Lane today.

In 1910 the **"Dovecote"**, probably the most prominent feature of the gardens, was designed by **Robert Atkinson**, together with the adjoining terraces. It consists of 4 rooms, accessible by a spiral stairway. The high-pitched roof, curving outwards from its base is an unusual feature of the tower.

It was restored in 1976 according to the original design at the NW Water Authority's expense.

Adjacent to the Dovecote (also used as a lookout tower) is a wall with arched windows in. Some of these have large stone slabs against them with holes that are semi-circular in shape. These enabled the doves or pigeons to fly in and out of the shed which originally occupied the site between the wall and the road.

Also in 1910 the **Gatehouse**, which spanned Roynton Lane with a hexagonal building at each end was built. It was demolished in the 50's but the two circular stone gateposts and foundations can still be seen. In 1913 Roynton Cottage was burnt down by Suffragettes to demonstrate against "use of capital". It was timed to coincide with a visit by George V and Queen Mary. It was replaced the following year by a more "fire proof" house of local stone (millstone grit) and glass.

Although only a one-story building, the **New Bungalow** was ornate particularly inside – on the dining room ceiling for instance was painted the position of the constellations on October the 23rd 1851, the day Lever was born. The First World War delayed part of the proposed building – an elaborate circular ballroom was not completed until 1920. The garden house in the north west of the gardens was also built at about this time.

In 1919 the gardens were opened to the public for the first time. Work on the gardens was begun again in the 1920's following its delay by the first world war. Many paths were laid out with irregular crazy paving, and flights of stone steps and archways constructed. The **Japanese Gardens** with a waterfall, large lagoon, garden ornaments and shelters, built to resemble Japanese tea houses, were completed. Also at this time the **Italian Gardens** were created.. A series of waterfalls and ponds were formed by diverting a small stream, and four inter-connecting caves were made partly by excavation and partly by construction. Rock ledges and steep pathways were made adjacent to the stream and two footbridges also crossed it. As in other parts of the gardens use was made of the horizontally-layered local rock.

In 1925 **Lord Leverhulme**, as he had then become, (having attached the name of his wife's to his own) died. The large death duties that his son, Viscount Leverhulme, subsequently had to pay, forced him to sell the various properties and to sack the 50 landscape gardeners hired from London and 50 local workmen that worked in the gardens. **John Magee**, a local brewery owner, bought the bungalow and grounds but the latter were kept open to the public and the bungalow was opened annually until his death in 1931. Even before Magee's death the gardens became neglected presumable because he could not afford to maintain them, and after his death and with the Second World War the situation became worse.

Leverhulme's footbridge over Roynton Lane

Liverpool Corporation bought the land from the Magee family, the local authorities being unable to afford it, despite Magee's wishes. During the 1939-45 war Rivington Bungalow was acquired by the army and much damage was done – the glass roof of the ballroom was smashed and the floor was ripped up. Vandalism became a problem generally in the Gardens. The cost of repairing and maintaining the buildings led to Liverpool Corporation's decision to demolish the Bungalow and the three lodges in 1948, after various other uses had been considered (including a hospital) and despite objections from local people. Today a small black and white tiled area can be seen on the Bungalow site but little else remains.

Nearby lie the **Kitchen Gardens**, their dividing walls still fairly high. Greenhouses once occupied the two northernmost walled areas. Further south, the **Potting Shed** can still be seen with the walls virtually intact, although they have long since lost their roofs. Opposite the Kitchen Gardens is the outline of a **Pagoda or Japanese teahouse** can be seen, adjacent to the ruins of a small garage. There was another garage further north which had a dovecote on top. The foundations and large building stones can still be seen here. Inset in the wall adjacent to the path near here are stone built shelters which contained wooden seats. These can be seen in several places in the Gardens next to the paths.

Since the 1970's beneficial changes have taken place in the Gardens, voluntary conservation groups have cleared the once overgrown paths and ponds and restored some of the stonework, so that people can enjoy the Gardens more fully and a variety of plants and animals can co-exist. *(this description does not give full credit to the massive amount of work done by the British Trust for Conservation Volunteers who totally transformed the Gardens from a total overgrown jungle to the beauty we now enjoy today, thanks!)*

Vegetation and Wildlife.

Introduction

Many different species were planted in the Gardens and many of them have survived despite the physical conditions. The soil is acid, the rainfall rather heavy (about 45 inches a year), and as the site is on a steep slope (from 220 to 320 metres above sea level) rather strong winds occur at times. Some species have been lost, through neglect and the rapid spread of some plants, at the expense of others, and theft. However over 150 of plants have been identified in the Gardens at the present time (May 1978).

In a short article such as this, only a brief account of such a variety of species can be given. The location of some of the plants is indicated by numbers in brackets which refer to the map.

Trees.

A large number of different trees can be seen in the gardens – there are about 40 species about which half are conifers , the rest being broadleaved. All the broadleaved ones are deciduous (i.e. lose all their leaves in winter) apart from **Griselinia**. Most of the tree species present are not native to this country. Some, such as the Monkey Puzzle (1), come from as far away as South America. There is a noticeable difference in the trees of the Lower and those of the Upper Gardens. In the latter, there are more exotic species, particularly conifers, as this area was treeless moorland until 1905, the oldest trees being therefore 98 years old *(in 2003)*.

Oak, Birch and Rowan are the most common deciduous **broadleaved trees.** Others are infrequently seen: **Elm** (2), **Willow** (3), **Alder** (4), **Whitebeam** (5), **Ash** and **Wild Cherry** are noticeable near the paths through the gardens. A cultivated variety of Ash, **"Weeping Ash"**, with drooping branches can be seen near the Japanese Lagoon.

Sycamore, introduced into this country in the 17th Century, has spread rapidly in the gardens and in the Lower Gardens particularly, the vast numbers of seedlings it is able to produce can be seen very frequently. Considerable numbers of Sycamores have been felled by Conservation Volunteers to allow other species to grow, especially native deciduous trees such as Oak. These generally have many other plants associated with them , dependent on them for food and shelter.

Beech is a common tree in the gardens, and in addition to the Common Beech there are two other varieties: **Copper Beech** with its dark purple leaves and **Cut-Leaf Beech** (7).

Exotic Cherry trees are also fairly common in the kitchen garden area. They have smooth shiny reddish bark and produce prolific blossom in summer.

Other introduced broadleaved trees present but rare in the gardens are,: **Lime, Horse Chestnut, Norway Maple, Laburnum** (a poinenous tree with long tassels of yellow flowers), and the **False Acacia or Locust Tree** (8). The latter is an unusual tree with rough channelled bark and paired spines on the twigs, pinnate leaves resembling Ash, and white flowers drooping like Laburnum. There are only two of these trees in the gardens.

Griselinia Littoralis (9) is another unusual and interesting tree found only in one place in the gardens. It comes from New Zealand and has evergreen untoothed leaves, bright and shiny above but dull below.

Conifers.

These are identifiable by their narrow, needle-like leaves and the fact that they bear cones. **Larch** is the only deciduous conifer and occurs in considerable numbers in the gardens (10).

Several species of **Pines** (Pinus spp.) are present, the most common ones (all of which have needles in pairs) are:- **Scots Pine** (with blue-green needles about 1.5 inches long), is very common particularly in the Lower Gardens. **Corsican Pine** has needles about 4 inches long; there are some large specimens by the south west garden house. **Mountain Pine** (pinus mungo) is a small bushy pine with many bright green needles grouped in whorls on the branches (unlike other pines), the bare twig can be seen between the whorls. This pine occurs in large numbers near the seven arch bridge.

Another group of conifers are the **Spruces** which have very sharply pointed, short stiff needles growing singly on small woody pegs which are left when the needles fall, thus the twigs are very rough when touched. **Sitka Spruce** is the most common, the underside of its needles are blue-grey. There are only three or four **Blue Spruce** trees (12) but they are easily noticeable as their needles are blue-grey all over, and they point in all directions from the twigs.

Silver Firs (Abies spp.) are quite common in the gardens – their needles are set in two distinct layers, the lower ones being horizontal so that the foliage looks flattened. The needles grow singly (unlike the paired needles of the pines) and leave a flat round scar when removed unlike the Spruces. The bark is dark and not channelled, but has small resin bubbles on it. Three very tall Silver Firs can be seen by the SW summerhouse (13).

Cedars (14) have needles set in tufts or dense bunches like larches but they are of different lengths and remain over winter. Also their cones may be8 cms long whereas those of larch are only 2 or 3 cms long. Only three ceder trees have been found in the gardens but all are adjacent to paths.

There are several **Cypress** (Chamaecyparis) trees in the gardens, their flattened spreading foliage of tiny leaves which overlap the stem, make them unlike any of the conifers mentioned above.

Another conifer which has overlapping small leaves but which does not have flattened spreading branches is **Cryptomeria japonica** (15) of which there is only one tree in the gardens.

Yew is the only native conifer besides Scots Pine present in the gardens, here it grows as a small bushy tree particularly between the kitchen gardens and the Japanese Lagoon. The leaves are soft to touch and often yellowish-green.

Shrubs.

Introduction.
Mawson planted thousands of **Rhododendrons** and many other shrubs including **Gaultheria, Kalmias, Vaccineums, Hollies, Berberis** and many others. Some of these species originally planted are no longer present, having been lost through theft and neglect with some shrubs such as **Rhododendron, Gaultheria** and **Pernettya** spreading rapidly at the expense of other species. However 29 different shrub plants are to be found in the gardens today, nearly all of them introduced species, some of them fairly rare. Many of the shrubs planted appear to have been chosen because of their hardiness and tolerance of, or even preference for, an acid soil, e.g. many members of the **Ericaceae (Heather)** family and Rhododendron. The latter, together with Gaultheria and Pernettya, are the most common shrubs in the gardens, having spread rapidly by means of underground suckers. A number of varieties of Rhododendron are present, all characterised by untoothed leathery leaves and trumpet shaped flowers of various colours. Some of them have unusually small leaves (only 0.75 inches wide and 2 inches long but the most common is **Rhododendron ponticum** with large tough dark green leaves. The **deciduous Azeleas** occur in several places in the gardens.

Pernettya mucronata, aptly called **"Prickly Heath"** is a shrub growing up to about 2 foot high with small toothed leaves alternately arranged on its red stem. Introduced from the extreme south of South USA, it is evergreen (like Gaultheria) and bears red berries.

Oleria hastii (16) is an unusual shrub from New Zealand and is found adjacent to the summerhouses in the Upper Gardens. It has curiously stringy bark and untoothed evergreenleaves which are felty and buff coloured underneath. In July/August it bears daisy like flowers – thus it is included in the group of shrubs called the "Daisy Bushes".
Bamboo (17), a plant found naturally in S E Asia is a plant one would not expect to find growing here but there are several plants in the Italian Gardens.

Above the swimming pool are two small **Quince** (18) bushes and adjacent to the square lawn by the bungalow site you can see the only site where **Dogwood Cornel** grows in the Gardens (19). It is a deciduous shrub easily recognised by its bright red stems and shoots.

At least two species of **Laurel** occur in the Gardens:- "Spotted Laurel" with yellow spots on its leaves, and the "Common" or "Cherry Laurel" with its large glossy evergreen leaves with prominent veins.

Holly is a fairly common shrub or small tree in the gardens and species present are: Broad Leaved Holly (whose leaves are up to 2 inches across) and the **Common Holly** of which there is also a variegated (yellow-margined) variety occurring here.

Two species of **Barberry (Berberis spp.)**, a very spiny shrub up to three feet high, can be found in the gardens. **"Rosemary Barberry" (Berberis stenophylla)** with small inrolled untoothed leaves, grows well in places, particularly near the Great Lawn. The other has small holly-like leaves and grows in only a few places. **Pieris taiwanensis** (20) grows abundantly above the Japanese Lagoon and is one of the first shrubs to flower in the gardens. It produces abundant white, lily-of-the-valley type flowers in early April, and has alternately arranged leaves, distinguished from small rhododenrons by their finely toothed edges, pale green colour and narrowly lanceclata (spear-like) shape.

Also in the early spring **Flowering Current** bushes are noticeable with their drooping red flowers unlike the **Red Current** (found in the Kitchen Gardens) which has insignificant greenish-yellow flowers. Other typical vegetable garden plants growing here include **Gooseberry**.

The other shrubs likely to be seen are native to the area, although some of them may have been planted: **Elder, Hawthorne, Hazel and Gorse.**

Ground Flora. (Flowers, grasses, rushes, ferns, mosses etc)

Although there are large areas of the gardens where there is little ground vegetation, particularly where not much light penetrates the tree and shrub leaf-canopy, a large variety of plants (over 70 species) are present. Although Mawson originally planted introduced species such as Alpine varieties, most of the ground vegetation now consists of native species that one would expect to find growing naturally in this area.

Some of these are typically English woodland plants e.g. **Bluebell** and various grasses, particularly the soft hairy **Holcus species** which are very common in the gardens; and **Wood Sage** and **Wood Sorrel** which are relatively rare. Others typically colonise bare ground; **Sheeps Sorrel, Chickweeds,** the small **Annual Meadow Grass** with its bright green leaves with keeled tips, and **Foxglove** all grow well on waste ground, on the edges of the paths and on slopes of otherwise bare soil (Particularly following Rhododendron clearance).

Other plants are characteristic moorland species; **Heather, Bilberry, Heath Bedstraw, Mat Grass, Flying Bent Grass and rushes**. In some places, such as the Great Lawn, they have re-colonised the area again. Of the **Rushes (Juncus spp.), Soft Rush** is the most common, forming large tufts about a foot high, and the smaller **Heath Rush** is common on the lawns. It is generally less than 9 inches high, does not form tufts and has small narrow leaves at its base. All the plants are abundant on the moorland surrounding the gardens.

Other plants are typically found in wet places – in or by the streams, ponds and boggy areas in the gardens: **Water Forget-me-Not, Marsh Thistle, Bittercress, Iris and Reed Sweet Grass (Glyceria maxima).** The latter has bluntly pointed folded leaves that may be 1 inch wide and grows up to several feet. It is found in "Neptunes Pool" (21). The flat basal rosettes of leaves of **Hairy Bittercress** are common especially near the stream in the Italian Garden.

Japanese Knotweed (Reynoutria japonica) is a Japanese species planted in the gardens and has spread rapidly by means of underground suckers. It is a tall, stout cane-like plant growing up to 6 feet high with large oval leaves and tassels of white flowers in summer.

Of particular interest are plants confined to the stone walls of the terraces and summerhouses in the gardens such as **Ivy and Berrillio Sandwort**, a tiny plant which produces relatively large white flowers in April. **Ivy-leaved Toadflax** which has purple flowers, can be seen growing on the seven arched bridge. **Epilobium nerteriodes** is a small creeping willow herb with round leaves introduced from New Zealand but which now grows wld in the UK. The plant grows well on the rock faces by the interconnecting caves in the Italian Gardens. Here also the moist shady conditions provide an ideal habitat for **mosses, the flat green liverworts**, and some Ferns, particularly **Lady Fern**. The ferns most frequently seen in the gardens are **Bracken, Broad Buckler Fern and Lady Fern**, which are common particularly in the Lower Gardens. **Hard Fern** with its lobed fronds only a few inches long, occurs in several places.

Animals.

The variety of plants and presence and shrubs offer food and shelter for many animals that otherwise would not be found here.

Birds.

Thirty species of birds have been identified. They include birds of prey such as the Owl and Kestrel; typical woodland birds like the Great Spotted Woodpecker and Wood Pigeon. Some birds such as the Goldcrest (a very small bird with a golden-yellow stripe on top of its head) have benefited from the planting of conifers in the gardens, preferring to nest in them rather than in deciduous trees.

The birds most likely to be seen apart from the above species are: Robin, Blackbird, Blue-, Great-, and Coal Tits, Magpie, and Chaffinch, Wren and Tree Creeper. The latter is noted for its habit of creeping up tree trunks looking for insects and its prominent white front in contrast to its mottled brown back. Other species present include Bullfinch, Redstart, Redpoll, Jay, Starling, Hedge Sparrow, Chiff-chaff, Carrion Crow, Cuckoo, Linnet, Fieldfare, Nuthatch, Long Tailed Tit, Willow Warbler and Redwing.

Mammals & Amphibians.

Rabbits, Hedgehog, Wood Mice, Fox, Weasel and Stoat have been seen and recorded in the gardens but only the rabbit is a common sight.

Frogs and Smooth Newts are the only amphibians to have been seen in the gardens.

Please Remember:-

A lot of time, energy and money has been spent (and will continue to be spent) trying to conserve the variety of features in the gardens which make them interesting for the large numbers of people that visit them now and in the future.

In some cases damage and erosion has occurred, therefore for everyone's benefit PLEASE:

- be careful not to start a fire
- don't drop litter
- keep to the paths so plants are not damaged and wildlife is not disturbed
- don't damage walls and buildings
- keep to approved vehicle/bike routs and car parks.

Kevin Eyles, one of the volunteers who are restoring Rivington Terraced Gardens has made a replica of a pagoda that used to sit in the gardens. (photo from the Lancashire Post)

Bolton Mountain Rescue Team

The 3 new Land Rover vehicles, pictured here as they were collected from Crake International, Cumbria, in April 2011.

History

Founded in 1968 by 3 Rossendale Fell Rescue Team members who lived in the Bolton area, the Team has grown from its small beginnings to be one of the busiest and best equipped teams in the country.

The early years, as with many foundling organisations, was one of sheer hard work to raise minimal amounts of money for essential equipment which was initially transported both for exercise and incidents in privately owned vehicles.

The first vehicles owned by the Team were all old "second-hand" ones past their best before date, they were cherished and nursed by the dedicated membership. Much is owed to these early pioneers, most of whom have long left but two remain in the team – Alan "General" James, one of the original founder members, now a life Vice President, only stopped active service in early 1999 due to a job move to the London area. (Alan moved back up North in 2003 and promptly resumed his service in the team). Geoffrey H. Seddon, currently Deputy Team Leader, joined within a few months of the

Team's inauguration and has served as Team Leader (7 years) and Chairman.

The 1980's saw consolidation of the Team with a gradual improvement in the quality and quantity of equipment and vehicles. During this decade we saw the implementation of structured training and the MRC casualty care course and certificate. By the late 80's and early 90's, training was based on a professional and formalized activity.

As a "fringe" Mountain Rescue Team based in an rural/urban area, the local moorlands generated few incidents. Even up until the early 90's fewer than 10 incidents per year were the norm. In the 70's and 80's 2 or 3 call outs per year were common.

The combination of a large urban catchment area for membership and low incident rate meant a very high level of training was able to be undertaken.

Morale was maintained by training weekends in the Lakes or North Wales with the added bonus of possible calls to assist local teams. At this time in the Team's development, Stewart Hulse, the leader of Langdale Ambleside MRT at the time, and Tony Jones, then leader of Ogwen Valley MRT were especially supportive and encouraging.

The advent of the West Pennine Moors Recreation Area, coupled with the fruition of years of liaison meetings with the Lancashire and Greater Manchester Police Forces and the Lancashire and Greater Manchester Ambulance Services saw a dramatic rise in call out activity from 1994 onwards as the professional expertise and resources of the team were recognised on a wider basis.

We can now expect upwards of 100 incidents attended by the team per year.

1999 also saw the team with its very first new vehicles – 2 Landrover 110″ County Station Wagons and a Landrover 110″ hardtop. The first two being first response vehicles and the hardtop van an Incident Support Unit. In Autumn 2003 the Team commissioned into service its fourth brand new Landrover, principally utilised as a personnel carrier.

In April 2011 the team replaced its 1999 purchased Land Rovers with three identical brand new Land Rover Defender Mountain Rescue Ambulance vehicles. As of June 2011 the team operates four Land Rover Mountain Rescue Ambulances, a Ford Transit Minibus (donated by GMP in early 2010), a 3.5m semi-rigid inflatable SAR Boat, a fully equipped catering trailer, and a control vehicle (the team maintains a cargo trailer which generally carries our two Aireshelta tents).

Team bases

2003 was the year that we lost our much loved home at the New Overdale Youth Training Centre, as well as the vehicle storage at the Carnaud Metal Box (CMB) factory in Westhoughton.

The Overdale base consisted of a modest garage, just large enough to fit a Land Rover into it, with a roof space just large enough to hold a meeting in. But, it was home and it had been home for 32 years since 1971.

Many of our Team members regarded it as their second home – Just ask the TL's partner, Ann! The New Overdale site had been sold for property development, and so, sadly, ended the lease of the garage there.

The CMB factory had served as a vehicle storage facility for 3 of our vehicles for many years, and the security staff had put up with our comings and goings at all times of the day and night!

Sadly, the factory was scheduled for closure and within the space of a few months, we were faced with not only the loss of our training base, but also with nowhere to store our 4 vehicles!

Fortunately, the reality of homelessness never struck. Thanks to our recently-established links with Greater Manchester Fire & Rescue Service, and the long-standing relationship with Greater Manchester Ambulance Service, we were offered 2 new homes.

The first came from GMFRS, in the form of a two bay garage at Bolton Central Fire Station. The second offer, from GMAS, gave us not only a place to garage our 2 other vehicles, but also offered an excellent training/base prospect, which we duly constructed.

To accommodate our ever growing fleet of vehicles, GMFRS came to our aid again with garage space at Bolton North Fire Station.

Team Leaders

Name	Role	Tenure	Duration
Michael Hope-Ainscough	Team Controller	1968-1969	
Mike Marshall	Team Leader	1968 to early 1969*	6 months
Derek Mottershead	Team Leader	Early 1969 to 13/09/1973*	4 years
Geoff Seddon	Team Leader	13/09/1973 to 13/03/1981	7 years 6 months
Bob Hutchinson	Team Leader	13/03/1981 to 12/03/1983	2 years
Howard Hill	Team Leader	12/03/1983 to 11/03/1989	6 years
Garry Rhodes	Team Leader	11/03/1989 to 16/03/2016	27 years
Alistair Greenough	Team Leader	16/03/2016 to current	

A bit about what we do and where we operate

Primarily, we exist to provide a voluntary search and rescue service for the West Pennine Moors, but besides searching for missing or injured hill walkers and people involved in mountain biking and climbing accidents, (which is usually the first thing pictured when the phrase "mountain rescue" is mentioned) we are also heavily involved in other happenings.

Our past callouts have involved crashed aircraft, hang gliders and parapenters.

Generally, however, where there is a problem locating victims, or the terrain surrounding a casualty is difficult to access, it is likely that your mountain rescue team is involved.

Several times a year we also provide standby rescue cover for events held within our area. We can often be spotted at orienteering events, fell races, sponsored walks, and mountain bike races.

We are a key resource to the emergency services, our specialist skills being recognised and respected by Greater Manchester, Lancashire and Cheshire police who utilise us (along with other teams) to help in search and rescue operations, alongside use by the Ambulance services. The team also works with Greater Manchester Fire Service.

Besides our upland moorland area, we also operate throughout the lowland areas of Bolton, Salford, Wigan, Trafford, Manchester South, and the western half of Bury. We are also called upon to assist other teams in North Manchester, the eastern half of Bury, Tameside, Rochdale, Oldham, North Cheshire and South Lancashire.

We cover an area from Darwen in the north to Manchester Airport in the south, Wigan to the west and the centre of Manchester to the east.

It's true – that sounds like a mainly urban area that you wouldn't associate with "Mountain Rescue" however our patch contains quite a lot of moors and open land which is full of walkers, climbers, mountain bikers and horse riders. And that's not the end of the story. Believe it or not many of the incidents we attend aren't on the moors at all.

Whether it's a 10 year old child who's fallen off a rope swing and is stuck in a stream bed, an elderly person who's been reported missing from home, or looking after stranded motorists on snowbound motorways, you'll find Bolton MRT working alongside the police, ambulance and fire services of Greater Manchester and Lancashire.

Take a closer look at our website and find out more!

https://www.boltonmrt.org.uk/

A new tunnel appears in Lead Mines Clough.

Near the end of 2018, Garry Rhodes and Derek Cartwright were walking in Lead Mines Clough in the mining area of the valley and spotted a newly visible entrance to a possible tunnel.

At the time of writing this tunnel has not been investigated or explored but it has been thought it may be a trial tunnel dug along the line of the fault to investigate whether or not any minerals may be present. Why did they dig along the fault? It's because mineral veins tend to form when mineralised warm liquids head towards the earths surface via areas of weakness in the rocks, such as cracks or faults.

Over a long period of time the liquids cool down, crystalise into all sorts of minerals, crystals and other substances

At the time of writing (Aug 2019) this tunnel has not been explored or documented .. leave it to the experts!!! Don''t wreck things.

Joe's Cup

On the approach to the ruin of Drinkwaters Farm from the white Coppice side a spring runs from left to right from the moors under the path with a small well on the right of the path, this spring is how Drinkwaters got its name.

Just on the left is a memorial to Joe Whitter (1939-1991), fell runner and good friend to many.

Removing the loose stone beneath the sign reveals an enamel cup. When Joe and his fellow runners were out on the moors they often stopped for a drink at the spring.

The cup is placed there in memory of Joe and for anyone else who needs a drink while out on the moors. These days the cup often contains small change left in respect for Joe.

Joe Whitter was a member of Wigan Phoenix club and was well known for his long distance runs over the Anglezarke and surrounding moors in the winter months. All reports suggest that Joe was great character to run with over the moors and many have stories to tell about their times out running with Joe, all agree that the Anglezarke moors are a poorer place without him.

Joe Whitter, 52 years, RIP

Farmhouses of the area.

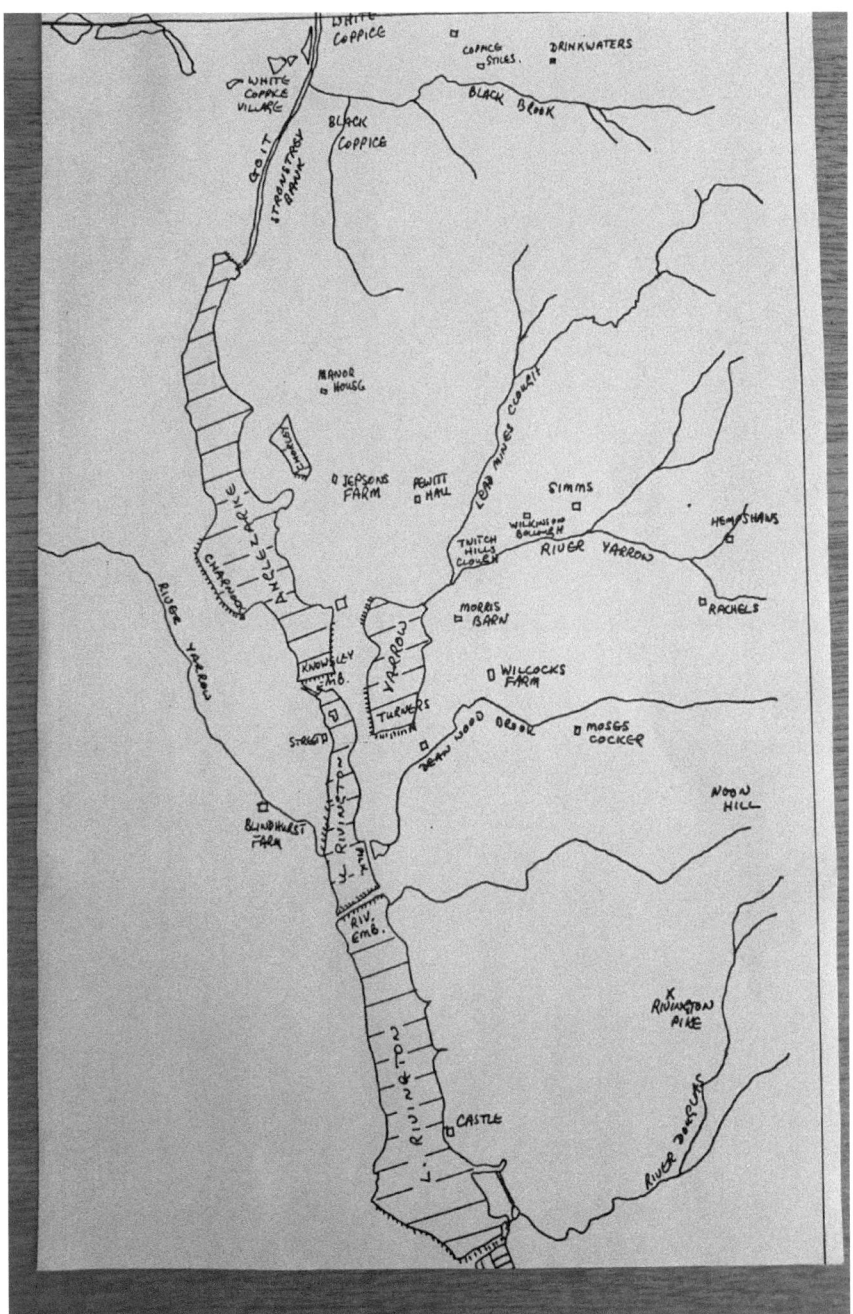

Map showing some of the major farms in the Anglezarke area.

Ruins

Drinkwaters Farm ruin, Anglezarke SD 6369 1907

Great Hill Farm Ruin, Anglezarke SD 6417 1887

Above and below, Higher Hempshaws Farm ruin, Anglezarke. SD 6489 1625

Above and Below, Cottage in the Moors, Winter Hill SD 6663 1412

Simms Farmhouse circa 1972 prior to North West Water bulldozing it circa early 1980's when stone surfaced fire access tracks were constructed in the area post major moorland fires on Anglezarke moor! (photo's by Dave Lane)

Geological Walk. The River Douglas North of Horwich. By Rodney J Ireland.

(This was, I believe just one of a number of walks around the area contained in a booklet published by the Wigan Geological Society - which seems to no longer exist.. I have been unable to obtain a full copy of this booklet, merely a photocopy of this article)

Introduction.

The excursion, which follows the course of the RiverDouglas, commences at Rivington School, Lever Park Avenue, Horwich and terminates on Rivington Pike. Most of the journey is made along the river bed itself in order to see the best exposures. It is therefore recommended that, if possible, wellington boots are worn. Although the walking distance between the school and the Pike is only 1.5 miles (3 kilometres) the valley is steep and travelling over much rough ground. Accordingly, it is recommended that the better part of the day is set aside for the excursion. It is also recommended that the excursion should not be attempted immediately following heavy rainfall since high flows in the river can result in the route being dangerous and, furthermore, renders several exposures inaccessible.

Despite the above cautionary notes, the excursion is both worthwhile and interesting. The valley affords numerous excellent exposures of the Lower Coal Measures (Westphalian) and Millstone Grit Series (Namurian). The geomorphology and faulting is also noteworthy and, in clear weather, a final reward is provided by the panoramic views from the Pike.

Itinerary.

Rivington School (SD 638127), may be reached by following Lever Park Avenue out of Horwich for a distance of about 1 km. There is ample parking space alongside the Avenue in the vicinity of the school. Take the footpath leading east from the south side of the large Sports Hall alongside the road. The footpath leads to Old Lords Farm Footbridge (639126). Hereabouts, upstream from the bridge, leave the footpath, climb through one of the gaps in the old iron fence, descend to the river bed and proceed upstream.

In the river banks and on the bed, exposures of shales, mudstones and siltstones with occasional thin sandstones (less than 0.2 metre) can be seen. These rocks form part of the strata between the Crutchman Sandstone and the Old Lawrence Rock (sandstone) within the Lower Coal Measures. Carefully note the stratal dips. Initially the beds are horizontal but some 200 metres upstream the same beds can be seen dipping at 20 degrees. Careful examination of the siltstone/mudstone sequences hereabouts reveals the presence of fossil plant debris. Another 10 metres upstream the siltstones, dipping even more steeply, are abruptly truncated by a fault. This can be clearly seen on the south side of the river and trends in a north-westerly direction. The fault surface contains a fault breccia consisting of angular pieces of sanstone and siltstone occurring within a matrix of sand and mud. The hade, or slope of the fault surface, indicates a south-westerly downthrow. Upstream the Ousel Nest Grit (or Horwich Grit) and its underlying shales and occasional flagstones are exposed. The stratal juxtaposition indicates a vertical displacement on the fault of about 250 metres. The increasing dips observed downstream are features common to many such displacements.

Continue upstream from the fault. Siltstones and occasional flaggy sandstones, both both much disturbed by the fault, can be seen. There, considerable variation in stratal dip and some folding also occurs. Above a small waterfall, the beds become horizontal again. Black and purple shales and siltstones crop out on the left bank of the river and become overturned at the waterfall. Such overturning is probably the result of "soil creep". Some 15 to 20 metres upstream from the waterfall a coarse-grained yellow sandstone (Ousel Nest Grit) can be seen. Many small faults with slickensides (the polished fault surface exhibiting striations which indicate the last direction of movement) are present. One fault, exposed on the right bank, throws shales against sandstones. For approximately the next 40 metres, the river is in a very narrow, steep sided and picturesque ravine containing a series of cascades and waterfalls. It is possible to traverse the ravine and observe the Ousel Nest Grit which is subject to much small faulting with associated well developed slickensides. However if you are not wearing wellingtons be prepared to get your feet wet!. Alternatively a detour around the ravine may be made, leaving the river bed and rejoining the river upstream. A small quarry on the right bank above the ravine displays a particularly well-exposed fault surface exhibiting white slickensides. Further upstream observe the feature created by the Ousel Nest Grit on the left bank. Here the sandstone is well-jointed and cross-stratification can be demonstrated. As the footbridge is approached note the sandstone is terminated against shales. Here again, faulting can be demonstrated.

Immediately upstream from here a careful examination of the 1 metre of mudstone and shale, overlying the compact, dark, flaggy sandstone in the river bed, reveals the presence of a Marine Band. This is best exposed on the right bank below the roots of a large tree. Goniatites (*Gastrioceras*), bivalves (*Dunbarella*) and brachiopods (*Lingula*) can be readily found. Most of the goniatites are flattened by the compactation of the sediments. However, detailed inspection shows them to be *Gastriocerous subcrenatum*. Some excavation below the Marine Band shows the presence of a thin inferior coal (0.015 metre), and immediately above this the non-marine bivalve *Anthraconaia bellula* has been found. The fossils prove the coal to be the Six Inch Mine at the base of the Lower Coal Measures. The former is separated by some 60 metres of stata from the overlying Ousel Nest Grit. Since the two horizons are faulted into juxtaposition immediately downstream of the footbridge, the throw of the fault must therefore be approximately 60 metres.

Continuing upstream, a high wall, the remains of an old dam, is passed on the left bank. A series of "terraced" sandy gravels clearly represents the partial infill of a former mill "lodge" impounded by the dam.

Upstream the valley bifurcates. Both tributaries enter over waterfalls caused by a north-westerly trending fault throwing the shales and mudstones, above the Six Inch Mine, against the Upper Haslingden Flags. The hard flagstones are resistant to erosion and hence form the lip of the waterfall. The shales and the mudstones on the downthrown side of the fault are soft and have been eroded to form "plunge pools" at the base of the falls. Take the left hand tributary, ascend around the waterfall and return to the stream bed. Here the river gradient coincides with the dip of the bedding surfaces in the Upper Haslingden Flags. Accordingly, one walks on a single bedding surface for some considerable distance. Sedimentary structures, including ripple marks, may be seen on the bedding surfaces. Joint frequency and direction may also be examined. (Great care is required as hereabouts much of the river bed is **very slippery**). Near the top of the gorge the overlying shales crop out and rest on the top of the flagstones. Above here, the base of the Rough Rock, a feldspathic sandstone, and the highest member of the Millstone Grit Series can be examined.

At the top of the gorge it is necessary to again climb through the old boundary fence. Upstream the stream bed is incised in the Rough Rock which, between the fence and Belmont Road, exhibits several well-developed pot holes.

Above and left of the stream two slope changes can be seen on the hillside. These represent the outcrops of the Upper and Lower leaves of the Sand Rock Mine. Both coal seams occur within the Rough Rock. However, only the upper seam was of workable thickness. Spoil heaps can be seen beneath Brown Hill where a drift mine formerly worked the coal. Crossing Belmont Road and continuing upstream, well developed cross-stratification occurs in the Rough Rock.

From here traverse due West towards Brown Hill. Immediately east of the hill a northerly trending fault is visible in the small stream. The fault truncates the Rough Rock and throws down the overlying shales. From the steam climb up the side of Brown Hill where the shales pass upwards into the Margery Flags.

These form the capping of the hill and dip at 8 degrees to the south. Descend Brown Hill on the north-west side towards Rivington Pike. In the saddle between the two hills, and to the right of the track, a circular depression with a surrounding raised lip can be seen.

This probably represents an old bell pit which worked the Sand Rock Mine. From here it is well worth completing the excursion by walking to the top of Rivington Pike. There are several limited exposures of the Marjory Flags en route.

From the Pike one can return to the School by descending through the plantations and the terraced gardens to Rivington Barn. Alternatively a more direct route may be followed by descending across the fields to Roynton Lane and thence to the rear of the school.

References.

JONES R C B et al (1938) Wigan District   Mem. Geol> Surv
Maps Geological (IGS)
1:63,360 (1 in to 1 ml) Sheet No 84 – Wigan (solid)
1:10,560 (6 in to 1 ml) Lancs. Sheet No 86 NW
Ordnance Survey
1:50,000 Series, Sheet 109
1:10,560 Series, Sheet SD 61 SW

Good Friday. The Pike Fair.

Good Friday at Rivington Pike is either a nightmare or a pleasurable annual event, dependent on how you see things. For me, it's a nightmare yet I still keep going back every Good Friday … and now I even go with my grandchildren!

Good Friday is the day of the "Pike Fair". On that day each year, the "fair" arrives at the Pike along with hot dog vans, children's entertainment's complete with bouncy castles and tacky stalls selling all sorts of things that we don't really want.

At the end of the day when all the traders have gone, the Pike area looks something like a giant rubbish dump. It must be the only "fair" in the country to be held near the top of a fairly inhospitable hill whatever the weather!

Nobody really seems to know when the Pike Fair originated, but it is undoubtedly of fairly ancient origin, possibly dating from the Middle Ages. It used to be held at the Whitsuntide weekend and in the early 1800's the fair seems to have been a rather rowdy event and - according to a local newspaper – the road round the Pike was filled with "nut stalls and drinking booths".

Add to this, the proximity of the public house, the Sportsman's Arms, just a few hundred yards from the Pike and it must have been quite a lively spot especially as the festivities lasted from the Saturday morning, through the night, through the Sunday finally closing on the Monday! Sunday was the day when people from all around always walked to the peak of Rivington Pike – and still do.

After the Sportsman's Arms lost its licence (I don't know the exact date or the reason but I believe it occurred around 1880), the fair seemed to calm down and local interest in it began to wane. An article in the Bolton Chronicle of 1884 commented that "Pike Fair has lost much of its rowdyism since the removal of the public house licence"

The fair was moved to Good Friday in 1900 and since that time the numbers of stalls and visitors have fluctuated wildly decade by decade.

According to one article I have read, it would seem that things were fairly quiet in the 1930's and 40's but by the 1960's, crowds of over 50,000 were reported (along with increasing crowd and litter problems). Nowadays, the fair seems much quieter than I remember it 20 years ago and the number of stalls is well down in numbers.

So why do I keep going to the fair if it that's awful? Pure habit and I love things that are a bit out of the ordinary – especially when it's a tradition.

Aerial view of the Pike, taken prior to the building of the southern "staircase". The photo is taken from my microlight flying about 800 feet above the Pike

The Tup Row Quarry Pumping station.

At the bottom of Georges Lane at Wallsuches, you'll find Curleys Trout Farm and Dining Rooms. Just across the rough track hidden behind the trees is Tup Row Quarry which was once the site of the Horwich Waterworks Pumping Station built in 1924

The Tup Row Pumping station

A borehole was dug to a depth of 346 meters to obtain water for Horwich to supplement that which was obtained from the bottom of the Montcliffe Colliery.

SD 61 SE 1

Horwich Urban District Council.

Surveyor's Department,
Council Offices,
Horwich,
Lancashire.

T. GREEN.
M. INST. M. & CY. E.
ENGINEER & SURVEYOR

IN REPLY QUOTE

25th February, 1941.

F. W. Cope, Esq.,
H.M. Geological Survey Office,
250 Oxford Road,
Manchester 13.

HORWICH BORE.

Dear Sir,

Water Supply - Lancashire.

In reply to your letter of the 22nd instant, I trust the following information in reply to your queries is satisfactory.

(1) Height above O.D. of top of borehole. ... 750'
(2) Depth and diameter of shaft... 14' 6" x 10' x 5'
(3) Diameter of borehole. ... 0 - 400' 16" Diameter.
    400' - 850' 15" Diameter.
    850' - 1172' 14" Diameter.
(4) Any available details of lining tubes. ... 168' lining tubes inserted.
(5) Rest water level. ... 100'
(6) Pumping water level. ... 495'
(7) Yield. ... 6500 gallons per hour.
(8) Hardness of water. ... Clarkes Method.
    Temporary Hardness 5.8
    Permanent   "   0.0

Yours faithfully,

Th. Green
ENGINEER & SURVEYOR.

The 2018 Fires and the aftermath

The fires that consumed much of the Winter Hill and Rivington Moor area during the hot summer of 2018 were disastrous for the wildlife, vegetation and peat. The fires also came close to occupied housing. The heroic efforts of the local firefighters supported by those from all over the country and many of our own volunteer groups stopped the fire causing even more damage. The fires and the activity to fight the fires have left their mark on large areas of our moorland.

The fires followed a prolonged hot and very dry spell. The water sources and reservoirs around the West Pennine Moors were low from mid-spring 2018.

Yarrow Reservoir, Anglezarke early Summer 2018

Although large moorland fires have happened over the years fires of the size of the 2018 event occur very rarely indeed and perhaps only twice in the same location in the average human lifetime. The fire removed grass, heather and in some places the peat itself was damaged. In many location the fire used coal outcrops and old mining waste as fuel.

Watching the moors recover and wildlife return once the fires were extinguished and the moors opened again is a very interesting

experience. Some areas recover quickly, others less so. The wildlife although back will take some time to rebuild to its former strength.
One of the consequences of the fires, indeed any moorland fire is the potential to observe the land and its structures covered for many years by foliage. This has happened on Winter Hill and Smithills Moor. Due to the rarity of fires of this magnitude few people will be around who will have seen the exposed land last time a fire of this size happened.

A smoky Anglezarke 2018, at this time the Winter Hill area was closed off to the general public to allow the Fire Fighting to continue. Thick smoke drifted in a westerly direction.

Fire Fighting Operations, West Pennine Moors. Helicopter with water. July 2018. Photo Henry Lisowski

Mysteries of the moors

Many of the features and items photographed below will have been seen before but the age and function of many are yet to be understood and academically described. Please let us know if you can offer an explanation or insight into anything we have presented.

Smithills Tunnel: Pictured below is the entrance to a tunnel and a view inside. The entrance is approx. 0.8m deep and 1.0m wide. The tunnel is made up of dry stone built walls and stone slab roofing and sits under an earth hill/mound. The construction appears to be one of cut, build and refill. The tunnel is around 34m long, it is above all water course and the ridge of a hill and is quite dry and, is stand-alone i.e. not visibly connected with any other structures. It had another rounded exit/entrance at the other end, now filled in.

It is understood that there are no chambers from the tunnel left or right. The tunnel is roughly level with no holes, depressions or other changes in the floor. On examination the tunnel appears to have had a roof fall or is angled to the right at some 7.4m in from the entrance pictured.

The tunnel does not appear on any maps scrutinised to date from 1846. Location: SD 68530 13681. 345m above sea level. In the vicinity of Wimberry Hill, Smithills

Tunnel, Whimberry Hill Smithills post fires 2018

Internal photo of the tunnel. There is more about this tunnel later in the book

Smithills Round Stone: This stone was found in an area with significant fire impact. The stone was found flat, as pictured, and is clearly round with grooves (coin-like) around the edge from front to back. The stone is approx. 450mm in diameter and 120mm thick. No centre hole exists and no other similar stone was apparent in the local area. The stone was found around 10m from the Tunnel above. Location: SD 68530 13681. 345m above sea level. In the vicinity of Wimberry Hill

Potential mill or grind stone, near the tunnel in the vicinity of Whimberry Hill, Smithills

Smithills Worked flint: Flint doesn't occur naturally on the West Pennine Moors with small glacial deposits being the exception. Therefore any worked flint found is very likely to been brought to the area from afar. This piece was found on Smithills Moor post the 2018 fires. dated 2000-3000 years BC

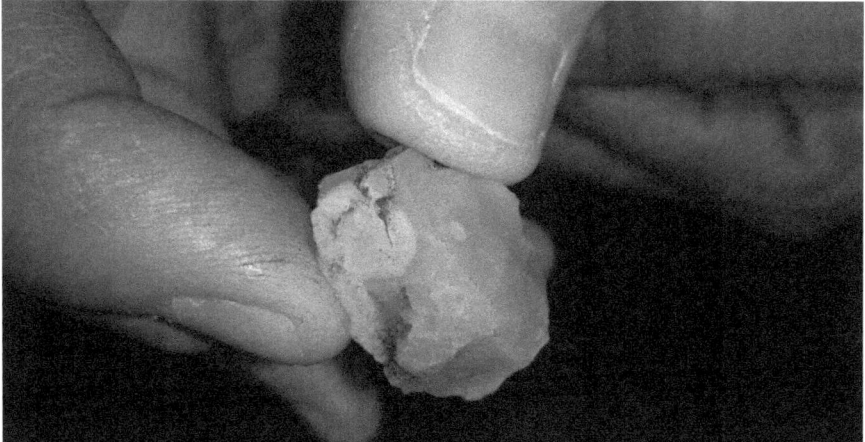

Worked flint found post fires, 2018. Smithills Moor (Garry Rhodes MBE)

Winter Hill Stone collections: The stones are separated from other stones in the area and appear to be the local grit stone. The drone picture demonstrates the separation of the stones from others in the vicinity.

Drone Photo of one of the stone collections, Winter Hill. Photo, Andrew Coward 2018.

The stones present evidence of being shaped by humans. Some stones are standing upright. Some have pieces cut out making the stone broadly "L" shaped or shaped as a shoulder. Locations: SD 67226 14174. 429m above sea level in the vicinity of Winter Hill.

Standing "shoulder stone" as part of the above collection

Ground shot of the Winter Hill stone collections pictured above. Post Fires 2018.

New vegetation growth following the 2018 fires have now once again covered many of these features making further investigations difficult.

Smithills Potential Stone Circle: This potential stone circle arrangement was spotted and photographed while the 2018 moorland fires were very much still active.

The photographer was a volunteer spotting fires for the fire fighters. Location: SD 687143 in the vicinity of Hampsons Pasture.

Potential Stone Circle, Smithills Moor

A further circle of stones has been observed post the 2018 fires in the Whimberry Hill area (SD 683 136).

This new discovery occupies the peak of a hill with many non-local and river worn stones seen scattered in the vicinity.

There is evidence that the stones sit upon a raised embankment which is visible from various locations. The circle is 10 meters in diameter.

The flint tool shown above was found in very close proximity to this circle in early 2019.

Vegetation growth since the fire is quickly masking the find making the circle less obvious.

Rivington Pike and the Tower.

When driving along the motorway past Horwich, two things immediately catch the eye, the Reebok Stadium and the Tower on Rivington Pike. I wonder how many thousands of people have driven past and wondered what the Tower is? Many local history books tell you all you could ever want to know about the Tower but any book about Winter Hill would be incomplete without a few words about the Pike and its Tower so I'll try to give a potted version of what you'll find in the other books.

Rivington Pike is the last high point at the south western edge of Winter Hill and is 1,198 ft or 365 metres high. A surveyors bench mark can be seen carved onto one of the large boulders halfway up the Pike on the main footpath leading from the Brown Hill area. Geologically the Pike is composed of gritstones, shales and several layers of the Margery Flags. The Pike is circled by two coal outcrops – but they are fairly speculative on the eastern side, although coal has been extracted there in days gone by.

There are three major routes up the Pike, the Brown Hill footpath, the paths from Winter Hill and that from the Terraced Gardens. There is a road going round the hill. Due to the erosion occurring on the Terraced Gardens Path (which was getting quite severe with the footpath forming an ever-deepening gully) a staircase was built up the Pike in latter years.

The summit of the Pike was once the site of a beacon. The first recorded use of it was in the 12th century when those awful Scottish people invaded our part of the UK. At that time, the whole country was linked with a chain of fire beacons to alert the population in times of crisis.

Apart from this occurrence, there seems to be only one other record of the beacon chain being lit in anger, this being on the 19th July 1588 when the Spanish Armada threatened our shores. The beacon was held in readiness for lighting at a time in the early 1800's when a French invasion was threatened, but the beacon was never lit. The beacon site has only been used since that time on the odd occasion to celebrate war victories or royal occasions.

The Tower.

The builder of the tower on Winter Hill was John Andrews in 1733 and it is reputed that he built it as a sign of his authority and ownership following an earlier land dispute with another landowner. The tower was built to function as a shooting hut and initially consisted of one

square room with a cellar underneath. One source says that the room was oak panelled and there was definitely a fireplace within the walls as early photos clearly show a chimney on the roof.

There was one door into the tower with windows in the other three sides. The roof was below the level of the walls and could not be seen from the outside. The stones for building the tower were obtained locally and those from the original beacon were utilised in the structure.

The Pike as it used to be (photo taken in 1979) before the building of the "grand staircase". The erosion was a great deal worse than this by the time the new steps were built.

Photo of the tower taken in the 1880's. Note the chimney!

In the 1890's, Rivington Hall and the surrounding lands were bought for £60,000 by William Lever - Vicount Leverhulme - who was a Boltonian who had made his fortune in soap manufacturing starting the company that was to end up as Unilever. After Levers death he bequeathed his lands to the "people of Bolton" on condition that it was preserved as a park with total public access. Liverpool Corporation objected to parts of this bequest as portions of the land lay within the Liverpool Waterworks water catchment area. As a result of various court cases, Parliament decreed that although the park remained as a gift to the people of Bolton, the property would be managed by Liverpool Corporation. As a result of this arrangement the tower started to fall into a state of disrepair.

Although Liverpool made general repairs to the structure from time to time, no real attempt seems to have been made to make it really presentable and in 1967 they announced that they intended to demolish the tower. Following massive local objections to this course of action which lasted for some years the ownership of the land was sold to Chorley UDC and the tower was finally repaired in 1973.

A few lesser known facts about Rivington Pike!

RIVINGTON PIKE AND TOWER. GOOD FRIDAY APRIL 13th 1979.

Vegetation.

The vegetation composition of the Pike is what is known as a "semi-natural upland acidic grassland environment" and is said to be "anthropogenic" i.e man modified.

Without mans interference (and sheep!) heather, bracken and scrubby plants would soon colonise the land and trees would start to regenerate naturally.

So what types of plants are actually growing on and around the Pike? By far the most dominant grass is Nardus Stricta (Mat Grass), but Molinia Caerulea (Purple Moor Grass/Flying Bent) becomes especially abundant in the southern half of the site, especially in the wetter south-western corner. Other plant species noticeably present are:

Festus ovina (Sheeps Fescue)
Deschampsia flexuosa (Wavy Hair Grass)
Agrostis canina montana (Brown Bent)
Poa annua (Annual Meadow Grass)
Agrostis tenuis (Common Bent/Brown Top)
Cynosurus cristatus (Crested Dog's Tail)
Juncus squarrosus (Heath/Moor Rush)
Juncus conglomeratus (Common Rush)
Vaccinium myrtillus (Bilberry)
Empetrum nigrum (Crowberry)
Callauna vulgaris (Heather)
Epiophorum vaginatum (Hare's Tail Cotton Grass).

The weather.

Due to its exposed and high elevation, the Pike does experience severe weather conditions with the prevailing strong winds coming from the west. Rainfall is heavy and frequent. Measurements were taken in 1977 and during that year a total rainfall of 1169 mm (approx. 46 inches was recorded. No month by month rainfall figures have been recorded for the Pike but they are available for Brown Hill, a few hundred yards to the south east.

These show that the monthly rainfall throughout 1977 was:

January	79.2mm
February	157.0
March	70.0
April	79.2mm
May	46.5
June	161.5
July	38.5
August	73.2
September	89.0
October	124.3
November	151.8
December	98.9 (source NWWA)

The Pike Geology.

"The underlying solid geology of the Pike is Carboniferous in age. Beds of the Millstone Grit Series are overlain by "marine bands" and Margery Flags. The latter here represents the base of the sandstones and grits of the Lower Coal Measures. The Carboniferous rocks are strongly bedded and generally sandstone and shales alternate. The rocks dip only very slightly to the south-east"

"The sudden rise of the land to form the oval shaped ridge on which the Tower stands can be partly explained by the Lower Coal Measures present which are also oval in shape, and the base coincides approximately with the 351 metre contour. At the summit of the Pike, some of the bedrock has been exposed and strongly bedded, fine grained, vertically jointed sandstone can be seen to be underlain by very easily disturbed thin shale bands which are readily fragmented."

The Soil.

"The soil profile generally consists of, in decending order: a thin layer of humus; a layer of peat which varies in thickness; a bleached, greyed, browny, clayey, very acidic alluvial horizon containing small fragments of sandstone and shale; a thin iron pan; a relatively thick, partly iron stained, darker brown, less clayey, more sandy alluvial horizon within which are larger fragments of sandstone and shale; the parent rock.

Extracts taken from "Rivington Pike. Erosion and Management Plan" by Christine Tudor for BTCV and NWWA . June 1978.

++

The Hole Bottom Area of Winter Hill.

"Hole Bottom". What a name! Don't expect me to explain why the place has this name because I haven't a clue! If anyone has any explanation then please get in touch then we can all share this invaluable and fascinating information!

90% of people reading this are going to ask where Hole Bottom is! It's no wonder you don't know where it is, for today it's one of the most insignificant spots on Winter Hill and is totally ignored by most walkers and drivers unless you happen to be a "local". To find the place, go up the road leading to the TV mast from Montcliffe, go

over the cattle grid and eventually you'll reach a left bend in the road with a metal crash barrier on the right side of the road. This is Hole Bottom! Welcome to one of the most fascinating spots on the hill!

If you stand at Hole Bottom and look around, what do you see? Not much .... for little now remains of what was once here. This was once a thriving, working small community with a brick & tile works, coal mines, houses (including an ale house – wish it were still there) and was on a major route from one part of the county to another. If you look carefully at the photo below, there are clues to the past history. Look uphill towards the mast. Over a century ago you would have seen a number of pit heads all the way up to the present TV mast.

There is a clear track leading up the hill that was once a tramway. Also on the hillside looking uphill there are a large number of blocked remains of adit entrances and a number of "collapsed" areas where the underground coal and clay workings have fallen in.

In the small "valley" to the right of the photo, there used to be three major adits leading from the valley into the Mountain Mine coal workings.

Two of these adits are now completely filled in and sealed, and the third one seems to have been commandeered by the water department as the entrance is covered by a modern brick built structure (which is just about visible from the road as it's surrounded by a fence).

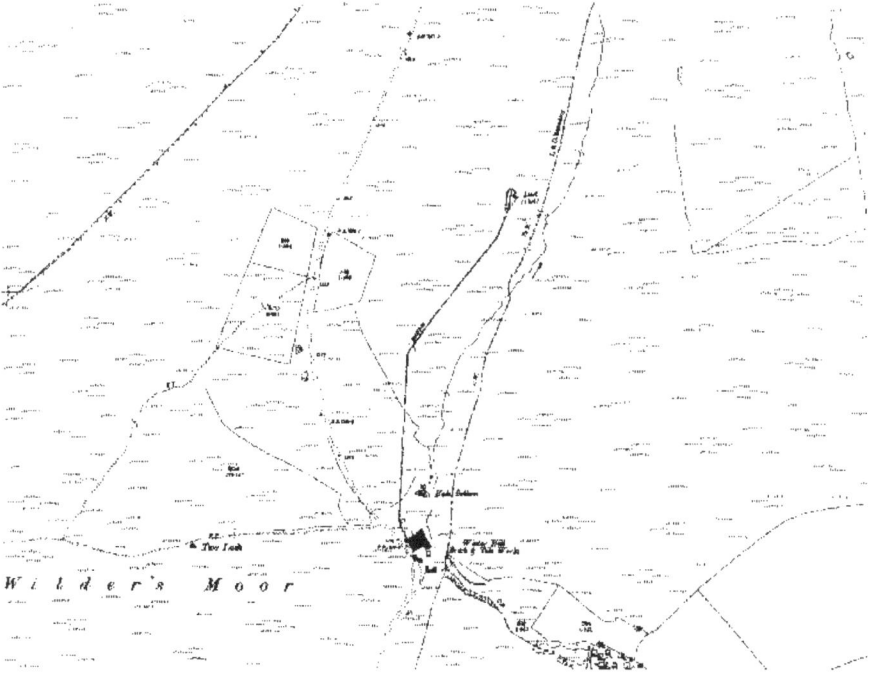

To the right of the photo and directly behind the crash barrier is the site of the old Winter Hill Brick & Tile works, now demolished. Less than 100 yards higher up the road on the left hand side there used to be a row of houses called "Five Houses". The Five Houses appear on many old maps of the area but are not shown on the 1894 First Edition maps.

The brick works were probably once known as "Five Houses Fire Brick and Tile works" as can be seen from an advert in the Bolton Chronicle on the 19th February 1849 which read:

TO BE LET.
An extensive and well established Fire Brick and Tile Works, situated at the Five Houses, Horwich Moor, the present proprietor being desirous of retiring from the business.

The works are complete with Steam Engine, Grinding and Crushing apparatus, Stoves, Drying Houses, Ovens, Moulds and every convenience for carrying out business.

The clay and coal being of superior quality, and are got on the premises at very trifle expense.

P.S. Any person taking the works can be accommodated with five or six acres of land and a few cottages adjoining.

For particulars apply to Mr Wm. Garbutt in the premises, or on Monday at the King's Arms and Four Horse Shoes Bolton.

I have been unable to source any photo of the Brick and Tile works so far - and I have not managed to find its date of closure or demolition.

The tramway mentioned early, and visible on the photo, was used to carry the coal and clay from a mine level situated higher up the "valley" transporting these directly into the brick works. Little now remains of the works apart from a few walls and various mounds of rubble.

It is however worth investigating the two "mounds" furthest away from the crash barrier, for these were obviously the site of the two kilns. The general design of the kilns can be clearly seen, along with some of the fused and once molten internal brickwork – caused due to the intense heat within the kilns. It would be interesting if someone could provide a plan of the works then we would all know what the various "mounds" around the site once were.

At one time there was, I understand, a cottage (illustrated above) near

to the brickwork known as the "Hole Bottom Bungalow" – or Bungalows as I've now ben told it was two bungalows! The bungalow/s were latterly used as a Scout Hut until some point in the 1960's when it was demolished.

The photo is merely a scan of a photocopy of the original photograph and I have no further information on the subject – although I presume this is a property which was marked as "Winter Hill House" on some maps produced around 1950.

Five Houses.

The earliest mention I can find of Five Houses is in connection with the 1838 murder of George Henderson (see an earlier article). Old maps indicate that this was a row of five houses as the name implies

. One of these properties was used as an "ale house" and it was at this house that the murdered man, the travelling salesman George Henderson, used to meet his fellow salesman Benjamin Birrell every other Friday for a drink at 11.am.

After Henderson was shot he was carried down to Five Houses where he was seen by a doctor but he later died.

The alleged killer, a James Whittle, miner, also lived at Five Houses.

Looking at the 1881 Census it is noted that two families lived in the properties at that time:

Dwelling: Hole Bottom, Horwich Lancashire

	Marr	Age	Sex	Birthplace	Occupation
William Thompson M	M	45	M	Leeds(Rainow),York	Burner, Terra Cotta works
Ann Thompson	M	44	F	Rainow, Cheshire	Wife
Fred Thompson	U	19	M	Rainow Cheshire	Terra Cotta works
Samuel Thompson	U	16	M	Rainow, Cheshire	Terra Cotta works
Fanny Thompson		11	F	Rainow Cheshire	
Sarah A Thompson		9	F	Horwich, Lancs	Scholar
Frank Thompson		8	M	Horwich, Lancs	Scholar
Ada Thompson		6	F	Horwich, Lancs	Scholar
George Wilkinson		11months	M	Bolton, Lancs	Boarder
Price Hampson	M	55	M	Flint, Wales	Terra Cotta Works
Harriet Hampson	M	54	F	Bolton, Lancs	Wife
James Hampson	U	26	M	Flint, Wales	Terra Cotta Works.

There is now nothing to see at the site of Five Houses.

The photo above shows all that is now left of the Hole Bottom Brickworks.

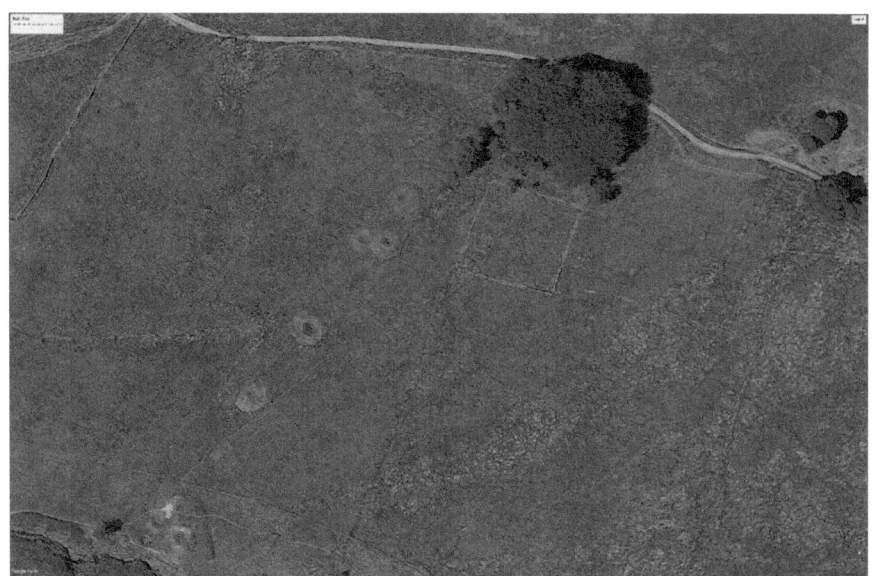

Bell pits between Drinkwaters Farm and Dean Brook, Anglezarke

Dean Brook Tunnel

The Dean Brook tunnel was constructed circa 1870 to divert most of the Dean Brook to feed the Yarrow Reservoir. The egg shaped tunnel runs around 400 meters from a weir in Dean Wood dropping 10 meters over its length before it reaches the banks of the Yarrow Reservoir. A ventilation shaft was made half way along its length which is approximately 25 meters deep and 2-meters in diameter. The tunnel passes close to the ruin of Andertons Farm on the eastern bank of the Yarrow, around half way between the embankment and Alance Bridge (D.A. Owen)

The egg shaped Dean Brook tunnel end at Yarrow Reservoir 2019

Inside the Dean Brook Tunnel

Limestone Brook.

Limestone Brook is the main water source for Lead Mines Clough and would have been responsible for powering the main aspects of the mining operation throughout its productive life. During this time the acquisition and management of the water supply would have been key to the success of the mining operation.

The vital water resource would have powered water wheels and would have been used in the processing of the mined minerals, settling/sludge tanks etc. The consistent supply of water, both in the winter time when too much water could disrupt the operation to the drought of the summer when mining would have to cease would have been a high priority for the mine management and owners.

Limestone Brook near Shooting Hut on a misty morning. The flat stones seen are thought to have once been stood upright, placed there to control the water flow at times of plenty (slow the water down) and drought (to create a series of mini lagoons).

Features are visible in the main section of Limestone Brook near "Shooting Huts" which suggests water management was in operation to possibly regulate the water flow. Add to this channels in the peat cut to funnel water into the brook and its tributaries which could include "Devils Ditch" demonstrates the lengths the mine owners were prepared to go to maintain a constant water supply.

More recently the Limestone Brook joins the Yarrow River at "meeting of the waters" and together form the main water course feeding the Yarrow Reservoir which became operational in 1867.

Possible water management features in Limestone Brook. Flat stones stood upright to hold the water. These were possible pushed over or removed when the brook became one of the main feeder water source for the Yarrow Reservoir circa 1867

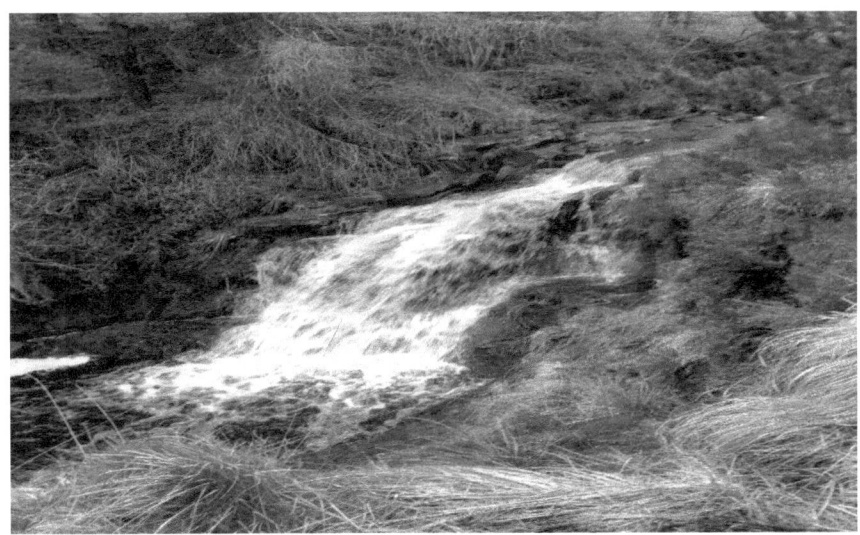

First waterfall in the Limestone Brook near the footbridge at the top of Lead Mines Clough

Second and the Major Waterfall of Limestone Brook mid ways in its travel down Lead Mines Clough. Garry Rhodes MBE and Andy Coward set up for a great photo shoot. 2019.

Limestone Brook continues its journey from the waterfall down the length of the Lead mines Clough

Lead Mines- Clough 2004 – before all the trees were planted!

Waterfall at the lower end of Leadmines Clough

Natural History in the Anglezarke area.

The natural history (trees, plants, ferns, grasses and wildlife etc) of the area is entirely dependent on the landscape characteristics. These can be grouped broadly into three landscape types:

The lower lying agricultural land on the West of the area with woods and hedges. It also contains most of the water area of the landscape

Poor agricultural land on the valley sides and upland fringe, where trees are un-common and hedges tend to give way to walls for some 30% of the area. Woodland occurs in the sheltered cloughs and are usually deciduous species.

The central upland block, which is mostly unenclosed moorland, poorly drained and largely grazed by sheep. Course grasses dominate, but some areas of heather are present mainly in the northern portions of the area.

Large parts of the area have suffered in the past from poor management and this resulted in an unsightly combination of impoverished vegetation, peat erosion and derelict dry-stone walls. Recently attempts have been made to "improve" the area with access roads appearing and a plethora of new fences, tree plantations etc being created.

The moorlands cover a large part of the area and much of the remainder of the land varies greatly in botanical interest. The zones of upper grassland, which are probably the most extensive type of moorland in the area, although a good "type" example are of little interest botanically. Much of the lower regions are in fact old systems which are reverted back to upland grassland. Extensive areas have been colonised extensively by soft rush.

The reservoirs of the area are all of some value as refuges for wildfowl and the Rivington and Anglezarke reservoirs are especially important in winter. Shallow water areas, such as the eastern arm of Upper Rivington Reservoir and parts of Anglezarke Reservoir, support dense aquatic vegetation which is important as a source of shelter, food and cover for many species of breeding and wintering wildfowl. The upper end of Anglezarke reservoir is an ideal sheltered refuge for ducks and grebes and a feeding site for wading bird. The north end of Upper Rivington provides a valuable natural refuge for wildlife and the wooded slopes around the reservoir afford undisturbed cover for many nesting woodland and waterside birds.

The Chorley and District Natural History Society keeps a close eye on the many different biological plants and animals of the area and for £10 a year membership is well worth investigating for anyone interested. Their web site can be found at: www.chorleynats.org.uk . Species lists for birds, butterflies, moths, Odonata, mammals and flora of the Chorley area can be found on the website, along with back copies of their Newsletters. A fascinating archive.

Some decades ago the North West Water Authority produced a report on the then natural history of particular parts of the area and some of these are reproduced below. These lists just scratch the surface but illustrate the wealth of wildlife and biological activity in the area.

Area 1. White Coppice and Anglezarke Reservoir.
Grid Ref SD 620 190

Industrial archaeology and geological interest. Type locality for witherite at Drinkwaters.

The Goyt is an important habitat for fish and insect life, and such notable bird species as Ring Ousel, Dipper and Stonechat nest in the vicinity. The reservoir acts as a refuge for wildfowl and a feeding site for breeding birds

Species List for White Coppice Goit.

Trees
Oak	-	Quercus sp
Rowan	-	Sorbus aucuparia
Alder	-	Alnus glutinosa
Willow	-	Salix spp
Holly	-	Ilex aquilifolium
Birch	-	Betula pendula

Shrubs
Blackberry	-	Rubus fructicosus
Bilberry	-	Vaccinium myrtillus
Heather	-	Calluna vulgaris
Gorse	-	Ulex europaeus

Herbs
Mint	-	Mentha spp
Sneezewort	-	Achillea ptarmica
Yellow Loosetrife	-	Lysimachia Vulgaris
Heath Bedstraw	-	Galium saxatile
Wild Tormentil	-	Potentilla erecta
Rose Bay Willowherb	-	Epilobium angustifolium
Great Willowherb	-	Epilobium hirsutum
Indian Balsom	-	Impatiens glanduifera
Bluebell	-	Endymion non-scripta
Foxglove	-	Digitalis purpurea
Yellowflag Iris	-	Iris pseudacorus
Hawkweed	-	Hieracium spp

Grasses

Mat Grass	-	Nardus stricta
Wavy Hair Grass	-	Deschampsia flexuosa
Tufted Hair Grass	-	Deschampsia caespitosa
Scented Vernal Grass	-	Anthoxanthum oderatum
Yorkshire Fog	-	Holcus lanatus
Sweet Reed Grass	-	Glyceria maxima
Purple Moor Grass	-	Molinia caerulea
Bent Grass	-	Agrostis tenuis
Red Fescue	-	Festuca rubra

Ferns

Lady Fern	-	Anthyrium filix-femina
Broad Buckler Fern	-	Dryopteris dilatata
Bracken	-	Pteridium aquilinium
Sweet Mountain Fern	-	Thelpteris limbosperma
Horsetail	-	Wquisetum spp

Rushes

Soft Rush	-	Juncus effusus
Sedges	-	Carex spp

Birds   **Invertebrates**

Birds	Invertebrates
Coot Kingfisher	Pond Skaters
Wren	Dragonfly
Blue Tit	Blue Damsel Fly
Willow Warbler	Ladybird
Great Tit	Cabbage White
Butterfly	
Blackbird	Grasshopper

Area 1A Sphagnum Flush, White Coppice

Grid Ref SD. 62 29 *(the full ref is not given .... see below)*

The Sphagnum Flush near White Coppice contains several bog plant species rare, or unknown, elsewhere in the area.

Species list for Sphagnum Flush, White Coppice

Trees
Alder	-	Alnus glutinosa
Oak	-	Quercus sp
Willow	-	Salix sp
Holly	-	Ilex aquilifolium
Hawthorn	-	Crataegus monogyna

Shrubs
Blackberry	-	Rubus fructicosus
Billberry	-	Vaccinium myrtillus
Gorse	-	Ulex europaeus

Herbs
Tormentil	-	Potentilla erecta
Common Sorrel	-	Rumex acetosa
Marsh Thistle	-	Cirsium palustre
Creeping Buttercup	-	Ranunculus repens
Mud Water Starwort	-	Callitriche stagnalis
Meadow Buttercup	-	Ranunculus acris
Marsh Marigold	-	Caltha palustris
Nettle	-	Urtica dioica
Wild Angelica	-	Angelica sylvestris
Bog Forget-me-not	-	Myosotis secunda
Valerian	-	Valeriana officinalis
Devils Bit Scabious	-	Succisa pratensis
Sneezewort	-	Achillia ptarmica
Ragged Robin	-	Lychnis flos-cuculi
Marsh Pennywort	-	Hydrocotyle vulgaris
Broad-leaved Willowherb	-	Epilobium montanum
Water Pepper	-	Polygonum hydropiper
Woody Nightshade	-	Solanum dulcamara
Water Crowfoot	-	Ranunculus petalus
Marsh Bedstraw	-	Galium palustre
Bog Willow Herb	-	Epilobium palustre
Marsh Thistle	-	Cirsium palustre
Red Campion	-	Silene dioica
Sheep's Sorrel	-	Rumex acetosella
Great Willowherb	-	Epilobium hirsutum
Lousewort	-	Pedicularis sylvatica
Marsh Birds Foot Trefoil	-	Lotus uliginosus

Grasses

Sweet Vernal Grass oderatum	-	Anthoxanthum
Common Bent Grass	-	Agrostis tenuis
Reed Sweet Grass	-	Glyceria maxima
Yorkshire Fog	-	Holcus lanatus
Purple Moor Glass	-	Molina caerulea

Ferns

Marsh Horsetail	-	Equisetum palustre
Sweet Mountain Fern Iimbosperma	-	Thelypteris

Rushes

Soft Rush	-	Juncus effusus
Jointed Rush	-	Juncus articulatus
Sedges	-	Carex spp

Mosses

Liverwort
Sphagnum recurvum

Area 2. Lead Mines Clough

Grid Reference SD. 629 162

Industrial, archaeological and mineralogical interest. Yarrow Valley of geographical/geological interest. Clough with oak woodland attracting good variety of nesting birds, much frequented by the public.

Trees

Oak,	-	Quercus petraea
Birch	-	Betula pendula
Ash	-	Fraxinus excelsior
Sycamore	-	Acer pseudoplantus
Rowen	-	Sorbus aucuparia
Alder	-	Alnus glutinosa

Hawthorne	-	Crataegus monogyna
Corylus	-	Corylus avellane

Herbs

Creeping Buttercup	-	Ranunculus repens
Wood Sorrel	-	Oxalis acetosella
Common Sorrel	-	Rumex acetosa
Chickweed	-	Stellaria media
Mouse Ear	-	Cerastium fontanum
Red Campion	-	Silene dioica
Spear Thistle	-	Cirsium vulgare
Creeping Thistle	-	Circium arvense
Foxglove	-	Digitalis purpurea

Grasses

Wavy Hair Grass	-	Deschampsia flexuosa
Yorkshire Fog	-	Holcus lanatus
Common Bent	-	Agrostis tenuis
Purple Moor Grass	-	Molinia caerulea

Ferns

Bracken	-	Pteridium aquilinum
Broad Buckler Fern	-	Dryopteris dilatate

Rushes

Soft rush	-	Juncus effusus
Horsetail	-	Equisetum spp.

Area 5. Dean Wood

Grid Reference SD 629 153

A valuable and little disturbed site in a very popular area. Little disturbed oakwood of special value for its ground fauna and breeding birds.

Trees.

Oak	-	Quercus petraea
Sycamore	-	Acer Pseudoplanatus
Wych Elm	-	Ulmus glabra

Beech	-	Fagus sylvatica
Birch	-	Betula pendula
Ash	-	Fraxinus excelsior
Larch	-	Larix decidua
Scots pine	-	Pinus sylvestris
Yew	-	Taxus baccata
Horse chestnut	-	Aesculus hippocastanium
Rowan	-	Sorbus aucuparia
Hazel	-	Corylus avellana
Hawthorne	-	Crataegus monogyna
Elder	-	Sambucus nigra
Alder	-	Alnus glutinosa
Grey Willow	-	Salix cinerea

Shrubs

Blackberry	-	Rubus fructicosa
Raspberry	-	Rubus idaeus
Rhododendron	-	Rhododendron repens
Honeysuckle	-	Lonicera periclymenum
Dog Rose	-	Rosa canina

Herbs

Bluebell	-	Endymion non-scripta
Golden Saxifrage	-	Chrysosplenium oppositifolium
Primrose	-	Primula vulgaris
Bog Violet	-	Viola palustris
Wood Sorrel	-	Oxalis acetosella
Red Campion	-	Silene dioica
Foxglove	-	Digitalis purpurea
Nettle	-	Urtica dioica

Grasses

Wavy Hair Grass	-	Decchampsia flexuosa
Common Bent	-	Agrostis tenuis
Yorkshire Fog	-	Holcus lanatus
Creeping Soft Grass	-	Holcus mollis

Ferns

Bracken	-	Pteridium aquilinum
Broad Buckler Fern	-	Dryopteris dilatata

Male Fern   -   Dryopteris Filix-mas
Lady Fern   -   Athrium filix-femina
Adders Tongue Fern
Hard Fern

Birds   **Mammals**
Kestral   Fox
Sparrowhawk   Stoat
Woodcock   Weasel
Redstart   Rabbit
Bullfinch   Hare
Heron   Hedgehog
Wood Warbler   Mole
Pheasant   Mice
Great Spotted Woodpecker   Voles
Spotted Flycatcher

Belmont Jan 2004 from 2,000 feet

The farms of Anglezarke Moor.

There were once a number of farms on the Anglezarke Moorlands but between 1902 and 1905 the whole area was taken over by Liverpool Corporation and to "protect the water catchment area" many of the farms were deemed as needing to be destroyed.

The website "Anglezarke.net" keeps a list of the farms once there - and the site is well worth keeping an eye on for news on the subject, an excellent web resource for anyone interested in Anglezarke. The current farm list on that site of ruins is as follows:

- Abbott's
- Anderton's
- Brook House
- Brown Hill
- Fogg's
- Hempshaw's
- Higher House
- Latham's / Wilcock's
- Lee House
- Moses Cocker's
- Old Brook's
- Old Knowle Farm
- Old Rachel's
- Parson's Bullough
- Peewet Hall
- Simms
- Stones House
- Stoops
- Turners
- Wilkinson Bullough

Richard Skelton has painstakingly compiled a list of once existing farms in the area from all the available mapping sources:

Abbots, Alance, Albion Villa, Bradley's, Brinks, Brown Hill Farm, Calico Hall, Cliff, Clump, Coppice Stile House, Coomb, Drinkwaters, Finch's Land, Gills, Gir' Nest, Great Hill Farm, Grimes, Grut, Heapey Moor Farm, Hempshaws (Higher and Lower), High Bullough, Higher Knoll, Hollinshead Hall, Jepson's, Keck, The Lord's Hall, Lyon's Den, Moor Edge, Moses Cocker's, Naylors, New Temple, Nightingale's, Old Brooks, Old George's, Old Isaac's, Old Kate's, Old Knowles, Old Lord's, Old Rachel's, Old Will's, Pall Mill, Parson's Bullough, Peewet Hall, Pendennis, Piccadilly, Pimms, Ratten Clough, Rough Lee, Siddow Fold (Gamekeeper's Cottage), Simms, Scott Hall, Solomon's Temple, Sour Mik Hall, Stone's House, Stoops, Turner's, White Hall, Wilcock's, Wilkinson Bullough.

An awful lot of information about these structures and remains can be found on Anglezarke.net. Well worth a visit.

Photo of the water wheel pit in Lead Mines Clough that was used to pump the water from the mine beneath (photo by "Jake of Winter Hill" at https://jakeofwinterhill.blogspot.com)

A double kerbed cairn?

Stones found **(SD 63025 17418)** between Pike Stones and Limestone Clough in the vicinity of Rushy Brow. Someone has mentioned it's a listed double kerbed cairn. The inner kerb (approx 3m in diameter) can be seen on the pics but the outer kerb can only be seen if you root around in the grass

TWO LADS HILL.

In between Rivington Pike and the road to the TV mast lies a small hill with an obvious cairn on top of it. This is "Two Lads", or "Twa Lads" as it has sometimes been called in the past (or still seems to be called this by some with a strong local accent).

There are several major routes used to get to the top of the hill, two from the TV mast road and the other starting next to Sportsman's Cottage on George's Lane.

There are many conflicting stories about the history of Two Lads and how it got its name. One tale has it that the cairn (an earlier one, not the present one) was built in remembrance of two boys who were lost in a snow storm some 400 years ago "their rigid bodies discovered frozen to each other in a final vain attempt for warmth".

The other tale goes back a lot earlier to Saxon times (the name Rivington is believed to be of Saxon origin derived from "The Town of the Ravens") when there was some sort of encampment on Two Lads.

It is said that the two sons of a local Saxon "king" had the monument built for the funeral of their father. As T Morris in the first issue of the "Rivington Review" pointed out, the latter theory for the name is quite credible, as Saxon funerals tended to be on higher ground where this was possible.

Just to confuse the issue, there is yet a third tradition of the story which has it that the two lads who perished in the snow were orphans of a Saxon King who was himself killed in battle.

Another writer has suggested that the name Wilders Moor derives from the fact that the "two lads" became "wildered" (bewildered) or lost on the moor. *Gladys Sellers in her book "Walks on the West Pennine Moors" says that "Two Lads Moor" used to have two Bronze Age burial mounds close to the track and not far from the top. In fact they gave the moor its name. They were excavated long ago and no records of their contents were ever made. Not even their sites can be seen today"* Anyone any other theories to add? We'll never know the truth but what a fascinating story - whichever of them might be true.

Although I've never found a thing on Two Lads, despite 30 years of searching, I understand that Mr John Winstanley carried out some excavations (date unknown) on Two Lads and "discovered items of pottery, tools and human remains some of which date back to pre-historic times".

The present cairns on top of the hill are not the original ones. These were reputed to have been located in a slightly different spot but no remains of them now exist.

One of the main mining tunnels underneath Winter Hill passes almost directly underneath Two Lads (about 50 yards to the North to be exact – there is a photo elsewhere in this book of that tunnel)) heading from the field in front of Sportsman's Cottage almost to the TV mast.

All the coal and clay from directly underneath Two Lads summit has been removed , half in 1919 and half in 1930. The surrounding areas of the hill were mined between approximately 1914 and 1957.

There is also a small quarry on the south-western flank of the hill, a most odd spot for such an undertaking unless the stone were needed extremely locally, Hole Bottom perhaps, or even for any early "encampment" on the hill itself.

The hill is part encircled by a ditch. Some folk claim this was once part of the hills ancient defences, but others tell me this is a modern development, and is purely to do with water drainage. Still others say it's a mixture of the two.

In the late 80's there was a local "storm" in the Bolton Evening News both in articles and especially on the letters pages.

Over the years the Two Lads cairn had virtually vanished and was in ruins. In 1988 a "mystery man" started to rebuild the cairn (I have since learned that the "mystery man" was David A Owen!).

This task was then taken over by amateur historian Robin Smith who took over the task of restoring the monument to its original glory and he added a further four feet to the structure both by adding to it in height as well as clearing away rubble from the base.

During the digging he found the remains he believed he could date back one or two centuries.

His most amazing discovery came when he dug to the bottom of the cairn and hit solid stone.

He believed this could be the top of another ancient construction, adding weight to many historians view that the cairn marks the site of a Bronze or Iron Age fortress.

The council took offence at this "new" structure (especially its 10 foot height) and claimed it was dangerous and proceeded to pull it down!

Undeterred, the mound was once again rebuilt by local people in 1989 but it was promptly pulled back down again by the authorities!

Two Lads became known as "the Yo Yo cairn"!

One reason for the council pulling it down is a bit rich – it is too big! A sketch of Two Lads was drawn by Albison of Bolton 200 years ago which clearly showed that even in those days it was about eight feet high and thirteen feet in diameter!

I genuinely don't know what to believe about all this story. Can we please have photo's of the "old pots, jars, pieces of leather and clay smoking pipes etc found there.

Springs and Dingle Reservoirs

Although this book was only intended to cover the main area of Winter Hill, as the Springs and Dingle reservoirs take all their water from the north-eastern flanks of the hill, it was felt worthy of inclusion. The reservoirs lie next to the A657 on Belmont road between Bolton and Belmont. The two reservoirs lie next to each other with Dingle being a little lower and near to Bolton. Springs holds 134 million gallons and has a maximum depth of 48 feet whilst Dingle can contain 79 million gallons and is 30 feet deep. The total length of the embankments of both reservoirs is over three quarters of a mile in length, quite an undertaking for when they were constructed in the early 1800's.

Springs reservoir takes its name from the source of its water, from the springs on Daddy Meadows and was Bolton's first major reservoir supplying water to the town. Dingle reservoir takes its name from Shaly Dingle where the stream was diverted in order to supply the water to the new reservoir.

There was a problem that had to be overcome before both these reservoirs could be built. In nearby Eagley Brook, there were a number of water powered mills who derived a considerable amount of the water needed for their power from the flanks of Winter Hill. Before permission could be obtained to build the reservoirs, the Bolton Waterworks Company had to undertake to build a further large reservoir at Belmont (on the site of a much earlier smaller one) from which water would be released daily to compensate the mill owners for the loss of water from the Winter Hill Springs.

As well as Springs, Dingle and Belmont there is also a smaller reservoir in the area, Wards, usually known as the "Blue Lagoon". This was built in the early 19th century to supply water to Rycroft Works which was at the side of High Street on the spot now comprising the Brookdale Estate. The reservoir was enlarged in 1893 by Deacons who used the water to improve the water supplies to Belmont Bleachworks.

The major water supply for Springs reservoir comes from a man made well on Daddy Meadows. A friend once commented that at one time he had come across an old map which indicated that in this area there were "wind pumps". I have never seen a copy of this map. He went on to explain that in the 1960's he had a vague recollection of seeing old metal "mast type" structure (old USA style wind pump perhaps) in the area. Whilst looking through some photo's lent to me by to this person, I found the photograph shown below (I think it came from an old Bolton Waterworks publication). When checking on a 1947 Waterworks plan I note that "Springs Well" is the direct feed point for Springs reservoir – along with "Daddy Meadows Springs". The date of the photo is unknown.

SPRINGS WELL BORING PLANT

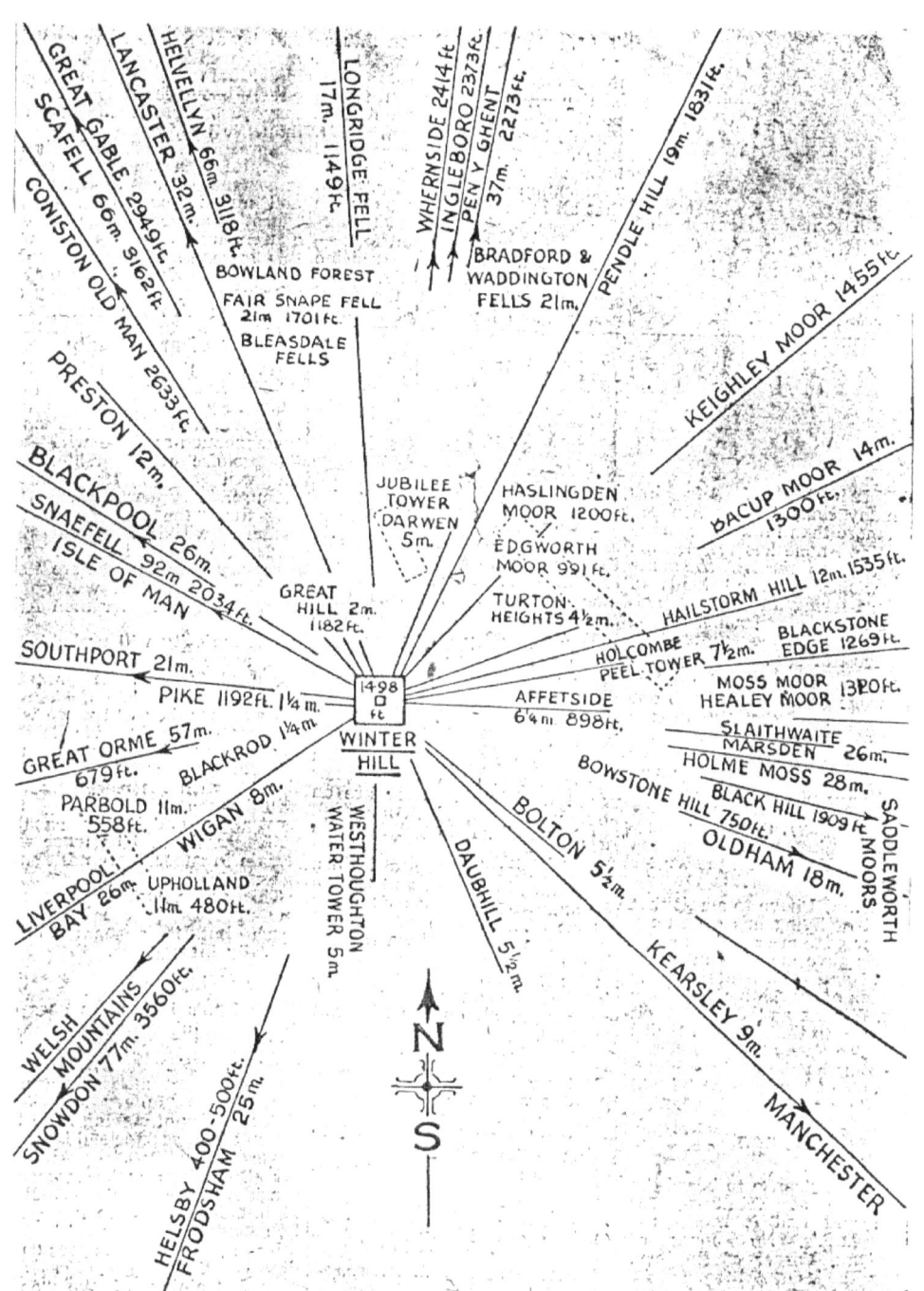

More Winter Hill Mining Remains.

Since writing volume 1 of this book, I have received many enquiries about the coal mines and tunnels under Winter Hill. A large number of people have asked "Are there any other mining remains other than the things you have written about". A very difficult question to answer! As explained earlier, it would be foolish to fully describe ALL details of mines under Winter Hill because this would merely encourage every adventurous minded person in the area to descend on them and to explore them. I am however tempted to give details of a few other finds in the area just to educate people as to what is there. So here goes. I'll give a few more brief descriptions of other interesting things to see – but please don't pester me via email for any EXACT details other than what is written below. All workings mentioned below are either fully sealed up, have a blockage near to the entrance (rockfall, roof collapse etc) or have been filled in by the explorers after finding nothing of interest.

Another "Montcliffe area" mine.

Apart from the main Montcliffe Mine and the associated Margery Drift, there is another rather odd mine in the same general area. Entrance to this mine was effected by squeezing through a small hole at the top of a wall and for this reason (and because it was VERY wet) I declined to enter and so my description is merely what I have been told. I nearly always decline to physically explore tunnels these days!

Dropping through the hole you enter a concrete roofed flooded area with man made stone walls and after a few yards there is a passage on the right hand side, the tunnel straight ahead being chest deep in water. The RH tunnel goes nowhere. Following the main tunnel, the water shallows and eventually becomes reasonably dry underfoot.

I am told that parts of this mine are somewhat "cave like" with a running stream in one section which heads off downhill.

Wilderswood area.

There are at least two old tunnels in this area which can be clearly seen by any passing walker so I am giving away no secrets. Both are a waste of time exploring internally for they are both totally blocked after a few yards with major roof falls – and I mean "major"!

Taking the path from Ormston's farm (from the bottom of Ormston Lane) that heads towards the bottom end of Wilderswood, you pass over a bridge spanning the stream. Look over the upstream parapet and on the right hand bank you will be able to see the entrance to a small tunnel. This is blocked only a few yards in and any attempt to excavate would probably collapse the roadway that passes over it. Nothing is known about this tunnel and I have seen no maps or charts relating to any underground workings under Wilderswood.

Carry on up the path and after 100 yards or so, pass through the hole in the right hand wall (where a "cabin" once stood, reputedly to record the amounts of coal coming out of the local workings) and go up the steps to the footpath. After a few yards drop down to stream level and head upstream and soon you will find another tunnel entrance. This one is strange and nobody has so far been able to explain its purpose. The size of the tunnel indicates a fairly major mine entrance, but in order to enter it, you first of all have to drop down into a sort of well about 3 feet deep. Whether this "well" is a later development is not known, but for this to be any sort of working mine entrance, there should not be a well or wall there which would have prevented any easy coal extraction from the mine. Yet another of this areas mysteries! This tunnel is also blocked after a few yards and the site of the collapse can be seen from the banking higher up the slope.

There are other suspected mine workings in the area but all are either totally sealed, collapsed, or can no longer be found despite being marked on early maps. In a later volume I'll try to get round to giving a step by step guide to this general area so to make a visit here more interesting.

A bricked up adit entrance at Hole Bottom

Winter Hill & Noon Hill Burial Mounds.

(The following is an article was written by J Rawlinson and published in the Chorley & District Archaeological Society Bulletin Sept & Dec 1961. It describes the discovery and excavation of the Winter Hill Barrow.)

The barrow is marked on modern maps as "Tumulus" or "Cairn".

In the district of Central Lancashire there are several authentic burial mounds. On Anglezarke Moors there is a large round barrow called "Round Loaf". It is possible this covers a stone chambered grave.

On the same moor there is a site called Pike Stones, a ruined chambered grave from which the farmers have taken a lot of stone. Both these are marked on the OS maps.

On Rivington Moor there is a saucer tumulus called "Noon Hill", famous locally for more than 400 years, and Winter Hill Round Barrow which was discovered by Mr Tom Creear and myself in March 1957.

On Horwich Moor, there is "Two Lads", a site encircled by earthworks, which once contained two stone cairns surrounded by a stone wall with an entrance from the east.

Nearer Bolton just outside the Horwich boundary is a barrow with the interesting name of "Priests Crown". This mound and Two Lads are marked on the OS map.

To return to the Winter Hill Round Barrow. On Sunday afternoon 24th March 1957, whilst searching for a possible Roman signalling and observation station on Winter Hill, Mr Creear and I discovered a curved line of stones about 20 feet long just peeping out of the turf.

Investigation proved these to be part of a stone circle about 63 feet in diameter. Inside the circle there was a pile of stones forming an inner circle with a slight depression in the centre.

The site commanded a wonderful view of Lancashire and its surroundings, only a small section of about 30 degrees to the South of East being obscured by the hills. Just north of east the southern slopes of Pendle Hill were to be seen with the way into Yorkshire through Burnley and Colne. West of Pendle, on a clear day, Ingleborough, Penygent and Whernside come into view.

Continuing West, Longridge and Bleasedale Fells can be followed bringing the sea coast into view near Pilling.

The coast is visible to Great Ormes Head at Llandudno in North Wales including the estuaries of the Ribble and the Mersey and in an arc from SW to SE the view continues to the Peak District of Derbyshire …. Including the industrial sprawl around Warrington and Manchester, and occasionally above all Snowdon and the Carnedds peep out of the clouds.

On Friday evening 21st June 1957 I took Mr Rosser to the Winter Hill Barrow site and he was very impressed. Mr Creear and myself revisited the site on 29th June.

Mr Creear exposed about 30 feet of the outer wall whilst I dug a trial hole in the west side of the circle, here I found the wall 25 inches high resting on the cleared surface of the moor.

I took two photos, one from the west and two from the south-west before starting work on the site. This work was reported at the Society meeting on July 4th and another visit arranged for Saturday July 6th to expose more of the outside wall.

Nineteen members of the Society visited the site as arranged and about fifty feet of the outer wall was exposed, the work was then stopped and we reported the situation to Mr Rosser. On Tuesday 6th August Professor A Whallet, Dr Bulock and Mr C EP Rosser visited the site and stated that it was a Bronze Age Barrow and would be scheduled by the Ministry of Works.

Later it was decided to excavate the barrow the following summer. On Friday afternoon the 18th July 1958 together with Mr Ron Rigby, our Society Vice Chairman, I met Dr Bullock and Mr C E P Rosser on the site on Winter Hill. We pegged out the south-west section and arranged for work to commence on the following Monday the 21st. I also arranged for hot lunches to be delivered on the site for the week from Rivington Hall Barn.

On Monday and Tuesday the excavation went steadily on without any outstanding incident. The pattern formed on the vertical face of the excavation was very interesting, the mixture of clay about four different colours from cream to brown with the network effect of the turf lines produced a design almost like a continental cheese.

This basket filling continued all the way through the mound but about halfway to the centre there was a plainer sloping turf line as though the centre cairn had been covered first and the space left to the outer wall filled in later.

On Wednesday afternoon a flurry of excitement was caused by the discovery of a squarely cut piece of wood (birch) lying on the last layer of turf at a depth of 3 feet from the surface and 13 feet from the centre of the mound.

The wood was very soft and wet and to prevent it drying out and crumbling after measuring, it was covered with a wet sack. The stick was 2 foot 2 inches long by 2 inches wide and almost one inch thick.

I suggested to Mr Rosser that perhaps it had been used as a measuring stick. Later two samples about 3 inches long were taken for tests. I was promised one of these at some future date with a report.

On reaching the centre portion we found a large quantity of stone which had been a central cairn and a thick almost vertical turf line which led one to believe that the centre had been disturbed. Dr Bullock said this was probably about 200 years ago.

Another section of the north east of the mound was commenced and later two square holes 6 ft by 6 ft near the centre were dug.

Nothing more was found but the two professionals said that they were perfectly satisfied with the excavation which had proved that the site was a burial mound and the stick of wood would eventually give its age.

Personally, I was disappointed I thought that the whole mound should have been excavated. The following month, August, the newly formed Bolton Archaeological Society under the leadership of Mr J Winstanly commenced to excavate Noon Hill, Rivington, in the Chorley Rural Area and about three-quarters of a mile from the Winter Hill Mound.

We had photographed and measured Noon Hill two years ago and I had taken Dr Bullock and a small party there whilst we were working on Winter Hill. Dr Bullock gave the opinion that it had been dug. I visited Noon Hill on the Wednesday of the second week of the excavation and found a south-eastern quadrant excavated to the inner wall.

In the south-eastern quadrant the inner wall had been completely taken out and evidence of three burial found there. One had a shattered urn but only a small heap of burnt bones were found to mark the other two.

Two tanged and barbed flint arrowheads were unearthed and a small flint knife blade with one edge fine toothed like a saw and the other a straight sharpened edge. All probably votive from the burials. The bones had apparently been broken up to go into the urns, and some of these were later found to be a child's.

The shattered urn of a dirty yellow colour has now been rebuilt and is on exhibition at Bolton *Museum (it is now no longer exhibited but is held in the museum storage area).*

The excavation showed an outer circle formed of a double ring of large stones, this circle is about 52 feet in diameter, an inner wall of smaller stones, mostly boulders, was strengthened by several buttress stones. The wall is three feet high and forms a ring 33 feet in diameter, the burials were found built into this wall.

The filling of this mound was much darker than that on Winter Hill, more loam and less clay so the turf lines were not so plain. The urn is 10 inches in height, 9 inches in largest diameter, base 4 inches diameter and a simple design of straight lines covers the top half. The excavation was stopped soon after my visit to be resumed next summer under C.B.A. direction.

Two Lads is a hill 1275 feet above sea level and almost a mile south east from Rivington Pike. On the summit is a large pile of stones and between the summit and the 1150 feet contour there are 1 mile & 1500 yards of earthworks. In places these have been altered and adapted for water conservancy purposes but sufficient can be seen to lead one to believe that they constituted a breastwork and trench system of defences.

The cairn on the summit has been built from two cairns, and a surrounding wall around the year 1800 by a local lord of the manor so that it could be discerned from his residence. The famous antiquary Durning Rasbotham visited this hill in 1776 and our reconstruction is from his description. The hill has been a prolific source of flint finds for a long time. I cannot find any mention of an excavation here but I hope to take a Yorkshire Archaeologist who has had experience on Pennine Sites over the hill.

John Rawlinson.
Chorley and District Archaeological Society Bulletin.

An unexplained mystery.

Since the writing of Volume 1 of this scrapbook, I have received a number of e-mails from various people around the world who have all added a little bit to my knowledge of Winter Hill. One such person lived for a period at Sportsman's Cottage in the mid 1950's and I repeat below exactly what that person wrote because not only is it a fascinating story, but I also wonder if anyone has had any other "strange" experiences either on Winter Hill or on the nearby moors. Any similar information received will be most welcome for us all to share (e-mail me at d.lane@btinternet.com).

"I would like to tell you something that happened on the moors one night. My Grandad was a no-nonsense man who had been a policeman in Liverpool for many years before his retirement to Rivington. He was not a fanciful man nor a liar. I was staying with them, as usual, and when I got up this particular morning I knew something was wrong....my Nan packed my stuff and some for her and Grandad and took me home to Liverpool.......they never went back to Rivington, to

Sportsmans Cottage !! It was not until many years later that I found out what made them abandon their home overnight.

My Grandad had got up in the night to use the toilet and, as you would, had looked out of the window over the black moors. He saw something out on the moors that made him tell my Nan he wouldn't spend another night there and they came to stay with us until they could find somewhere to live. They never went back there to stay, only to pack up and move out.

My Grandad would never tell anyone what he saw, not even my Nan, and the secret died with him. All I know is that it scared him to death and made him move out straight away. I missed Rivington a lot. Do you know of anything that my Grandad could have seen? Are there any tales of strange things up there? I have wondered about it all my life and if anyone else has ever seen anything that affected them" .

Can you add anything to this recollection? Have you experienced anything similar?

Another "ghostly" occurrence in the vicinity.

Although not strictly on Winter Hill, Anderton is near enough to the base of the hill to include the following snippets!

They are taken from the Bolton Evening News dated December 4th 1982 and from a letter written in the same newspaper on Thursday the 23rd December 1982.

Pub's spirit gives staff the shakes*. Licensee Mr Richard Calvert reckons there are more spirits in his pub than behind the bar. A catalogue of strange sightings and weird experiences by members of staff at the Millstone Hotel, Anderton, near Horwich, over three years has convinced Mr Calvert that a "grey lady" exists. The latest incident centred on the coffee lounge. Mr Calvert said "We showed a couple in there and asked them to sit near the fireplace. Almost immediately the woman came out shaking, saying there was a ghost. She was gasping for breath and trembling".*

But most reports of mysterious presence at the Millstone focus on the main restaurant, known as "the back room". Mrs Lynne Edwards, of

Mary Street East, Horwich, worked at the Millstone as a cleaner for two years.

She said "The first time I saw something strange was one morning when we had all been sitting in the bar area having our coffee break.

I felt a strange sensation that there was someone watching me from the back restaurant. I glanced up and saw this grey outline."

Mother of two, Mrs Janice Tyrer of Wright Street, Horwich, confesses to be "terrified" of being alone in the back room. She has worked as a cleaner at the Millstone for the past four years.

Mr Calvert spoke of other strange happenings at the pub, like the burglar alarm going off in the middle of the night.

He said that the previous licensee had an alsatian, which refused to go in the back room and in an upstairs bedroom.

One of the questions now being asked is could the Millstone Phantom be the Phantom of Headless Cross?

Headless Cross is 200 yards from the pub and there have been many reports of a monk crossing the road. The sightings are based on an age-old story about Father Bennett who was head of Lady Chapel – now covered by Lower Rivington reservoir.

During the Reformation Father Bennett, fearing that valuables in the chapel would be plundered, decided to hide them. He entered a tunnel that was supposed to lead to the chapel and was never seen again.

The latest reports of ghostly goings-on centre on Headless Cross House. Mr Anthony Samuels and his family live there.

Mr Samuel's runs a business in St George's Road, Bolton, said they returned from their summer holidays last year to find all the lights on. Yet there was no shred of evidence of any intruders. He said: "Every so often, my wife can see a face on the door of the bedroom wardrobe".

++

Was it the "ghost" of priest daughter said. *Sir ...I was very interested to read your report of the ghost of the "grey lady" seen in and around the Millstone at Anderton, Lancs.*

My daughter Tracy, who was then eight, saw her in May 1978. The "lady" was standing in the centre of a small stone hump backed bridge in Grimeford Lane, leading from near the Millstone to the A6 at Blackrod.

We had been to the Millstone with my parents and two children and were taking my parent's home to Blackrod at the time she was sighted. It was about 10 o'clock on a lovely summer night as we were driving down the Lane.

As we approached the bridge Tracy saw a lady dressed in a long grey dress, a cape and with something on her head, which she could not describe properly at the time, standing as if waiting to cross the road.

As we drove past her she suddenly disappeared. You should have heard Tracy's reaction when this happened. She just could not believe it as she thought she had seen a real live person.

No one else in the car saw her except Tracy insisted she was there and started to describe her in great detail.

At this a cold shiver ran down my spine as I remembered my parents telling me of a ghost that used to haunt the lane when I was a child.

She said she was rather tall and seemed old but she did not see her features clearly.

She also wanted to know what a lady was doing down a lonely lane on her own at that time of night. She said that the dress was so long that "I thought she'd been to a party".

Later I started to draw pictures of what she said she had seen and, after drawing lots of different headwear, the thing she wore on her head turned out to be a barreta, the small four cornered cap that priests wear.

Tracey has maintained all along that what she saw was a lady but when the Pope visited Britain in May and she saw a full length shot of him on television she said "that lady" was wearing exactly the same clothes but they were grey.

Last year we got a book from the library about Rivington and the story of Father Bennett was in it. We think this is what Tracy saw as he used to travel round from village to village blessing the people.

We were also told by someone that priests around those times used to stand at the crossing of a ford and bless the travellers as they went by.

The bridge where Tracy saw the ghost was across a small stream which probably many years ago could have been the crossing of a ford.

I hope this letter sheds a little more light on the mystery as it certainly gives us food for thought knowing that someone else has seen the "grey lady" besides our daughter… Mrs Brenda Smith, Horwich.

Horwich Journal 23rd December 1927. Yet another ghostly occurrence!

An account of a ghost story – 25 years ago Mr and Mrs W H Lever were returning from Chorley to their bungalow in a coach and horses when, on the steepest part of the old road leading up from Lower House Farm to the Pigeon Tower, the two horses stopped and refused to go any further.

Mr and Mrs Lever had to walk the rest of the way.

The horses and carriage were turned with great difficulty and taken home another way.

Both the coachman and servants averred that the road was haunted and would not travel the road again after dark.

Aeroplane Crashes on and around Winter Hill

There have been a remarkably large number of plane crashes either on Winter Hill itself or in the surrounding area. Various people have compiled lists of these crashes and more information has come to light following articles in the Bolton Evening News. Unfortunately I can't give credit to the people who have provided this information for all I have are unsigned sheets of paper with the information on them. Below is a list of the crashes I am aware of:

Date	Type	Location	Remarks
1915		Bob's Brow, Horwich	Single seat fighter RFC
		Nr Nab Gate Harwood	
Apr-20		Ramsden's Meadows	Sir Alan Cobham & passenger unhurt
7.28	Atlas biplane	Winter Hill/Belmont Riv Rd	FO Walker. From Sealand to Catterick
3.4.29	DH Moth	Markland Hill Lane	R Taggert
15.11.35	Puss Moth	Crowthorne Hill	Lancashire Aero Club
6.6.36	DH Rapide	Nr Dean Golf Club	Pilots & passengers unhurt. IOM to Barton
37	Moth type?	Crowthorne Moor	Mail plane. IOM to Mc/r
17.8.37		No 50 Mornington Rd	Sgt Blackburn killed
		Little Hulton	RAF plane force landed
38/39	Roc	Stocks Park, Horwich	
13.2.41	Spitfire	Ashton Field, Little Hulton	Pilot had severe facial injuries
5.41	Skua	Golf Course Horwich	Fleet Air Arm
1.9.42	P 38	Sowall Farm, West/ton	Williams
7.8.42	Argus	Winter Hill. North side	5 ADG. 5 occupants uninjured
3.2.43	Skua	Dunscar Lodge	776 Squadron, RNAS, Stretton to Speke

Date	Aircraft	Location	Notes
16.11.43	Wellington	Hurst Hill, Anglezarke	28 OTU. All crew killed
24.12.43	Oxford	Winter Hill	410 Squadron RAF
13.1.44	B 7G	Crowthorne Hill	
44		Bryan Hey Reservoir	On flight to Burtonwood
2.2.45	Hurricane	Horrocks Field Farm, Scout Rd	N T Huddle Flt Sgt killed
2.2.45	Hurricane	Whimberry Hill	P S Taylor Flt Sgt killed
29.7.45	Mustang 3	Cadshaw Bridge/Bull Hill	W O Hoga Polish Squadron 12 Group killed
1946	Spitfire	Darwen Moor	
14.9.53	Meteor	Crowthorne Hill	2 planes crashed. 610 Squadron. Hooton Park
27.2.58	Bristol 170	Winter Hill	35 died, 7 survived
22.12.65	Chipmunk	Smithills Moor	Manchester UAS flying from Woodvale
8.68	Cessna 172	Winter Hill	Pilot survived, Pleasure flight Blackpool, to Barton
29.9.77	Horizon	Whittle Pike, Scout Moor	2 killed, Yeadon to Barton
21.1.78	Piper TriPacer	Georges Lane, Horwich	3 killed. Flew into wall in rain & mist
C 1944	Spitfire	Nr Bay Horse, Heath Charnock	One cow killed!

The most disastrous crash on Winter Hill occurred on the 27th February 1958 when a Bristol Wayfarer of Silver City Airlines crashed on the summit of Winter Hill with 35 people losing their lives. The aircraft had left Ronaldsway on the Isle of Man with a party of motor traders on board who were on their way to the Exide Battery Works at Clifton Junction. It was mid morning when the crash occurred following a navigation error.

When the Silver City Airlines plane took off from Ronaldsway all was in order. Charlie Sierra, flew over the Irish Sea at 1,500 feet, with the crew expecting a lift in altitude when they reached the Lancashire coast. It never came and Captain Edward Cairns was asked if he could maintain the same height by Air Traffic Control at Preston. He agreed, and was told by his First Officer William Howarth that the planes radar compass was tuned to the beacon at Wigan. What the crew did not realise was that through an elementary mistake they had picked up the wrong beacon call sign. Instead of being on course for Wigan – call sign MYK, the ill-fated plane was heading for MYL – the Oldham beacon.

Watching the radar screen at Ringway Airport was zone controller Maurice Ladd. It was 9.44am when he picked up a faint radar signal to pinpoint Charlie Sierra somewhere over Chorley. Immediately Mr Ladd gave the order that Charlie Sierra should turn right on to a course of 250 degrees. Despite his split second decision, it was too late. The Wayfarer, already heading straight for the range of hills – and with the odds-against chance of flying "blind" through a gap in them – altered course. Unfortunately, through no-one's fault, the advice came vital seconds too late. The plane, by now in the cloud, veered to the right, but instead of open airspace her two-man crew were confronted by the bleak rearing hillside.

A total of 35 people lost their lives in the crash and there were seven survivors including the crew. The planes First Officer staggered the 350 yards from the scene of the crash to the Winter Hill ITA transmitter to raise the alarm. The aircraft had broken into three pieces, with only the tail recognisable as part of a plane

Conditions on the hill were appalling and rescuers had to struggle through snow sometimes six feet deep to get to the crash. Fog brought visibility down to almost zero and although ambulances were sent from nearly every nearby town they were held up until a bulldozer had cleared a path for them.

Three RAF helicopters were sent to the scene, one with a doctor on board but fog prevented them from landing. The survivors were taken to Bolton Royal Infirmary.

There is now a plaque commemorating the crash mounted on the side of the TV station and is visible from the road.

The commemorative plaque on the wall of the TV station.

The 50th anniversary plaque of the crash.

A Service of Remembrance
to mark the 50th Anniversary of the

Winter Hill Air Disaster
(Thursday 27th February, 1958)

IN MEMORIAM *(Kathleen Faragher)*

Oh tragic isle, how anguished is thy weeping
for those lost sons returning home no more;
Snatched from thy breast to Death's grim, silent keeping,
on alien hills beyond their native shore.
Perchance their farewell glimpse of thee, O Mona,
was Snaefell's cap – Barrule light laced with snow –
Green glens deep scored against thy rolling uplands –
impatient waters frothing far below
As they set forth, encircling their loved homeland
on eager wing; then heading out to sea,
Were borne away upon their last long journey;
swept from our sight – but not from memory;
For surely when the heather spreads her glory,
when curlews call, and summer breezes play,
These island hills will sing their joyous story:
"Our friends of yester-year have passed this way!"

Wednesday 27th February, 2008, at 11.00am

in Holy Trinity Church, Horwich

RECENTLY COLLAPSED MINE ENTRANCE, CATTER NAB, RIVINGTON MOOR. STEPS LEAD DOWN TO BASE AT 20' DEPTH, SLOPING ENTRANCE SUPPORTED BY WOODEN BEAMS. ENTRANCE SUBSEQUENTLY CAPPED BY NCB. JULY 27th 1980.

Rivington Pike 1938

Access to the Moors

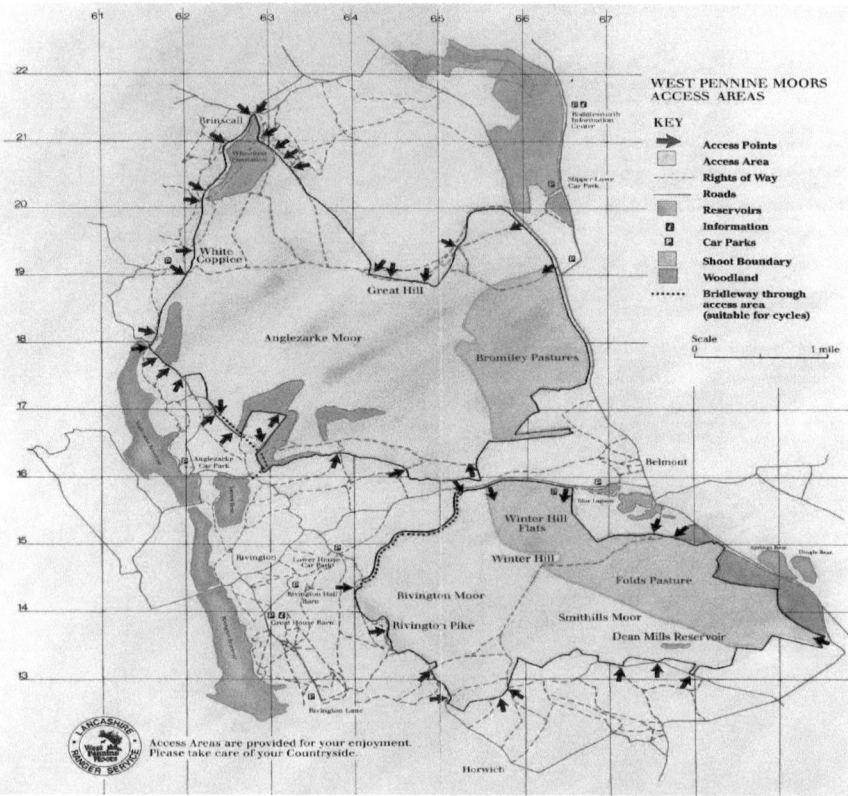

All of the land is owned by "someone". Winter Hill and the surrounding areas are all owned by somebody whether this be a private landlord, a water authority or a local authority. Although large areas of Winter Hill, Anglezarke Moor etc are open to the public there has to be some control over access to these areas so "access agreements" have been drawn up with all the local landlords involved. Apart from all the usual "rules" regarding how one should behave on the moors, there are clearly defined "access" points to get on to the moors (i.e. no climbing over walls, no crossing farmers fields etc in order to get onto the moors). The official map of all officially agreed access points is shown above .... **PLEASE STICK TO THEM**

RIVINGTON BUNGALOW TO GO
House and Gardens Everyone will Miss

FUTURE generations of Bolton folk, enjoying the splendid heritage of Lever Park, made theirs by the generosity of the first Lord Leverhulme, will probably look with puzzled eyes at the wooded slope of Rivington.

They will recall that the generous donor of an industrially-romantic day had a residence perched eyrie-like atop that hill. They will muse: "It has completely disappeared—pity!"

From the point of view of the lover of unusual things whether in houses and gardens, or jewels and music, it is a pity. But it seems inevitable. Liverpool Corporation have all along placed the unquestionable purity of the water collected on their great and beautiful gathering ground before the things of the spirit. And they, the last owners of The Bungalow, have this week signalized the last chapter of the strange story by proposing to hand the place, lock, stock, and barrel, as the saying is, to a demolition gang.

Soon then it will be gone, with all its striking characteristics that reflected the taste of its builder, and the hillside will return to the whispering solitudes, the wind, the rain, and the cry of the curlew.

Beautiful Tapestries

There was formerly at the Bungalow a collection of characteristic things—Lord Leverhulme's own almost monkish apartment, open mostly to the winds of heaven; his collection of beautiful tapestries in the hall, an attractive library of books beloved—almost a Lancashire anthology—and furniture worthy of a connoisseur; electric horses to take the place of flesh and blood mounts when years began to tell upon the busy Viscount.

He loved dancing, and it is no surprise to learn that he had a circular ballroom built whose perfect proportions and polished floor have delighted thousands of those to whom he so frequently threw open his house and grounds.

There was another feature that those who knew him understood. Although he was no great astrologer or astronomer he had his dining-room ceiling illuminated with the stars and planets as they were in their courses at the moment of his birth.

After his personal treasures no feature of the estate could so well reflect the man as the perfectly-proportioned gardens, green lawns and a miniature lake on levels carved out of the rock, waterfalls tumbling down the tree-clothed hillside, nooks and crannies filled with choice plants. And the Japanese gardens. These were planned in princely style. They were a romance of the landscape art, and nothing pleased their owner so much as to know his personal friends and his fellow townsmen of his beloved Bolton were enjoying them with him.

The Bungalow story is inseparable from that of his purchase in 1899 of the Rivington Hall estate from the agents of Mr. J. W. Crompton, of Rivington Hall.

He was living at Hillside, Heaton, at the time and as his son, the present Viscount, recalls in his memoirs, the proposal appealed to him. At Rivington he could make a "garden" in which his imagination could have full play.

"The rest of the estate he could offer to his native town as a park and so ensure the preservation of its beauties for the public, for Rivington Pike, some 1,200ft. above sea-level and one of the highest landmarks in this part of Lancashire had long been a favourite resort of the people of Bolton and the surrounding towns"

He fully realized the position and responsibility of the Liverpool Corporation Waterworks Committee, and it is noteworthy that at every stage he offered them first choice before he purchased the estate to fulfil his less utilitarian dreams.

Refused to Make Profit

And when Parliament decided in his favour and a commission fixed generous terms, he scrupulously refused to make a profit, devoting the surplus to Liverpool charity and to broadening the basis of the work of the Liverpool University, particularly in the study of architecture and civic design.

This bungalow scheme began as it has ended. On an unusual note. The first building was a bungalow of wood of simple design. This was replaced by a rather more elaborate residence—the one which it has since been admitted was burnt to the ground early in the morning of July 8th, 1913, by women suffrage extremists.

Then the Viscount built one, chiefly of local stone. One which he said could not be burnt down. Its terraces, garden houses and picturesque dove cotes we know. And in 1905 he started his garden scheme to plans drawn by Mr. Mawson, the eminent architect of Beautiful Bolton fame.

It is said that £250,000 was spent on the making of this attractive property.

After his death in 1925 the Bungalow and gardens were acquired by the late Mr. John Magee who, like Lord Leverhulme, welcomed visits of the public.

When Mr. Magee died, the property was placed on the market and conferences of representatives of local authorities and the Council for the Preservation of Rural England suggested that it would be acquired for the benefit of the public.

Negotiations were still proceeding when the Bolton Corporation Parks Committee surprisingly announced their retirement from the entire business, and whilst the Liverpool authority expressed sympathy with the project they did not give it any favour.

The war came so the remaining local authorities could not obtain a financial backing from the Government, and after unsuccessful efforts to defer the sale, the property went to the Liverpool Corporation at a cost, it is said, of £3,000.

To-day they are inviting offers for its demolition. Soon it will be gone. But the things it stood for, the love and preservation of the beauty that is so essentially ours, must not disappear with it.

BOLTON EVENING NEWS.
30TH MAY 1947.

The Natural Dangers of Winter Hill

All high moorland should be treated with respect, and Winter Hill is no exception. Whilst researching material for this scrapbook, I have come across numerous references of people who have had their lives at risk purely because they were "there". The bulk of the cases involve broken or twisted limbs or joints but a large number are due mainly to either the extreme weather or the pure physical conditions which exist at times and in certain places on the Hill.

There are reports of groups of youngster's entering old mines and getting lost – this was one of the prime reasons why mine shafts and collapsed entrances on Winter Hill are immediately filled in and sealed when they occur. People always refer to the day "those youngsters got lost down the tunnels"! It really happened!

There have been a number of cases of exposure on Winter Hill when ill-dressed folk have headed for the Hill in atrocious conditions. The weather in winter on Winter Hill can, on occasions, be just as extreme as one finds in the Scottish Mountains. I well remember one day on duty as a Ranger years ago in the Pigeon Tower/Rivington Pike area. A thin layer of snow had fallen the previous day, which had frozen solid overnight. A gale was blowing and ice particles were being ripped from the ground and blown in the air. To look around in any safety one had to wear goggles. The weather deteriorated and heavy snow fell, soon reaching the top of fence posts in places. At 4pm just as night was falling a call went out. Cries for help had been heard from the Pike. The weather conditions going up to the Pike were appalling with a snow blizzard obscuring all visibility – especially when carrying a stretcher! I forget exactly who was rescued or brought down that day but I write this just to illustrate how unforgiving Winter Hill can be at times. When I arrived home in Swinton that evening my wife looked uncomprehendingly at me as I explained my day …… as we had not had ANY snow in Swinton since the previous year! I'm sure she didn't believe a word I was saying! Winter Hill seemed a million miles away.

It is not always the weather or broken bones that can cause problems. In some isolated parts of the Hill the ground underfoot is not always as it seems! There are boggy areas and many people who love to get away from the recognised tracks have tales to tell …. me included! I am not referring to merely getting feet wet in a bog. Frequently one can go in up to the thighs. An article in the Bolton Evening News on Monday January 5th 1987 illustrates the dangers:

Moor ordeal man thanks rescuers. *A walker who cheated death by an hour after a "quicksand" ordeal on a bleak moorland has thanked police for saving his life. Mr John Gill, aged 27, was found unconscious, 1,500 feet up on the access road to the TV mast on Winter Hill. He collapsed exhausted after struggling for two hours to free himself after falling into a ditch in the hill's peat bogs. The alarm was raised when a CB radio user spotted what he thought was a body on the tarmac road. Police searched by torchlight in a gale before finding Mr Gill, who lives at Ridgeway, Blackrod.*

Speaking for the first time about his ordeal Mr Gill said "I would like to thank the teenager who saw me and the police. I apologise for any trouble I have caused. I was up to my waist in the bog and was stuck completely. I struggled for hours to get out. I shouted for help but it was useless at that time of night and in a gale. When I got out of the bog by pulling at tufts of grass, I was exhausted and could not feel my hands or feet. I thought I was going to die. The bog was like quicksand – I was sinking fast the more I struggled"

Mr Gill, set out for a walk at 8.45pm but was found close to death nearly five hours later. He said "I remember the police finding me and the next thing I woke up in hospital and was being brought round with tea and an injection. I had suffered severe hypothermia"

Although Winter Hill is a wonderful "playground" and a place of great beauty and fascination for many of us, we should always be aware of the hidden dangers at all times, and do all we can to minimise them.

Unfortunately, many of us like the bleakness and solitude of the place, and often go wandering around on our own - and at times when there is perhaps nobody else around on the moors – and in the most appalling weather conditions! Some would call us foolhardy, but this is our choice and what we choose to do - and we would defend our right to do just this – so long as we are all aware of the possible dangers and we dress and equip ourselves to minimise the risks.

In poor weather never underestimate Winter Hill. The bogs really ARE there. The visibility really CAN vanish totally within 60 seconds. The body surface temperature plus the chill factor for those unsuitably dressed, really CAN drop to −10C or more on top of the Hill.

DO take care on Winter Hill ….. but enjoy it! Remember. It CAN bite!

Liverpool Castle by the side of the Lower Rivington Reservoir. Photo taken from a rather low flying microlight piloted by one of the authors of course!!!!

The "building" of Scotsmans Stump circa 1912. (Photo copyright of Paul Lacey).

Winter Hill. A magnet for all UFO spotters!!

One of Winter Hill's claim to fame is that a remarkably large number of people claim to have spotted UFO's in its vicinity. The 1950's 60's and 70's local newspapers often commented on the latest "sightings". At times it seems to be getting very busy with UFO's in the area and in 1988 a local "ufologist" said that "over the past 5 years I have had about 100 calls about the Belmont area. When you think that many people are embarrassed or afraid to admit seeing UFO's, the number of sightings could be in the thousands". He went on to say "there is a concentration of sightings in Belmont and Horwich especially around the reservoirs. One theory is that they could be taking on water".

This photo is perhaps one of the most famous of all the "sightings" as it was taken in 1996 by a professional photographer who spotted the "object" after he had his slide's developed! He passed the information

over to the "Direct Investigation Group on Aerial Phenomena (DIGAP) who were convinced that British Aerospace at Wharton were developing a secret craft.

Another UFO "incident" occurred on the hill in 1999 which has been widely publicised on the Internet:

(http://www.maxpages.com/mapit/THE_WINTER_HILL_MIB_CASE).

The excellent Winter Hill website at: http://www.winterhill.org/ufos.htm carries an article on the 1999 subject which describes the claims better than I could ever do and is reproduced below.

Thanks to Stephen Mera of "MAPIT" for his help in compiling this page.

The case of the "Winter Hill MIB UFO" sighting is one of the great mysteries of Winter Hill. In 1999, a farm worker by the name of Murphy spotted a strange object hanging over his cattle field. When he came out to investigate, the object seemed to move away towards Preston. So odd was the sighting that Mr. Murphy decided to telephone the police and report the incident.

He then returned to the field to check on the cattle, only to find the object return and hover over the area for several more minutes. He became very distressed and, the story goes, called the number for MAPIT (the Manchester Aerial Phenomena Investigation Team) - apparently provided by the police. He left a disturbing message stating that he had witnessed a UFO and was scared.

MAPIT spent weeks investigating the incident, during which time they found themselves being followed by a man in a 4x4 jeep and later discovered that Mr. Murphy had been warned off by officials who claimed to be from the MAFF (Ministry of Agriculture, Fisheries and Food). Mr. Murphy disappeared and has never been traced, making it impossible to corroborate the story. The farm still remains, although the owner has always been reluctant to speak out on the issue.

So famous is the incident that television companies from Britain, America and Japan have all visited MAPIT's HQ to interview the organisation's president, Stephen Mera. He is yet to uncover the full story, although he has also investigated the use of high-tech military equipment - including so-called "black helicopters" which can regularly be seen in the area.

I'm afraid I have no real views on the subject of any Winter Hill sightings only to comment that after a decade of flying a microlight around Winter Hill in all weathers and at all times of day I have never spotted a thing that could not be fully explained. Whilst walking on the hill however, I HAVE spotted a number of people who obviously come from another planet.

You can spot these "aliens" all over the place, causing damage, dropping litter, causing general problems for the more normal inhabitants of the area. There must be an invasion of aliens on the Easter weekends!

Wilderswood and Rockhaven Castle.

On the southern flanks of Winter Hill, lies Wilderswood, a heavily wooded area on the side of the hill south of Georges Lane. To look at the area nowadays one would think that it had always looked like this but this is not the case.

The bulk of this area was once bare moorland with few trees (except for the nearby wooded cloughs) and must have been fairly busy with local coal mining activities.

At some past date - unknown to the writer - a house known as Rock Haven was built on the top of the hill which lies behind Brinks Row

cottages and in 1840 a Richard Brownlow, a Bolton attorney moved into the property. Over a period of years he rebuilt parts of the house and added various embellishments to it including castle-like parapets and the dwelling eventually became known as Rockhaven Castle, or "Torney Brownlow's Castle.

Richard Brownlow lived at Rock Haven until his death in 1899 but in his latter years he became something of a recluse rarely appearing in public and suffering from a "terrible disease" which involved some form of facial disfigurement.

He is reputed to have worn a mask to hide his illness on occasions and local people thought he was suffering from leprosy - but in fact he seems to have had a severe case of eczema.

After Brownlow's death the "castle" passed to the ownership of Lord Leverhulme and eventually in 1940 Blackrod Council put forward plans to turn it into a Youth Hostel but this idea was abandoned and in 1942 it was sold to a local quarry company who eventually demolished it in May 1942.

One rumour that I keep hearing, is that the Castle was a prominent landmark for German bombers who were trying to bomb the Horwich Loco Works and this was the reason for its eventual destruction.

The whole site was planted with trees and although I am no great lover of "forestry-type" plantations, a walk through parts of the woodland is a delight today.

When walking in the woods one often comes across the remains of parts of the castle along with small quarries where the stones were obtained for the original building. In M D Smith's book "About Horwich" he mentions that after the demolition, some of the stonework was used "to build a bungalow in Lytham whilst the remainder was carried as ballast in grain ships travelling to America". Fascinating!

Coal mining took place in the vicinity and as mentioned in an earlier article there are several tunnel entrances (all blocked or collapsed) to be seen especially in the clough on the north western side of Wilderswood.

This valley is well worth a visit especially if one follows the stream uphill. There is an excellent variety of mosses, liverworts and ferns clinging to the banking - and the upper reaches, just south of Georges Lane, are a mecca for whimberry lovers in autumn.

An interesting hour can be spent exploring this area of the clough, starting at the bridge on Dark Lane (also known as Cole-Fire Lane and Rothwells Clough) just inside Wilderswood, which is at the end of the track leading from Ormstons Farm.

Mention has already been made earlier to the two collapsed tunnels which can be seen in this vicinity, but as one walks up the main track there are in fact other mining remains, but these have all been totally sealed, some with brickwork and others with cement blocks. A shaft in the area known as Cabin Pit still exists but again, this is sealed. Don't bother searching for it, it is well secured and I can assure readers that there is nothing of interest down it!!

Carry on up the path. On the left hand side is another track. On the small hill in between the two tracks is another old pit shaft, now completely filled in. Nearby are the huge blocks of stone used as engine beds and supports for the machinery involved in winding the coal up the shaft.

The counterbalance (a large circular stone with a central hole) for the pit head gear now stands in Ormstons farmyard. The remains of Holden's Bleachworks can be found just to the north west of the pit shaft. Return to the main track in the bottom of the clough.

Go uphill on the main path. Where the path goes to the right through the gateposts, go straight on up the smaller path (i.e. leaving the main track) for a short distance. On the right hand side of the path you will see a large diameter metal pipe sticking out of the ground. This was an air vent to the mines below.

Although clearly marked on mining maps, the base of this pipe has never been found (it is a bit of a maze underground so it is no surprise that the bottom of the pipe has not been found – yet!). Carry on up the path.

There is a prominent large holly tree on the left hand side of the track. Behind the tree lies the remains of Higher Meadows Farm, the foundations of which are still visible in the undergrowth. Careful searching will reveal half of what appears to be the bottom section of an old grinding wheel.

Opposite the holly tree but down in the bottom of the clough, is a magnificent clump of wild iris growing in the waterlogged ground, a beautiful sight when in full flower. "Somewhere" in the clough is the entrance to an old mine marked as "old level" on old maps.

Despite frequent and extensive searches, this tunnel entrance has never been found despite its map location.

Carry on up the path until you reach another main track which leads up to Georges Lane. On the left hand side of this track, beneath Georges Lane are two "valleys" which look very artificial and are repeated many times on this hillside if one headed towards the Pike. These are thought to be old surface workings for either coal or clay although no proof of this has yet been found. This hillside is a magnet for whimberry pickers every autumn!

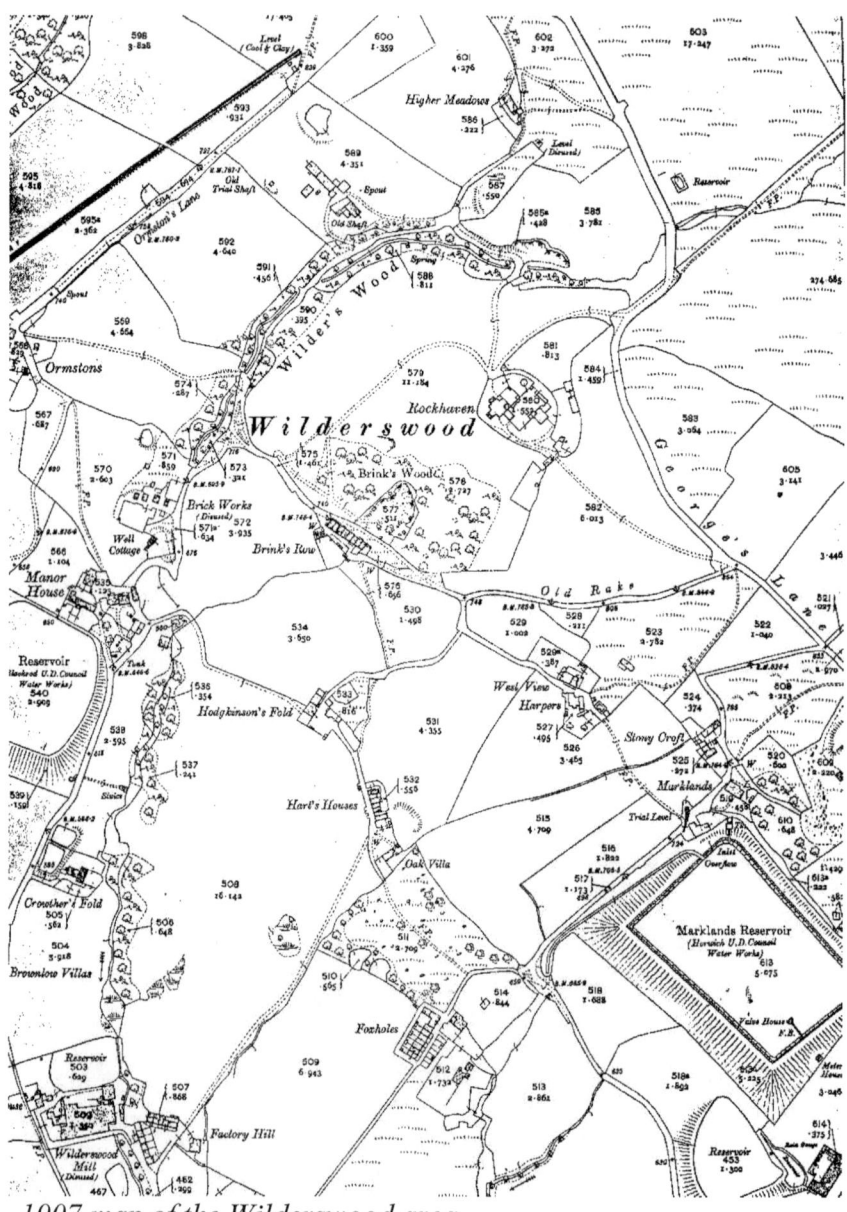

1907 map of the Wilderswood area.

The old or "disused" level mentioned in the last article can be seen just to the right of Higher Meadows Farm – clearly marked on the map but now vanished! The dark diagonal line at the upper left hand corner is the tramway to the Wilderswood Mine Drift entrance.

The Royal Wedding Beacon. Winter Hill. July 21st 1981.

Rivington Pike and Winter Hill have been used as beacon sites for hundreds of years. Perhaps the most memorable beacon at these sites was in 1981 at the time of the wedding of Charles and Diana. A chain of beacons was planned around the country

On the night of the beacon, the two-mile uphill track from Horwich to the Trig point on Winter Hill (where the bonfire was located) was jammed with revellers who slogged to the top of the hill for the official lighting time of 10.19pm. The beacon was "officially" lit by 10 year old spina bifada sufferer Janet Lomax of Hillfield Drive, Bolton. She was given VIP treatment and driven through the crowds of walkers to the site along with the mayors and mayoresses from surrounding towns. Many people arrived late – or even missed the lighting of the fire as it had been wrongly announced in the Press, that it was at Rivington Pike! This caused total chaos on the Rivington/Belmont road which was blocked till the early hours by trapped vehicles.

The beacon was built by the Royal Institute of Chartered Surveyors and was around 30 feet in height.

The beacon was no "jerry-built" job as can be seen by the photo of the frame.

It was estimated that over 5,000 people made it to the top of the hill in time to see its lighting only a few hundred yards from the TV mast. The sight of the flames ended a nail-biting 24 hours for the beacon builder Peter Veevers and his helpers who camped out on the moor to ensure there was no premature lighting. The team had brought wood up the hill twice every week over a two-month period to prepare for the bonfire.

It was an enjoyable and memorable occasion for all those who were there.

Flying at Winter Hill

A great deal of flying takes place on, around and over Winter Hill!

There are the commercial flights that pass high over Winter Hill. The LOWEST height they are allowed to fly over the Hill is 3,500 feet.

Smaller general aviation aircraft (such as those from Barton Aerodrome) have to keep BELOW this height and can often be seen in the area along with microlights and the occasional powered paraglider. In theory, these aircraft must remain above 800 feet from the ground.

Flying from the hill itself are hang gliders and paragliders, usually on days when the wind is in a northerly direction and not too windy and they fly on the northern side of the hill, overlooking the Rivington/Belmont road.

On a busy weekend in summer I have seen up to 40 people flying at the site and if the thermals are good an awful lot of them seem to fly in close proximity to each other vying for the best updraughts!

Most of the pilots belong to local hang or paragliding clubs with details easily found on the Internet via a search engine.

The hill was also once the "home" of the Rivington Soaring Association, a group of model glider enthusiasts who used both the Southern slopes of Rivington Pike and the Northern Slopes of Winter Hill.

I have heard no mention of this group now for many years

Fireclay on (and under) Winter Hill.

In earlier volumes, mention has been made of fireclay (sometimes known as Seat-earth) being found below (and sometimes in a tiny layer above) coal seams.

This material is especially relevant as in earlier days, it played a considerable role in the industries and ventures that sprung up on and around Winter Hill.

Fireclay is a grey muddy clay. It usually lies below most coal seams and on Winter Hill many of the mining ventures were specifically for fireclay - with coal being almost a by-product.

Coal was formed by compression of decaying vegetation existing in swamp-like areas. The fireclay represents the sediment or soil in which the swamp vegetation grew.

The clay is rich in alumina content and is an excellent material for the manufacture of firebricks used in kilns and smelting. The clay was also used in the making of salt-glazed pipes and sanitary-ware until the late 1950's when it was superseded by more modern materials.

There were a number of sanitary product manufacturers in Horwich earlier in the 19th & 20th centuries all using the clay mined from underneath Winter Hill.

You can still find the remains of some of the brickworks on the Hill, with perhaps the one at Hole Bottom being the most easily accessible. Firebricks still remain there, all made from the local clay.

An excellent example of locally made firebricks can found right at the summit of Winter Hill where a number are stacked next to - and on top of - the boundary wall adjacent to the most southerly radio mast.

A photo of the wall can be seen on the next page.

In several places on the Hill, the fireclay can be seen on the surface.

The best example I have recently seen, is in a small "shakehole" (formed by the collapse of an underground adit tunnel) about 300 yards to the rear of Sportsmans cottage and around 50 yards from the boundary wall on the top bank of the nearby stream.

The grey clay can be found on the sides of the hole and can be taken home, moulded and baked.

The collapsed adit tunnel used to exit on the on the banks of the nearby stream but is now totally filled in and covered in vegetation. It is clearly marked on mine abandonment plans.

There is also another clay outcrop near to the TV mast on top of Winter Hill (see the article about the "other Brickworks" elsewhere in this book).

All of the coal seams on Winter Hill are underlain with a seam of fireclay.

Firebricks near the most southerly radio mast on top of Winter Hill

The layer of grey fireclay can be clearly seen below the coal seam. This picture was taken under the summit of Winter Hill fairly close to the moorland road leading to the TV mast. This tunnel is now not accessible and this may be the last picture you ever see of it.

The Cranberries …. Where are they?

Since writing the earlier editions of this book, a number people have contacted me enquiring about the exact locations of various types of plants growing on the Hill. Where specific plants are numerous, I have given exact locations, where they are rare, I have been deliberately vague! By far the most asked question is "Exactly where are the cranberries on Winter Hill"? I'm still not prepared to disclose exactly where they are - but the photo below of the flower of the cranberry may help. Bear in mind that the flower and stem are only just over an inch high. Once you've seen a cranberry flower in real life you'll recognise it instantly anywhere.

The flower of the cranberry. The petals curl backwards towards stem. The leaves are those tiny insignificant things on the bottom left of the photo.

The flowers appear between late May and early July ….. and if you often walk on the very top of Winter Hill I'm willing to bet that at sometime or another you'll have passed within 10 foot of them! When you've found the cranberries, then you can start looking for the Cloud Berries!

If you can't find the cranberries OR the Cloud Berries, then there are simply acres of whimberries for you to pick! Bon Appetit.

More about the Lichens of Winter Hill.

Probably one of the most ignored organisms on Winter Hill are the lichens in all its different guises. The grasses, mosses, shrubs and trees are all too obvious to most observers, but somehow the lichens get overlooked or ignored by most folk interested in the plant life of the area. You tend to only take note of them, once they've been pointed out.

Lichens can exist in the most unlikely places even in spots where no other plant life grows - such as directly on the surface of rocks or bricks. They are complex plants rather than being simple as most people imagine, and are something of a mini ecosystem consisting of at least two life-forms, a fungus and a photosynthetic partner which is usually an algae (but can be others things as well). Lichens can exist in extreme environments and often grow under conditions that other plant life cannot tolerate.

"Weathering" on walls and rocks usually turns out to be lichen growth on closer inspection. Carrying a tiny hand lens when you go walking on Winter Hill can prove more interesting than you imagine - although you sometimes feel a real fool kneeling down to use it near other people.

There are many different types of lichen, a number of which can be seen right on the very top of Winter Hill, the most obvious ones being the "crustose" or "parmelia" ones growing on the walls and stones. These come in many colours, usually grey, slightly green, brown or even orange, perhaps even black dotted - and different species seem to inhabit different areas on different parts of the hill. Most of the ancient walls on the Hill seem to have coloured blotches - usually put down to "weathering" - are in fact lichens upon closer inspection.

Forms of the "reindeer moss" types of lichens, "pixie cup" lichens are all to be found on top of the Hill. Perhaps the most colourful variety to search for is the "British soldier", a bright red tipped member of the "cladonia" family which is easily spotted from June onwards on Winter Hill. All of these types of lichens can be found within 100 yards of the Hole Bottom brickworks. In this vicinity I have also spotted a lichen I have never ever seen anywhere else in the area, it grows on one of the bricks which once formed the inside of one of the brick kilns, a sort of melted looking stone.

If anyone can identify this lichen for me I'd love to hear from you!

Two photo's of "British Soldier" types of lichen - fairly common in the Hole Bottom area. The name originated with the red caps worn by British soldiers in earlier centuries. The plants red caps are actually the sexual fruiting structure of the lichen, the apothecia. British soldiers are members of the "Cladonia" family of lichens.

A lichen similar to those found on Winter Hill - although the maximum size I have ever found right at the top is about 1 inch in size. The usual variety found on Winter Hill is "Cladonia Arbuscula".

One of the Pixie Cup varieties, extremely common amongst the heather in many places on Winter Hill. Often grows in close proximity to the British soldiers.

One of the commonest lichens growing on the lower flanks of Winter Hill, Hypogymnia Physodes, usually on tree bark.

The sheep of Winter Hill.

When most people think of a sheep, they think of ... well .... a sheep! They all look the same don't they? Actually no they don't - and there are hundreds of different types of sheep in the fields, on the hills and mountains of the British Isles. Different varieties of sheep are grown for different purposes (some for meat, some for wool, others for breeding) and some types fare better in different environments.

Sheep are both a blessing and a curse on Winter Hill. They are a blessing because they look nice, they sound nice, they eat what's left of my butties to save me taking them home and most importantly, they provide a livelihood for local farmers. They are a curse because they seem to eat everything and the Hill looks as it does now, mainly because of the sheep. Unless an area is fenced off, no trees or shrubs grow, they are quickly devoured. Where sheep are present, the vegetation is usually very short and certain plant species are unable to survive the continuous close grazing. The presence of sheep maintains the generally deforested top of Winter Hill.

There are three main varieties of sheep grazing on Winter Hill.

"Derbyshire Gritstone", a mountain and hill variety which is found mainly in Derbyshire and the Pennine Districts of Lancashire & Yorkshire with a few also found in Wales. They are distinguished by their faces and legs being white with black markings and there is no wool growing on these parts either. They are hornless. Their wool is one of the finest of all grown by the blackfaced type of sheep and it is extensively used in the high quality hosiery business.

Also seen on the Hill is the Swaledale, dark upper face with grey muzzle and a tuft of wool on the forehead.

Both sexes are horned. It is found in the fells, moorlands and high ground of the six counties of Northern England and it lives easily in exposed places.

Many Swaledale ewes are used for breeding the very popular Mules, and the finer quality wool from this breed of sheep (the Swaledales that is!) is used for the manufacture of tweeds, rug wool and some of the thicker hand-knitting wools. Much of the wool is of coarse quality but this is ideal for the making of carpets.

The final variety found on the Hill is the Cheviot.

The Cheviot is distinguishable by its erect ears, white face and legs with a ruff of wool behind the ears. There is no wool on the face or legs below the knee or hock.

The males are occasionally horned. The wool quality varies from fairly course to quite fine and is used for manufacture into clothing - ranging from rugged sportswear to lighter town suitings.

Cheviot wool is also used for making blankets, rugs and hosiery yarns.

You need never again wonder what type the sheep are on Winter Hill! However, just to confuse you, the breeds listed are only those you will find on the Hill itself - in the fields on the lower flanks of the Hill you will also find Mules, Dalesbred and Lonks plus a few other crossbreed varieties.

The sheep on the upper parts of the hill are free to roam and are brought back down the hill several times a year for mating (known as "tupping") usually around October/early November, lambing around April and for clipping in June/July.

They may also be brought off the hill for dipping and worming although some farms dip the flock at clipping time, whilst others delay the dipping for a month or so until a little fleece has re-grown.

Don't forget .... whilst on the hills, KEEP YOUR DOG under control especially at and prior to lambing time. Your dog's hour of freedom could mean the death or abortion of a lamb and a financial loss to the farmer. Be considerate!

Dalesbred - distinguishable by its black face with distinct white mark at either side of its nostrils. The legs are also black and white and they have a rounded low set pair of horns. The fleece is tough and springy and is ideal for making carpet yarns. Dalesbred can survive in the bleakest conditions and on the roughest pastures.

Moorland Water Channels

A network of moorland water channels became visible after the 2018 moorland fires. Although sections were visible prior to the fires the full extent of the network became clear after the fires which burnt away significant amounts of foliage and heather. These channels were seen on Smithills Moor in the vicinity of Whimberry Hill.

The channels are set out in a herring bone arrangement with the side "feeder" channels angled and about 10 m apart. The water from these feeder channels enter a central spine of the herring bone layout. From this central spine the water is channelled via Shaly Dingle to the Springs and Dingle Reservoirs on the opposite side of Belmont Road

Side "feeder" channel, Smithills Moor post the 2018 fires. This network of channels would have been a considerable undertaking to construct.

The side feeder Channels are approximately 400 mm square 10/15 meters long and made from rough stone, bottom, walls and top stones. Water enters the channels from the surrounding moorland via gaps in the rough stone and construction. The central "Spine" is larger approx. 600 mm square and built the same as the feeder channels. The central spine is of considerable length running in the bottom of a small valley running in the direction of Shaly Dingle .

The Springs and Dingle reservoirs became operational as late as 1927. The network of moorland water channels appear much older than this so their original function was probably different than to feed the reservoirs.

Another "feeder" channel partially uncovered with evidence of a roof collapse

The central spine with sections of its roof collapsed with running water visible

More ancient remains from Winter Hill.

In an earlier volume I mentioned that someone had written to me saying that some years ago they had found a flint spear or axe in the vicinity of the Winter Hill Burial Mound. Thanks for the info John McDonald. Several weeks after receiving the information - and after the last volume had been finished a computer scan of the object turned up in my mailbox. Wow ….. what a magnificent find.

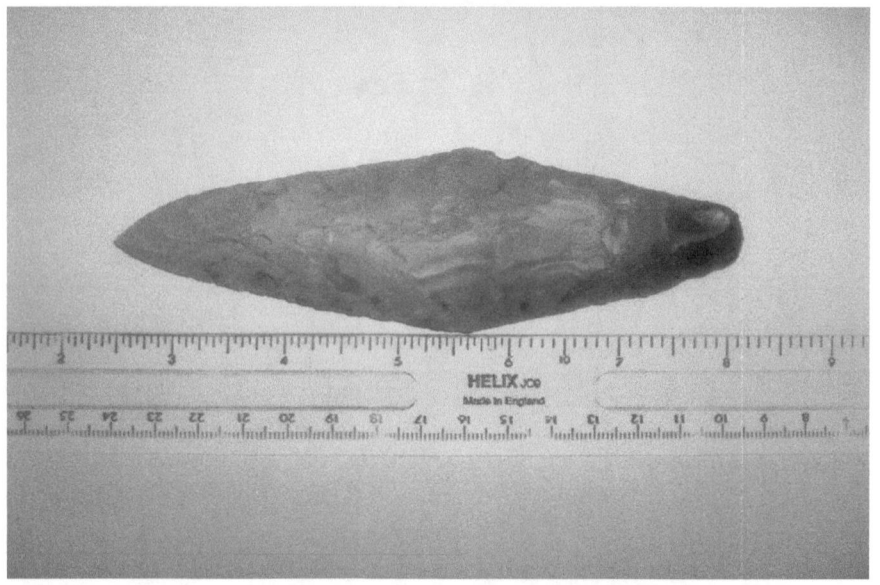

This is a five and a half inch long axe head, in what looks like excellent condition. Why is it that everyone else seems to find flint chippings, flint arrowheads, flint axes etc on Winter Hill ... except me! Thanks for the excellent photograph John, you lucky devil!

There are by the way, several well known sites (at least they are well known within archaeological circles) on Winter Hill where flint chippings have been found in some quantities. These would be areas where someone once sat whilst working on a block of flint producing arrowheads, spears, scrapers etc. These sites are marked on copies of a few privately produced maps. I have still found nothing! Any additional photo's of other peoples "finds" would be appreciated.

Gritstone - what is it - and how was it formed.

When you look at rocks on the summit of Winter Hill, they all look the same, a dark coloured, rough textured, gritty or sandy rock. The term "grit" is a useful - if non-scientific" - term for a course sandstone. There are of course other types of rock around, but by far the most predominant one is the substance some people call "millstone grit". The term "millstone grit" does in fact (in geology) refer to a whole "series" of massive and different layers of sandstone's, grits, conglomerates and shales. The type of rock - or the "species" of gritstone - you find on top of Winter Hill is known as "Rough Rock", a coarsely grained stone containing large amounts of feldspar and is sparsely pebbly. Lower down the hill you will find a different type of Gritstone…. the "Haslingden Flags".

The dark colouring of the rock is due mainly to "weathering" - and the pollution in this industrial area - break a piece open and inside it's a much lighter colour. This is a grittier type of the rock than that usually termed "sandstone". Take a look at it under a small hand lens. Are most of the grains are rounded? - if they are, this indicates that they were almost certainly transported by water (or in some cases by wind) which quickly removed the rough edges. If the sample contains only jagged or rough grains, then this indicates that the granules have only been transported by the water over a very short distance without being subjected to "rounding".

The rocks of the area were formed during the Carboniferous period (especially during the Namurian phase of that era), that is somewhere around 290 to 363 million years ago. How do we know this age? We know it by the study of a mixture of geological evidence, the study of the stratigraphic structures, the fossil remains, the study of the radioactive decay rates of rocks and finally by the modern technique of paleomagnetic studies.

Gritstones consists of rock particles transported by water. Different areas of Winter Hill show massive differences in the sizes of the grains transported and deposited, the size usually indicating the relative strength of the current - the larger particles usually being deposited in strong current flows, with the finer particles settling as the current strength decreased. Different sandstone's or Grits at different places on the Hill show a wide variety of colours and grain sizes. The "Rough Rock" on the top of Winter Hill almost certainly originated as sands or mineral grains - probably brought from as far away as Scandinavia and Greenland - were deposited near the mouth of a massive delta.

Park your car in the **upper** car park at Lower House car park (that's the one below the Pigeon Tower at the end of the road leading from Rivington Road). Take the footpath going north from the car park and on the right hand side of the path, drop into the small dry valley. After a few minutes walking, you'll spot some small gritstone or sandstone/mudstone outcrops on your right hand side. Take a look at the rocks.

The first thing you'll notice is that the rocks appear to be layered horizontal beds of sediment. This indicates repeated "floods" of varying strengths over a period of time, maybe years - or even centuries, maybe millennia. Different floods deposited different sizes of granules and these can all be seen in the revealed strata.

In this particular example, the flows seem to have been of different strengths at different times. Some strata contain large rounded rocks amongst the small grains, other layers are totally graded fine granules. Some layers are very thin, some are much thicker. Perhaps each "layer" represents a major "flood" each year ... your guess is as good as mine as to what the layers actually represent.

The layers of sandstone (or "grits") in this locality show conspicuous signs of "current bedding", indicating that they were deposition in deltaic environments i.e. at a place where a large river delta was depositing the solids brought down by its waters.

How did the granules turn into "rocks"? The various layers of silt and granules were endlessly covered by yet more layers. As they became thicker and thicker, the pressure on them increased, and they became compressed. There were still spaces between the grains or granules. These spaces were however often filled with moisture or water and this, combined with the increased pressure and its associated heat, caused chemical changes in some of the substances within the sediment. The quartz grains remained the same, but if there was any $CaCO_3$, $Fe(OH)_3$ or SiO_2 present, then the warmth and the pressure would precipitate these chemicals and "glue" the deposits together. That is how the "rock" was formed - through compression, water, heat and chemical action.

The major "cement" is silica (a form of quartz), others "cements" include calcite (only recognisable with a chemical test) and iron compounds (shown by their rusty red colour). The strength of the "cement" governs how easily grains may be broken away from the rock. Most Winter Hill cements are strong!

Occasionally (VERY occasionally!) plants or trees were swept down these torrents, and these remains formed fossils, but these are rare in most forms of sandstone (or gritstone) in this area. After years of searching

I have only found only one such sandstone fossil, this being part of a tree trunk - found at Black Hill, north of Anglezarke. It is course possible that "my" fossil came from Winter Hill and was carried to Anglezarke by later glacial action - although as the local glaciers tended to go from North to South this possibility fairly remote!

Don't bother looking for dinosaur fossils …. Dinosaurs would appear on earth 100 million years later than "our" rocks were formed - and the rocks containing dinosaur fossils were (if they ever existed) in this area, eroded away millions of years ago by either wind, water or ice!

Oh one other thing. Right now, the UK lies at about 53 degrees north of the equator. When our carboniferous and millstone grit series of rocks was being formed, our country lay ON the equator, Winter "Hill" would have been really hot!

Over the period since then, plate techtonic movements have moved our Hill (and most of Europe) about 5cms a year northwards, until today - when it reached it's present location.

How time flies!

A Victorian engraving of Rivington Pike. The date is unknown, but it appeared in a book called "England in the Nineteenth Century" page 280. Note the church with the small steeple at the left hand of the Pike

Another Winter Hill Brickworks.

In an earlier volume, a description was given about the Winter Hill Brickwork's at Hole Bottom. This is not the only brickwork to have been located on the Hill and in past centuries there were several, many working at the same time. The Hole Bottom brickwork is in an easily accessible place - but some of the other ones are in fairly remote locations.

One of the remote ones is much higher up the hill. To find what remains of it, go up the moorland road from Montcliff towards the TV mast. A few hundred yards before reaching the TV station you will spot a wire fenced off area on the left hand side of the road (this used to be the site of a small wooden hut where the TV station employees used to move to in inclement weather many years ago).

Take the track behind the fenced off area, cross over the battered wooden bridge across the ditch and head straight ahead to the brow of the hill. When you get there, look down and you will spot the mounds of the brickwork below. It is easily recognised as the

The view of the brickwork's from half way down the hill. There is no sign of any path or track leading to the site.

vegetation of the site is different from the surrounding moor.

Taking a look around the site gives a few clues to exactly what may have been there years ago. There are two mounds on the site, both covered in vegetation. Whether these are both the remains of brick kilns or whether the site had only one kiln plus one building cannot be determined without considerable digging.

The smaller mound on the left of the picture was almost certainly a kiln for traces of fused brick (those forming the inside of the kiln) can be spotted nearby. There are also two spits of raised earth heading downhill from this mound which I had long suspected as being where the kiln ash and cinders were tipped. On my latest visit to the site a large rabbit/fox or other large animal had very kindly dug a hole into the side of these raised areas exposing solid ash, clinker and cinders. My theory was proved right without having to do any digging around.

The site appears to have manufactured common bricks and perhaps

stoneware items as well. There are several piles of bricks lying around and a number of either complete or broken sinks can also be seen.

It seems from looking at the site, that the clay was obtained from the immediate area surrounding the kilns and in several places the rather poor clay is exposed. I can find no traces of any underground entrances although from the surface collapses I suspect that some of the clay may have been taken from just beneath the surface. I have not checked the geology maps for this exact site but there were surface coal outcrops in this vicinity so the brickwork would have its own clay and coal almost on its doorstep this probably being the reason for its isolated position.

The biggest mound on the site, whilst it "may" have been a kiln shows little real evidence of it so far - despite someone having had a dig into it at some time (it wasn't me). Without striping some of the soil and vegetation off it is impossible to guess any more.

If you have "Google Earth" in your computer, look at Winter Hill at its largest magnification and you'll clearly see this brickworks.

The Bog!

One area of Winter Hill seems to get few visitors whatever the time of year even during the warm days of summer. This is not perhaps surprising for this area appears to have nothing whatsoever to offer anyone and even a map shows nothing more than the words "Winter Hill Springs". Thousands of people walk the footpath between Rivington Pike and the TV mast, and lesser numbers travel between both these places via the Winter Hill Trig point and Noon Hill. Virtually everyone ignores the "empty area" between the two routes.

If you're just intent on getting from point A to point B then there is of course no reason to visit the "empty-quarter" but I have to admit to having a fascination for the place. I love the solitude, the views, the weather, the plants, mosses and lichens that grow there ..... and of course ..... the Bog!

Bogs on Winter Hill come in all shapes and sizes. There is the real muddy bog, the one where one second you're walking on firm ground then within a split second one foot sinks to the thigh in glutinous mud which often has a powerfully bad odour as well. **This** is a normal bog - a trap for the unwary!

Then we have the other type of bog, the "sitting water" bog. This is a place which is an obvious bog, a place where you know that you're going to get your feet wet unless you carefully try to step from one bit of dry or raised grass to the next. The worst that will happen in this type of place is that you just could get wet up to mid calf. This type of bog is also a normal bog!

There is however a different type of bog in many areas surrounding the Winter Hill Springs in the "empty-quarter". This type of bog I class as the "quivering bog" and is an experience not to be missed! I kid you not! These are areas which tend to be fairly flat, well populated by cotton grass in summer, the ground surface appears to be damp or wet and there are considerable clumps of sphagnum moss all over the place. Now this is still a "bog" but you CAN walk on it without getting your feet wet even though it feels decidedly dodgy and a bit "iffy". There is one acid test to see if you've found a "quivering bog". Stand still, keep both feet on the ground but move your BODY up and down fairly rapidly. The surface of the ground around you will start moving up and down in time with your body movements. If you've chosen a particularly good area to do your strange body movements, the ground ripples will appear all round you to a distance of perhaps up to 10 feet away. It's quite a sight, and boy, does it feel odd! The exact location of this bog is at SD 65063 14753.

The explanation as to why this "quivering" or "rippling" happens just may put you off trying in the first place, but what the heck, live dangerously and try it! The quivering bog is liquid glutinous mud but this is topped by a thin layer of fairly firm peat and plant life. The surface is safe enough to walk on and jump up and down on, but your body movements are enough to start movements in the liquid mud beneath, and these movements can affect a considerable area of surface peat around the spot where you are gyrating! This then is the "quivering bog"!

I do all MY gyrating at the edges of this type of bog. I take no responsibility whatsoever if any 20 stone person decides to test the quivering in the MIDDLE of such a bog, just so see if he/she can extend the quivering area to a **20** foot radius! Such a person has to be mentally deficit

Whilst you're in the area take a look at the sphagnum mosses. You can't confuse sphagnum with any other type of moss. They are "mat" plants the topmost, live part, consisting of rosettes of densely packed branches facing upwards. The "mat" builds on itself, accumulating an underneath branch depth of several inches or feet, browning and dying close to the surface, decaying lower down. The only "live" part of the plant is the green (they can be other colours too) bit at the top, the dead part of the "stems" are merely used to "wick" up the water to the living part of the plant.

Sphagnum moss can store or hold large amounts of water - if you grab a small handful and squeeze it tightly, large amounts of water will run from it - even in the dry seasons sometimes.

Sphagnum moss acts as a sponge and can hold 10 times its own weight in water both internally and in the spaces between the dense foliage. There are 30 different species of sphagnum moss in the British Isles and if you keep your eyes open in the "empty quarter" you should be able to spot at least 6 different types purely from their visual

appearance alone, size, colour, composition of rosette etc.
Sphagnum Cristatum

A single sphagnum moss plant is very small but it grows packed together with other sphagnum plants and they provide support for each others tiny stems.

This produces a soft spongy carpet which can, on occasions, look like a colourful patchwork, as each kind of sphagnum moss has its own shade of colour ranging from light green, through orange, pink, white and red.

The Coal Mines of Rivington Pike!

In the first part of this Scrapbook, mention was made of two coal mine shafts to the north of Rivington Pike plus a nearby level - all now long since filled in and virtually unseen today.

There are however, other coal mining remains nearer to the Pike - and you can still see the remains!

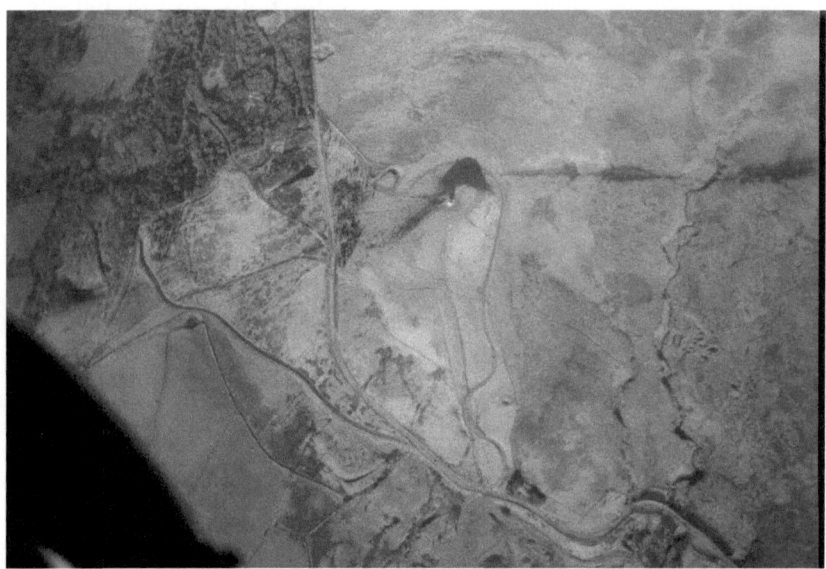

The photo is a rather poor quality winter aerial view of the area surrounding Rivington Pike, the Pike being upper centre. On the right of the picture can be seen mining remains on the right hand bank of the stream. The "crater" on the right hand side of the road going up to the Pike at the base of Brown Hill is an old mine shaft. Just to the right of extreme bottom centre of the photo are what looks like 3 more pits - but these are in fact the remains of an old farmhouse!.

Surrounding the Pike is a coal outcrop, an area where the coal seam emerged at the surface. In the early 1800's (or even earlier) this coal would have been worked using "bell pits" and it is this type of pit which is clearly evident on the banks of the stream on the right hand side of the photo. The dark oblong shape near the pits is the remains of a stone structure, probably a sheep fold. A further photograph taken at ground level (on the next page) clearly shows the sheepfold (or whatever it was) with the heavily mined ground at the rear of it.

I have no details whatsoever about the pit shaft visible near to the road up to the Pike, nor the ones next to George's Lane at the bottom of the photo.

The "sheepfold" with the coal workings at the rear.

Just when you thought you'd heard everything there was to know about Winter Hill ……….. well, now I've found THIS on the UFO Information web page at:
http://www.ufoinfo.com/news/humanoid1950.shtml

Location. Winter Hill, near Bolton, England
Date: 1950
Time: night
The witness, R Chapman sees a dark flat iron shaped object hovering close to the ground. Suddenly out of nowhere a "majestic" being appears. He is tall, well built, with black hair and beard, dark eyes and very pale skin. There is telepathic contact between Chapman and

the humanoid for several minutes. The humanoid then turns around and glides back to the UFO apparently decreasing in size as he did. After he enters the craft the UFO leaves leaving a vapour trail behind. The witness apparently encounters the same being again at the same location. (No details on that).
HC addendum
Source: Gemini Vol. 1 # 2
Type: B

Not much one can add!!!!!!

This photo is said to be taken on Winter Hill – but I suspect it is the Chipmunk which crashed on Smithills Moor.

Winter on Winter Hill!

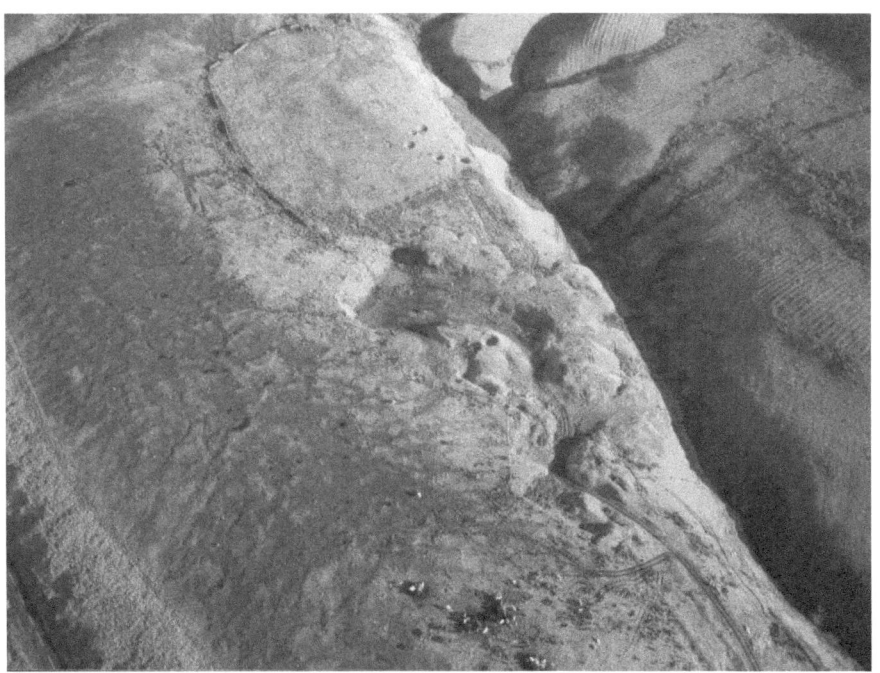

More Winter Hill mining remains! This view shows the "quarries" at the side of the Rivington to Belmont road (which can be seen at the extreme bottom left of the picture). Pit shafts everywhere! Notice the "tilled" field on the right hand side ... what on earth could have been grown there ………And when?

This site housed a gun emplacement during WW2 used for target practice - firing straight across the road! Hundreds of mortars were recovered from the fields across the road about 20 years ago! Someone once suggested that the green rectangular area could have been a Roman fort. Tread carefully!

Matchmoor Riding Centre.

Hidden away on the flanks of Winter Hill is a real "treasure" of the area, the riding school on Matchmoor Lane (Matchmoor Lane is the first road on the right hand side of Georges Lane after leaving the main Horwich Road. It's about 100 yards up the lane hidden away on the left hand side of the road. It's no use looking for the stables for they are partly sunken below the road level and you could easily drive past the place.

After almost two years of watching my grandchildren learn to ride there, I can assure you that this is a real friendly place and everyone seems to be welcome there both adults and children, total beginners and experienced riders. It's been in existence for over 20 years and they a large number of horses. You can take horse riding lessons there or you can join a "hack" going out in a group into the countryside surrounding the riding centre. On a clear day the views are superb.

They seem to run rides and courses in just about everything, from hacks, class lessons, private lessons, stable management lessons, children's holiday courses, BHS Riding and Road Safety courses and Stage 1, 2 & 3 career courses. They even cater for children's birthday parties.

The horses and ponies used range from Shetlands through to throughbreds with many sure-footed Mountain and Moorland ponies.

The Riding Centre is open all day, every day and you can book a lesson on **01204 693323**. The emphasis is on enjoyment - whether you just want to learn to ride or to improve your existing skills.

The one thing that has always struck me about this place, was the friendliness of all who worked there - and I take my hat off to the instructors who tought my grandchildren, they remained cheerful, offered constant encouragement and praise whatever is happening and whatever the weather.

The prices have always been reasonable over the last decade and my granddaughters used to love their Saturday mornings there.

Yet another ancient find on the Hill!

Following publication of Volume 2 of the Winter Hill Scrapbook I received an email from David Aspinall, who is the person who discovered and wrote about the stone rows on Winter Hill - which are described in this volume of the Scrapbook.

David kindly sent me the pictures shown below. These illustrate a

stone scraper found in the vicinity of "his" stone rows. The stone was found by someone else … who unfortunately does not live in the Bolton area …. So this picture is probably the only record of the item which will be seen by Boltonians. If YOU have found anything … send me a picture!

A wonderful old painting of Rivington Pike and Two Lads

(Many thanks to Wigan Leisure and Culture Trust, Dept of Heritage Archives for permission to show this copyrighted picture)

Sportsman's Cottage now known as Pike Cottage .... Date unknown

An imminent large shaft collapse just above the bridge in Lead Mines Valley. This was probably the major shaft in the Clough which produced the bulk of the spoil in that area. I believe this was the "main" shaft of the whole area

The "GeoCaches" of Winter Hill.

What is a Geocache? ...... "The basic idea is to have individuals and organisations set up caches all over the world and share the locations of these caches on the internet. GPS users can then use the location co-ordinates to find the caches. Once found, a cache may provide the visitor with a wide variety of rewards.

All the visitor is asked to do is if they get something they should try to leave something for the cache". That's the official description as laid out on the official geo-caching web site at:
http://www.geocaching.com/

In practice geo-caching involves the finding of hidden containers of various types and sizes by using a hand held GPS (Global Positioning System) unit.

These caches are hidden literally all over the world and there are thousands of them all over the UK. Some of them are merely 35mm film canisters with a really TINY visitors book inside .... These are usually known as "mini cache's". Other caches are substantial plastic containers or old ammunition cases which contain all sorts of gifts and other assorted junk! If you TAKE an item from the cache you MUST replace it with something.

Almost ALL cache's have a visitors book to sign and when you've found a cache it is good manners to log on to the www.geocaching.com web site to leave a message there also. In this way the person who hid the cache in the first place can get instant feedback on his computer as to who has visited it.

There are MANY caches both on and around Winter Hill but you'll have to go to the "View Map" page on the Geo-caching web site and have a root around to see what is available. As this is being written, I can see caches listed on the top of Winter Hill, Rivington Pike and many more nearby. New one's pop up all the time so any list given here would soon be out of date.

Take a look for them! It's great fun, a real excuse to get out in the fresh air and see new places and kids just love it.

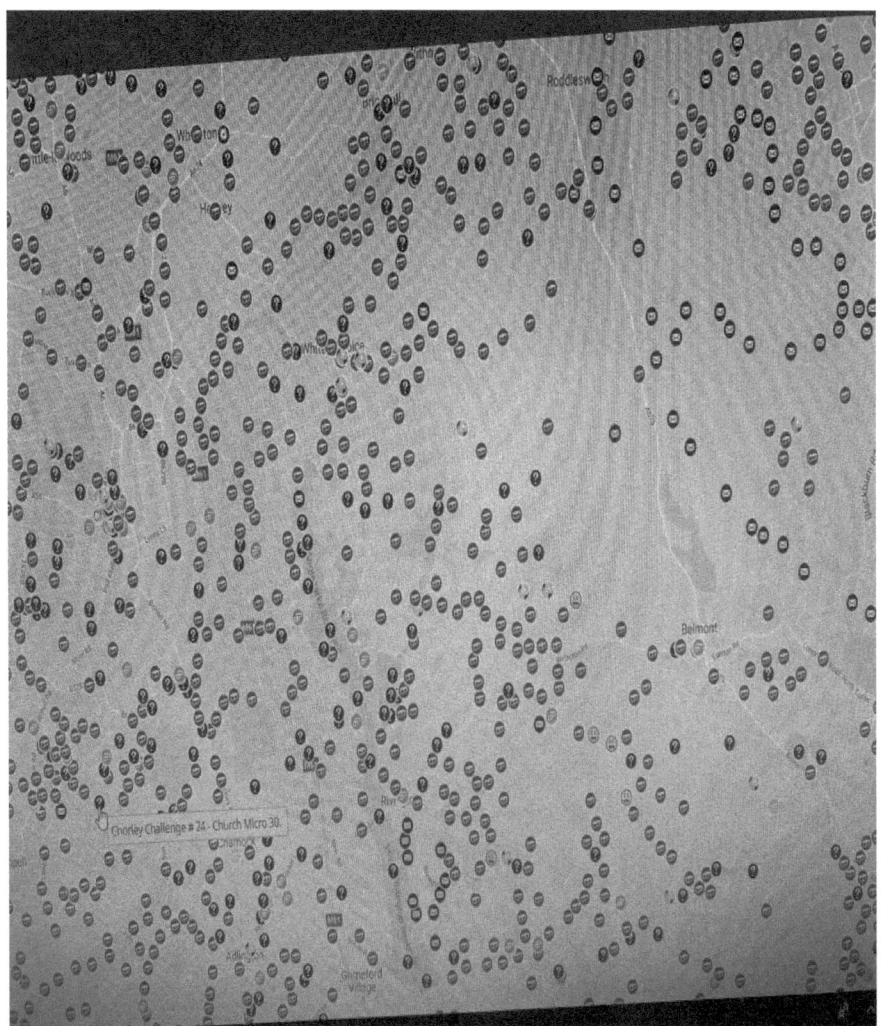

This map gives you an idea of the vast number of geocaches in the Winter Hill/Anglezarke/Belmont area

The caches are simply everywhere. The above map is available on the main geocache map website at
https://www.geocaching.com/play/map

Searching for these caches is a great way of learning about this area, it will take you to places you never knew existed. Hidden spots, unusual places, it's all there to discover and it can become quite an addictive hobby .... especially for families.

And all you need is a GPS or a smartphone!

A documentary film called "Scotsman's Stump" has been made about the murder of George Henderson on Winter Hill. Further details can be found at: http://reelvisionfilms.co.uk/shop.html

One of the Winter Hill tunnel entrances. Do NOT attempt to enter this lethal mine (photo courtesy of David Swain).

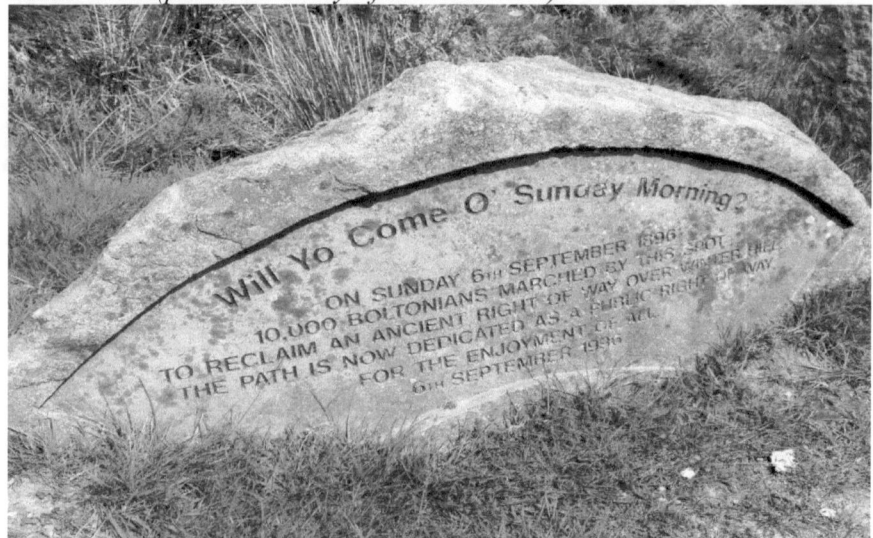

The Memorial Stone erected in 1996 to commemorate the centenary of the Winter Hill Mass Trespass of 1896. (photo courtesy of Eric Hewis)

Shown below is a QSL card (a confirmation that someone has either heard or seen transmissions sent by either a radio amateur or an experimental station) concerning experimental TV transmissions from Winter Hill. The experiments were conducted in 1956 and the card is from "Experimental TV station G9AED located on Winter Hill map ref 34/660149". The card quotes "Channel 9" as being used with vision on 194.75 Mc/s and audio on 191.25 Mc/s.

Past Vegetation on and around Winter Hill.

An earlier article tells the geological history of Winter Hill and many mentions are made throughout the book of how the plant life of the area has changed over time. However, no real mention has been made of the major vegetative changes that have taken place on and around Winter Hill over the last 10,000 years or so. This information can be obtained by the study and dating of pollen grains found within peat and in peat bogs.

The following extract from an article entitled "Past Vegetation, Future Global Warming?" by Robert Yates, Chairman of the West Pennine Moors Conservation Committee from 1983 to 2000.

"In Chorley, we are fortunate to have on our doorstep at Red Moss, Horwich, *(which is adjacent to the Middlebrook/Reebok Shopping Centre)* one of the best studied sites of peat deposition in the whole of the British Isles. Pollen analysis from Red Moss gives us a picture of the vegitational history of the area and therefore an understanding of past climatic changes. Perhaps they can give us a clue to future developments.

Since the end of the Pliocene, some 2 million years ago, we have had four ice Ages in the Northern Hemisphere, known as the Gunz, Mindel, Riss and Wurm, separated by three interglacial periods. Each glacial period was interrupted a number of times by a period of ameliorated conditions. The Wurm Ice Age had two such periods of slight improvement of the climate. We are now in the Flandrian - either the fourth interglacial or a past glacial period - only time will tell. This post-glacial period began about 10,000 years ago as the ice caps melted.

The Red Moss shows six major assemblages of tree pollen after the improvement from the first tundra type vegetation following the slow change in the climate and the gradual movement of the ice sheet north. These are:

a. A birch, pine, juniper period. About 10,000 to 9,500 years before the present. Birch is the dominant pollen type with considerable poplar and willow. Grasses and *Cyperaceae (the Sedge family)* are the dominant herb vegetation.
b. A birch, pine, hazel period. About 10,000 to 8,800 before the present. Juniper and willow decline and grasses and Cyperaceae remain dominant herbs
c. Hazel, pine period. About 8,800 to 8,200 before present. This period is marked by the arrival of the first elm and oak pollen.
d. Pine, hazel and elm period. About 8,200 to 7,100 before present. Birch declines and pine becomes dominant with elm exceeding oak.
e. Oak, elm, alder period. About 7,100 to 5,000 before present. Birch and pine decline and alder increases dramatically. Lime and ash become common and ericaceous pollen is present in large amounts.
f. Oak, alder period. About 5,000 before present to the present day. Elm, lime and ash decline and oak becomes dominant. There is a marked increase in pollen from plants of open and

disturbed land such as Nettles, Dock, Ribwort Plantain, and compositae such as Artemesia and Wild Chamomile.

Note that the above dates are derived from radiocarbon dating and are necessarily approximations.

Man, 10,000 years before the present, was still in the Palaeolithic or Old Stone Age and had little impact, as a hunter-gatherer, on his environment. It was only about 5,000 years before present that man entered his Neolithic stage and slowly introduced farming and stock rearing. The Bronze Age began roughly 4,000 years before the present and so, with improved axes, did the felling of trees and the slow clearance of the forests. This accelerated with the coming of the Iron Age, about 2,500 years before the present, and the combination of a slowly increasing human population with increased tree felling and increased grazing intensity from domestic stock, reduced tree seedling regeneration, and led to the treeless moors now so familiar to us".

Robert Yates.

++

Anyone any information about this?

I received the following email from Alan Foster of Atherton who wrote:

"I grew up in Smithills Bolton as a kid and remember seeing a map once, that showed a tunnel starting in the hill at the top of Smithills Dean Road and exiting at the back of Belmont Road.

If I remember correctly, it was a pretty straight tunnel, we were going to investigate it at one point but never got fully round to it."

Is there anyone else out there that can throw any light whatsoever on this tunnel as I have never come across it before. Although I was aware of the coal mines up on Smithills Moor I've never seen any maps of diagrams of any locations nor have I met anyone who remembers any open drift entrances.

If anyone can help ….. please get in touch - dave@daveweb.co.uk

Interesting and attractive map of the panoramic view from Winter Hill can be found at: http://www.viewfinderpanoramas.org/panoramas/ENG/Winter.gif

---

Coal Seams on Winter Hill.

As mentioned earlier, there are two major coal seams on Winter Hill which were widely exploited. They were known as the Upper Mountain Mine and the Lower Mountain Mine.

There are however other coal seams in the locality and several of the outcrops can be clearly seen on the surface.

One to outcrop right next to the road, can be found in the stream by the side of the Rivington to Belmont road about 200 yards past the Moses Cocker farmhouse.

The coal seam can be seen jutting out from the bank at water level about 10 yards from where the stream passes beneath the road. There are at least two further coal outcrops further up the valley. According to some geology books there were levels in the stream banks to extract the coal. These are all part of the Holcombe Brook Coal Seam which is also known as the Margery Mine.

On Rivington Moor and Smithills Moor, lie the Sand Rock Mine Coal seams which formed a "double seam". These seams plus the associated fireclay were extensively used in the Horwich area in the stone-ware industry.

South of Belmont village can be found the Brooksbottoms Coal seam. I presume it is the Brooksbottoms seam that was worked in the Shaly Dingle (see an earlier article) area near the main Belmont Road.

There are other coal seams - but they're so thin they're not worth mentioning!

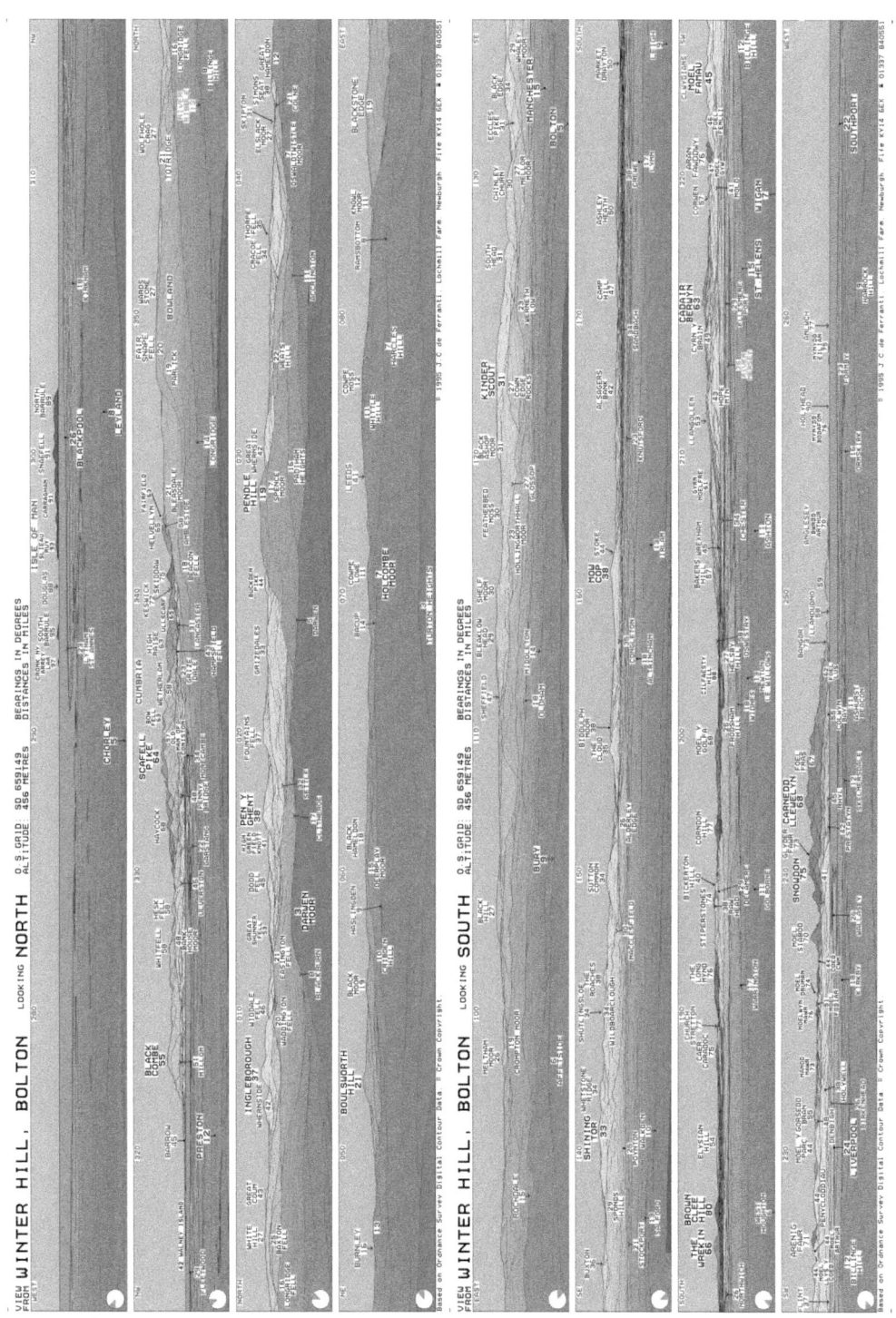

The panoramic view below is courtesy and copyright of Jonathan de Ferranti at: http://www.viewfinderpanoramas.org/

TEENAGERS SAFE AFTER MINE ORDEAL

SIX Lancashire teenagers were rescued by Coal Board safety men early today after a 13-hour ordeal in a disused coal mine near Chorley.

The six, four boys and two girls, were safe but frightened. They took only a torch, a cigarette lighter and an apple with them on their adventure.

A police spokesman said: "What a survival kit! They are lucky to be alive."

The six were: Janet Fishwick, 13, Brazley Avenue, Horwich; Mark Wilkes, 14, Chorley New Road, Horwich; Lester Pearson, 14, Panton Street, Horwich; John Anthony, 14, Sefton Lane, Horwich; Patricia

By CLIVE NAISH

Lester Pearson

Quilliam, 15, Brazley Avenue, Horwich and Anthony Stott, 14, Beech Avenue, Horwich.

It was 2 pm yesterday when eight youngsters crawled through a three-feet wide hole into the disused Winter Hill Mine at Rivington, near Chorley. The hole had been closed but re-opened by rains.

Two turned back but the other six went on to explore old workings which run for miles.

The two who turned back told their parents and when the six had been underground for six hours they were reported missing.

Police called out an NCB rescue team which toiled in the night and brought the youngsters to the surface and safety early today.

One of the girls trapped spoke today of her 13-hour ordeal.

Thirteen-year-old Janet Fishwick, was one of six people who got stuck in the old mine shaft they went exploring on an afternoon's ramble.

They were rescued from the mine shaft on Wilderswood Moors at 1 40 am this morning after a massive rescue operation had been launched by police from the Lancashire and Greater Manchester forces who also called in a mine rescue team.

Janet who attends Rivington and Blackrod High School said as she was comforted by her father today: "We were just walking round and round in circles, and in the end just decided to sit down, huddle together and keep each other warm. All we had was one torch and an apple.

"It was frightening. We just hoped that somebody would come and find us. Everybody was asleep except me when I thought I heard something. I woke them up but they said I was hearing things. Then we heard somebody shouting as we shouted back. We were all so relieved. It was very cold."

RAMBLE

The group of teenagers set off for an afternoon's ramble which turned into a nightmare. The alarm was raised by Patricia Quilliam's brother Mark and Peter Elliot, of Brunswick Avenue, Horwich, when the teenagers failed to return home.

Tanker driver William Fishwick and his son-in-law John Hurst, of Derwent Close, Horwich, were first on the hillside when they became worried after Janet had failed to come home for tea.

"We went up first but didn't have any proper clothing on and so came back," said Mr Fishwick. "We went up again and went into the cave and started shouting but nobody could hear us."

The rescue team from Boothstown, near Manchester, were then called in and warned civilians to keep out of the old mine workings because of the possibility of dangerous gas. While police and rescue workers awaited the arrival of the pit rescue team searchlights were set up and the mine workings sealed off.

Police were led by Supt Ian Hunter.

The teenagers were found soon after the pit rescue team entered the workings and after a check at Bolton Royal Infirmary were allowed home at about 3 am this morning.

John Anthony said: "We went in once to explore, but came out to go home, but then decided to go back to look at a lake inside. We got to the lake and decided to come out a different way, but got lost, we were going round and round in circles.

LANCASHIRE EVENING POST, NOVEMBER 15TH 1976

A view, circa 1905, of George's Lane (as we know it today) under construction. The view is taken soon after passing Sportsman's Cottage heading towards Rivington Pike. Note the "old" moorland road on the left hand side of the picture.

Photo below shows exactly the same view today!

More stone axes!

And yet ANOTHER stone axe has been found in the area to add to the two already found on Winter Hill. The latest find is shown above and was found in April 2006 by Ian Harper on the banks of Anglezarke Reservoir near to the Waterman's Cottage.

It is a highly polished axe, posssibly intended for ritual or ornamental purposes and is in near perfect condition except for one small chip

which can be seen near the bottom edge. The tiny flint arrowhead found by myself (and illustrated earlier in this book) was found within a mile of the axe .... so who knows what else is lying there to be found. Needless to say, if you DO make any new finds in the area PLEASE let me know so that we can ALL share in the history of our area.

++

The Horwich Borehole.

Whilst walking around the lower flanks of Winter Hill, especially in the stream valleys, those of us who like looking at rocks are often aware that the nature and of the fabric of the rocks changes when we are heading either up or down the hill. Some rocks are grey and fine grained, others have a very rough texture and are large grained

The different permutations seem endless, and the sheer variety of rocks over fairly small distances often surprises some people. Different layers of rocks were formed at different periods of time. Most of the Winter Hill rocks were formed (or "laid down") around 300 million years ago. The different layers were formed in differing "environments". Some were laid down in fast moving water, some in stagnant swamp-like conditions etc. Most (but not all) of these different layers or different types of rock have been given names such as "Haslingden Flags" or "Holcomb Brook Grit".

Just across the road from the entrance to Curleys Fisheries (near the bottom of Georges Lane) is a pumping station hidden in the bushes. Prior to this being built, a borehole was drilled to over 1,100 feet to test the rock strata and all the different rock layers were identified and their depths and thicknesses recorded.

Horwich or Ousel Nest Grit	0-90 ft
Margery Flags	124-198 ft
Six Inch Mine Marine Band	at 276 feet
Rough Rock	302-338 ft
Sand Rock Mine Coal seam	at 340 ft
Rough Rock	346-375 ft
Upper Haslingdon Flags	384-624 ft
Haslingden Flag Marine Band	at 730ft
Lower Haslingden Flags	Not found
Holcombe Brook Marine Band	at 860 ft
Holcombe Brook Coal Seam	at 872 ft
Holcombe Brook Grit	884-950 ft
Brooksbottoms Coal Seam	at 979 ft
Brooksbottoms Grit	984-1170 ft

The "gaps" in the depths given, are composed of mudstones and shales and do not have any "names".

Another small free book about Winter Hill now available on the Internet .... "Carboniferous Fossils of Winter Hill and surrounding areas". To download a copy go to the Facebook files section of the group "I belong to Winter Hill & surrounding district"

It is also available in printed book form at:
http://stores.lulu.com/microlight

The Date Stone of Winter Hill.

Boyd Harris brought to my attention a rather strange stone in the Shaley Dingle/Martha Tree Delph area on the Northern flanks of Winter Hill – see the map of the area – the Whimberry Hill area - earlier in this book.

In the earlier article I mentioned the causeway in that area. If you continue walking up the right side of the river, with the causeway on your left (at this point the stream has three tributaries – take the centre one - you will come to a large boulder with 3 dates cut deeply into it. They are 1805, 1912 & 1922. The GPS location is: SD 68144 14356

Has anyone ANY idea what these dates represent? Who might have engraved them? ANY information would be welcomed!

Montcliffe and quarry

Pikestones Neolithic Burial Cairn (3400-2400 BC), Anglezarke Moor

The funerary burial mound site is approximately 45 metres long and 60 18 metres across at its widest point. It consisted of one burial chamber constructed of large upright slabs. These would have been capped by two lintel slabs, forming a chamber of 4.5 metres long, 0.9 metres wide and 0.9 metres high. The Chamber would have been covered by a huge mound of stones and turves.

Artist Impression of the Pikestones burial Cairn

The cairn was aligned almost exactly North-South, with the burial chamber under the wider northern end. At the northern edge of the cairn, a double wall could be made out, curving inwards to form an entrance to a forecourt.

Today the cairn has been badly robbed and the main features are the five large gritstone slabs, the remains of the burial chamber.

Surprisingly, evidence suggests that the bodies were not interred directly in the tomb, but were left outside, perhaps at the entrance to the cairn, for birds and wild animals to consume the flesh and then, probably after elaborate ceremonies, the bones were placed inside the chamber.

Pikestones is the earliest man-made structure in the area and only one other chambered tomb has been found in Lancashire.

The monument must have taken an immense amount of labour to construct and like most long barrows was erected in a prominent position, located on a ridge at a height of just over 276 metres. This gave the Neolithic builders excellent views, and made the structure visible from a wide area of the Lancashire plain, perhaps warning other people that the land belonged to the builders.

Schedule History
First included 12/06/195
Details: No 120, Pikestones NMN 23731
Name: Pikestones Chambered Long Cairn
Revised: 01/08/1994

Pikestones late 1990's

Pikestones 2019

Pikestones 2019

Pikestones 2019

Example of a Chambered Cairn, how Pikestones might once have looked

Millstones – West Pennine Moors

Millstones have been seen at various locations across the West Pennine Moors from including Smithills, Black Coppice and Wilderswood. Some of these stones have been taken for use as garden features by local people and can be seen very well preserved and presented in private garden settings.

Millstones have been made an used in the British isles for thousands of years from the Neolithic use in grinding nuts, seed, grain and pigments to the 16th century and beyond when millstones were made for grain grinding and with mineral refinement, various materials including lead/clays etc.

During the 18th and 19th century British made Millstones were exported to Europe and even North America.

Unfinished Mill Stones one the Moors, Black Coppice. 2019

Most millstones made from indigenous rock in England were made in one piece and was almost always millstone grit. Occasionally Limestone or Granite was used to make the stones. For example limestone was usual in gunpowder mills as it was much less likely to spark than grit stone. For corn-grinding the diameter of the millstones reached almost 2 meters but eventually settling down to an established size of between 1-1.3 meters.

One method of moving the completed Millstone from the hill side and its place of manufacture and onwards to the customer

The Millstones were made in the quarries or on the hill side where the stone had been found as at Black Coppice. The rock was rarely transported to a building for work to be carried out. This meant that the work would need to be carried out to shape the rock in the most extreme wild and exposed places.

Unfinished Mill Stones with centre hole on the Moors, Black Coppice. 2019

It would appear that the millstones at Black Coppice (pictured 2019) were simply abandoned before completion and have remained in situ amongst the parent rock from which they were made.

Firm dates don't exist but the making of millstones at Black Coppice both in the quarries and on the moorland probably occurred at least in the 17th and 18th centuries if not before.

The transporting practice of the Millstones from where they were made to their final destination appears very variable across the country.

Unfinished Mill Stones amongst other stone on the Moors, Black Coppice 2019

There is little doubt that in some circumstances the millstones were simply rolled down the hillside to a river and then onto a boat (see below). Four wheel carts were used were possible, the etching copy of this practice is at Duxon Quarry, Lancashire with Houghton Tower in the background, early 19th Century.

Plate 6 Photograph of engraving of 'Houghton Tower', included in Edward Baines's book of 1831. Duxon Hill millstone quarry in foreground. Reproduced by permission from copy of second edition (1836) held by Birmingham Central Library.

Withnell Explosives Works
(also known as the Bellite Works or Colliery Explosives Works).

Withnell Explosives Works was operational between 1894 and 1920. The works was situated on Bolton Road (A675), approximately half way between the Hare and Hounds in Abbey Village and Tockholes Road.

Site of the explosive works along the A675, Abbey Village is upward and Belmont Village down

The works produced two explosives, Bellite and Withnell Powder. Bellite is a mixture of ammonium nitrate and dinitrobenzene. Withnell Powder is a mixture of ammonium nitrate, trinitro-toluene (TNT) and flour.

Eight buildings were situated on the moors with separate offices, changing rooms and canteen by the road side **(see map)**. Some of the buildings had double walls to ensure safety and dryness. Three large mounds of earth were also built for baffles in case of an explosion, these still remain and can be clearly seen from the road.

The buildings were connected by a tramline to convey the explosives to the various stages of processing - a truck would be pulled up and down the hill by a rope worked by a steam engine and windlass. On the other side of the main road was a tip for ashes and an area where the explosives were tested.

The works employed 50-60 employees. All workers wore overalls with the pockets stitched to prevent matches being taken into the works. Large overshoes were also provided with copper nails in the soles to prevent sparks. Boys, age 14, received 10 shillings for 56 hours per week and men earned 18-22 shillings per week.

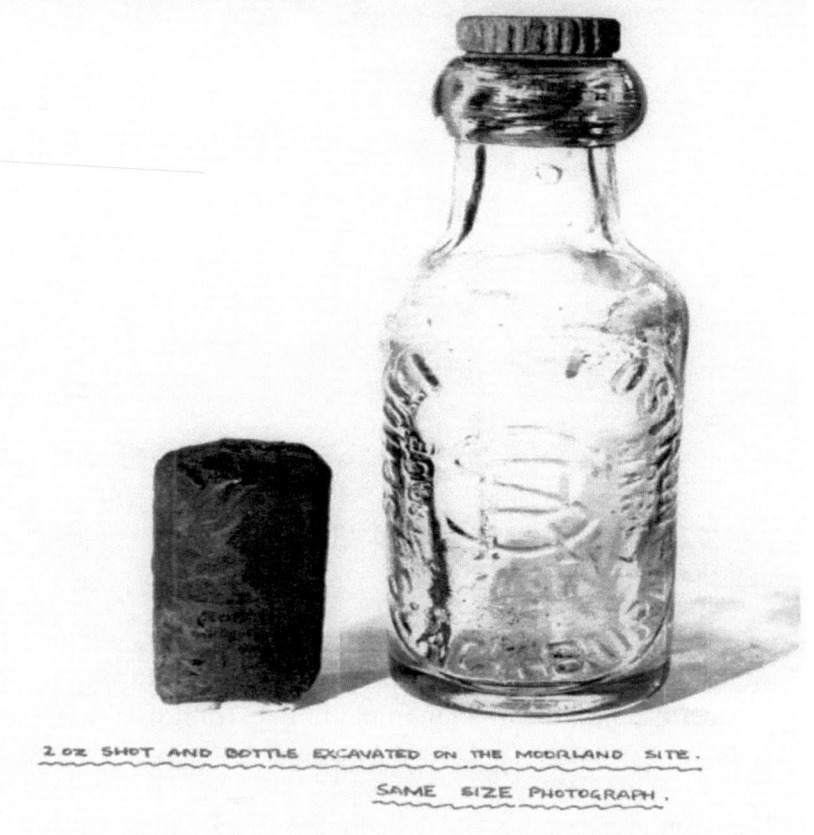

2 oz SHOT AND BOTTLE EXCAVATED ON THE MOORLAND SITE.
SAME SIZE PHOTOGRAPH.

These items were excavated at the site in the early 1970's. The 2-ounce shot would have been used for quarry and/or mine work.

Initially the works was owned by Carl Lamm, a Swedish Managing Director of the Rotebro Explosive Company in Stockholm (set up in the 1880s) and operating under the name of Lancashire Explosives Company Ltd. Lamm had invented and patented Bellite and had previously tried to set up an explosive works on the Isle of Man, but had failed to secure an operating licence. For a time, Lamm lived in Blackburn and travelled each day by train to Withnell Station (in Abbey Village) where he was met with a horse and trap which took him to the works.

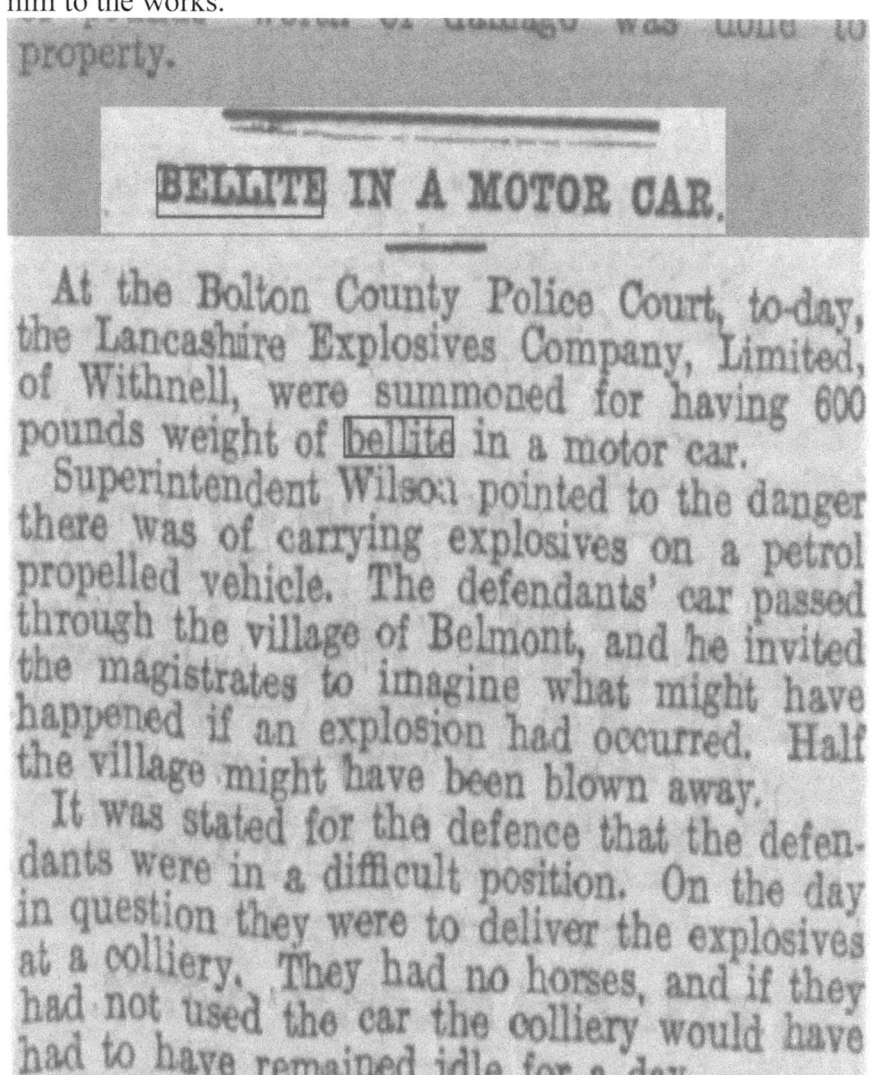

Piece from the Newspaper regarding the transportation of explosives from the works. 1915

The explosives were intended to be for blasting in coal mines and quarries, not in weapons. Surprisingly, Bellite was reported to be a powerful but extremely safe explosive;

"When subjected to the most powerful blow with a steel hammer upon an iron plate, it neither explodes nor ignites. A rifle bullet fired into it at 50 yards' distance will not explode it.

It cannot be made to explode by friction, shock, or pressure, nor by electricity, fire, lightning, and that it can only be exploded by means of a fulminate detonator…it is perfectly safe to handle and manufacture".

This however, was not the view taken by the court in 1915 when 600 lbs of Bellite was transported by car through Belmont (see newspaper report).

The risk of explosion, however, was not the major threat to the workers' health. Given the chemical composition of Bellite and Withnell Powder, the major risk was the inhalation of poisonous fumes and powder.

The dry ingredients, including nitro-benzol and ammonia crystals, were crushed under rollers and mixed in buildings 1 and 2. Number 1 building became known as the 'dead house', and workers could only work for 15 minutes before needing a break due to the fumes.

The explosive was then put into large tins and carried by the tramway to number 4, 5, and 6 buildings. The powder was put into hoppers and fed into tubes or powder shots of 3 different sizes (2oz, 4oz and 6oz). The shots were then made waterproof by wrapping in paper and dipping in hot paraffin wax (see photo).

Mercury fulminate detonators were brought from off site and carried to the store house on stretchers to avoid vibration, being inserted into the shots and ready to be transported to the coal mines.

Milk was supplied to the employees to neutralise the inhalation of the poisonous fumes and powder and muslin masks were also available to use over the mouth and nose. However, some of the workers, not surprisingly, became ill after a few weeks of working. Their legs went weak, their lips blue and their skin yellow – known locally as being 'Bellited'. Sometimes the workers were moved from job to job as a preventative precaution. One particularly nasty case of bellite poisoning, resulting in the death of 21 year-old, Lawrence Hardman, was reported in the newspapers in 1914 (see newspaper clip).

The works were closed in 1920 when the lease on the land expired. The contents and machinery were sold off and a farewell dinner was held for the workers in the White Bull Hotel in Blackburn. The Lancashire Explosives Company remained in business at other sites, being eventually incorporated into ICI Nobel, a division of Imperial Chemical Industries (ICI).

There are a few remains of gate posts at the edge of the A675, earth mound baffles and the twin walled buildings on the moors (see photo below)

Remains of a twin walled building as part of the explosive works. Pictured 2019.

POISONED AT GUNPOWDER WORKS.

Blackburn Man's Remarkable Death.

Remarkable evidence was given at an inquest at Blackburn Royal Infirmary, to-day, on Lawrence Hardman (21), of Quarry-street, Blackburn.

The widow said that the husband began to work at the gunpowder works of the Lancashire Explosives' Company, Withnell, about Christmas, and in January had to leave because of poisoning. He resumed in about three weeks' time, but had since complained of pains in the head, and once had to be carried out of the works. On the morning of July 19 he began throwing his arms about, rolling about the bed and screaming. He was unconscious for several days. The husband worked in what was known as No. 1 dead house. The men worked in that place for a quarter of an hour and then went out for 45 minutes.

Thomas Watson, another employe, said that on July 18 he came back to Blackburn with Hardman and told him he thought he had been poisoned by dust at the works. When walking home he rolled like a drunken man, and had to crawl upstairs to bed.

John Smith, manager of the works, said that when bellite was being ground dust arose, and was inhaled by the workmen. That was the only death they had had.

Dr. Peddie, medical officer under the Home Office, said he examined the men at the powder works once a month, and if the men showed deterioration in condition he was ordered to change his work. No man could start in the powder area without a certificate from him. One man had worked there twenty years, and was still hale and hearty. Bellite poisoning affected the whole nervous system. It was stated that death was due to cerebral poisoning and congestion, probably due to bellite poisoning.

A verdict to this effect was returned.

Piece regarding the effect of the work on the workers. 1915

Round Loaf Bowl Barrow Anglezarke

Round Loaf is located upon a gently sloping plateau on Anglezarke Moor. It includes an oval mound of earth and small stones 3.6m-5.5m high with maximum dimensions of 73m north-south by 66m east-west. Several flint flakes have been found on the eroded summit of the mound over a period of years.

Round loaf, Anglezarke

Despite some surface erosion to the mound's summit, Round Loaf survives reasonably well and remains a prominent landmark visible from a considerable distance in all directions.

It is not known to have been excavated and will therefore retain undisturbed archaeological deposits within the mound and upon the old land surface. Round Loaf has Scheduled Monument Status and was first scheduled in March 1954

Bowl Barrows

Bowl barrows, the most numerous form of round barrow, are funerary monuments dating from the Late Neolithic period to the Late Bronze Age, with most examples belonging to the period 2400-1500 BC.

They were constructed as earthen or rubble mounds, sometimes ditched, which covered single or multiple burials. They occur either in isolation or grouped as cemeteries and often acted as a focus for burials in later periods.

Round loaf with the spring Cotton Grass

Often superficially similar, although differing widely in size, they exhibit regional variations in form and a diversity of burial practices.

There are over 10,000 surviving bowl barrows recorded nationally (many more have already been destroyed), occurring across most of lowland Britain.

Often occupying prominent locations, they are a major historic element in the modern landscape and their considerable variation of form and longevity as a monument type provide important information on the diversity of beliefs and social organisations amongst early prehistoric communities.

Liverpool Castle, Rivington ... from 800 ft!

The Rivington Reservoirs looking north

The Lidar images of Winter Hill and Anglezarke.

You'll have probably seen many aerial photo's taken of this area either on the internet or even in local newspapers. You'll probably also have looked at the Google Earth images of this area. There is however another kind of image taken from "above" which is widely used nowadays by archaeologists to pinpoint ancient "structures" on the ground which may not be apparent at ground level.

LIDAR is a surveying method that measures distance to a target by illuminating the target with laser light and measuring the reflected light with a sensor. Differences in laser return times and wavelengths can then be used to make digital 3-D representations of the target. The name lidar, now used as an acronym of light detection and ranging (sometimes light imaging, detection, and ranging), was originally a portmanteau of light and radar. Lidar sometimes is called 3D laser scanning, a special combination of a 3D scanning and laser scanning. It has terrestrial, airborne, and mobile applications.

Using LIDAR it is possible to spot all sorts of things invisible at ground level.

The Lidar images of Winter Hill and Anglezarke are a goldmine for anyone interested in "what was once there". It's a stunning modern archive of the physical history of the area.

Try it for yourself - go to
https://houseprices.io/lab/lidar/map?ref=SD65881495

This link will centre itself on "round about" the TV masts at the top of Winter Hill. Using your scrolling control on your mouse you can zoom in and out and if you zoom out you'll soon see the Rivington reservoirs on the left hand side of your screen and if you look carefully you'll find the Belmont reservoir.

Using this photo you can zoom in and take a look at Round Loaf, mining shafts and other mining remains in the area. Ancient field patterns and their walls or ditches can be easily found along with the remains of old industrial sites.

Any photo's I put into this book of the images do not do them justice at all. You have to go to the original images on your screen and look for yourselves.

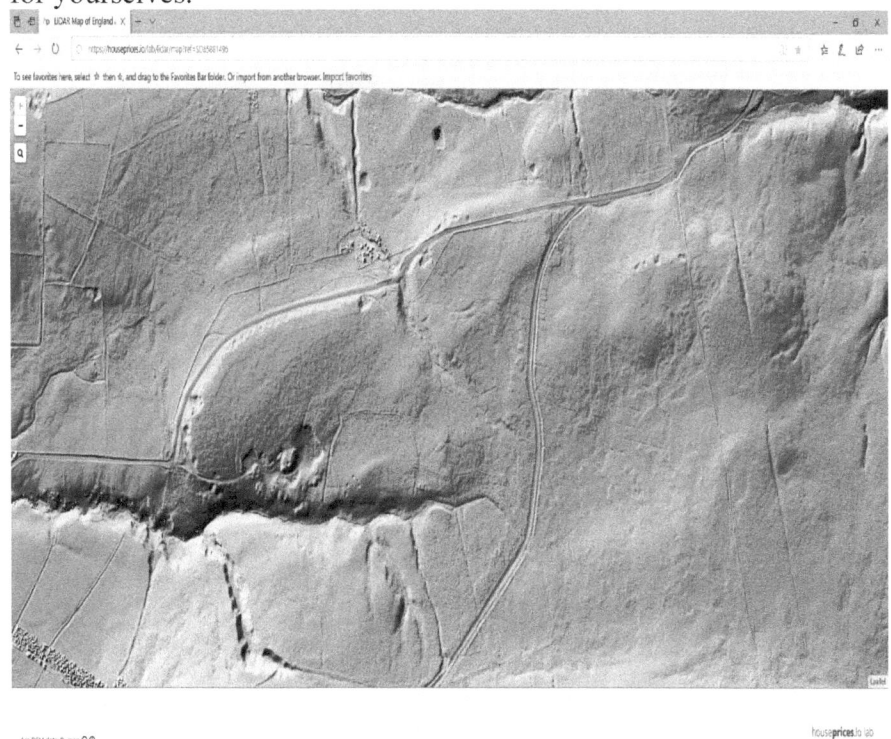

This Lidar image phoro shows the road from Rivington to Belmont running from the LH side of the image to the top right hand corner of it. The road from the bottom centre to the major road is the rough moorland track from the Pidgeon Tower. On your computer you'll be able to see things just not visible either on the ground nor on this awful black and white picture. There are at least 6 pit shafts on the RH side of the junction of the two roads plus at least 6 others on the banks of the valley at the bottom left. Just go look at the real images for yourself! Near the junction of the two roads the images hint that there just "could" have been structures of some sort on the sides of the rough moorland track.

To look at LIDAR images of other parts of the UK go to :
https://houseprices.io/lab/lidar/map and zoom in on areas of interest. If you click on any area of the image, a box will appear for you to type the name of the place, town or area of interest.

Using the Lidar web sites (of which there are many) you'll be able to search for unknown structures yourself.

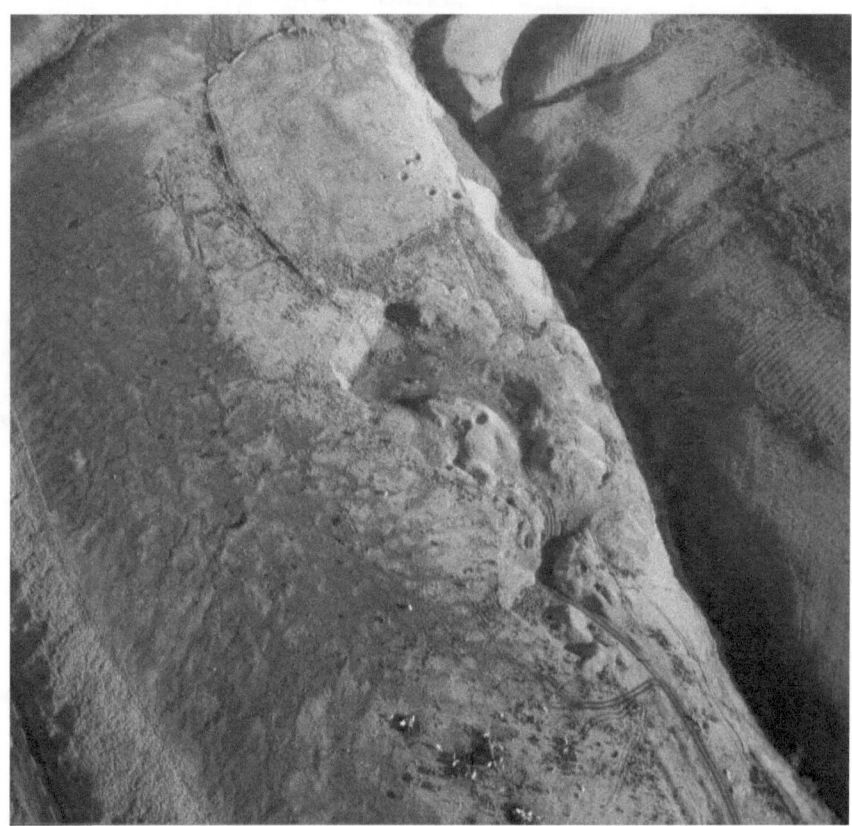

An aerial view of some of those same pit shafts. So what does it show? An enclosed area with a few pit shafts .... or even the remains of a Roman Fort!!!!! ... a perfect spot for a Roman fort!

RAF Hurricane PG472 Crash 1945, Smithills Moor

On the afternoon of the 2nd February 1945 two Hurricanes fighters, took off from RAF Calverley in Cheshire.

Flying these were **Flight Sergeant Thomas Stanley Taylor** and **Warrant Officer Norman Thomas Huckle,** both aged just 21.

The two pilots were cleared for local flying exercises, but some 20 minutes later they were flying over Winter Hill.

The crash investigators could not be sure what they were doing so far from their flight plan, but it was suspected that they had been flying in formation at some 6-7,000 feet over the Smithills area and collided in cloud.

Out of control they dived to the ground, one into the ground close to Horrocks Fold, the other – PG472 – diving into open moorland on the flank of Whimberry Hill.

The evidence found by the investigation teams suggests that PG472 hit the ground upside down, exploding on impact and creating a crater.

Fire consumed the plane and pilot with left to recover at the time, apart from the engine and remains of the pilot.

Investigators worked out that the two fighter planes must have flown directly to the area, instead of carrying out their training as planned over Cheshire.

The crash inquiry tried to find out what the Hurricanes were doing there and so appealed for any information through the Bolton Evening News, hoping to find a witness to the tragedy.

Someone responded saying that one of the pilots was engaged to a young woman who working in a Bolton factory and an impromptu air display had been arranged, but sadly the aircraft never turned up.

It is believed the wreckage from the other aircraft fell on private land with the final pieces removed in the 1990's.

What started out as a bit of fun and romance, turned into tragedy.

RIP; Flight Sergeant Thomas Stanley Taylor and **Warrant Officer Norman Thomas Huckle,**

Gary Rhodes at the site of RAF Hurricane PG472 Crash 1945, Smithills Moor. Picture, September 2018.

Please don't disturb or remove anything from the site, it is still a crash area and a pilot died there.

The Rivington "cup and ring" boulder.

In September 1999 a boulder with carved markings was discovered near the Lower Rivington Reservoir at Horwich. The markings were clearly of the "cup and ring" variety. Rocks with these markings have been discovered in many areas of the UK, although the bulk of them seem to occur in Yorkshire, Scotland and a few in Derbyshire.

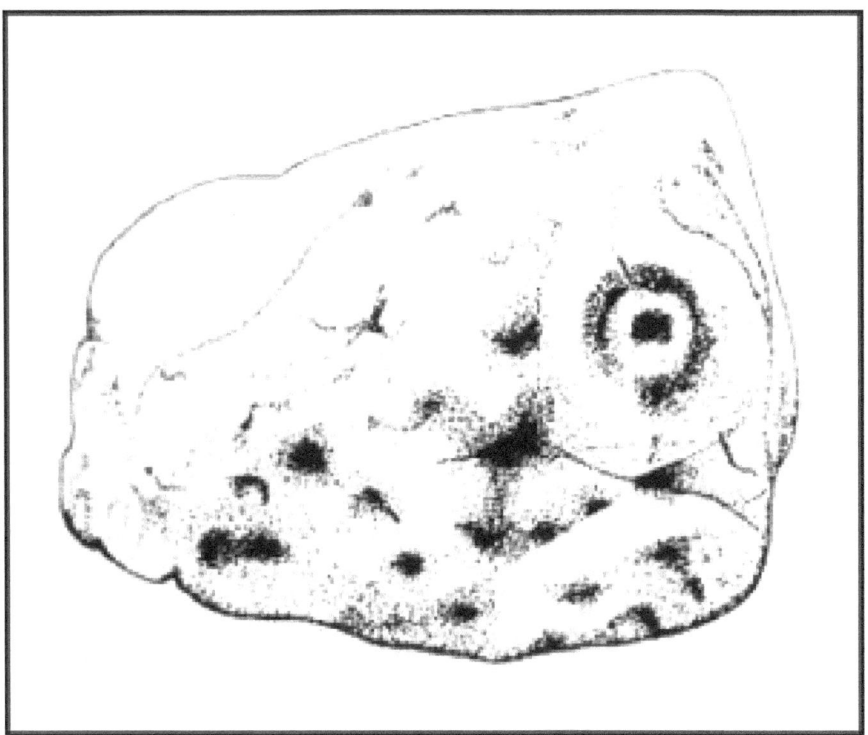

At the time of writing, (October 1999) the stone is on the grass outside Anderton Hall Conference Centre at Horwich.

It is hoped that the stone will soon be moved to somewhere more accessible by the public, such as the Rivington Information Centre. It should NOT be moved to Bolton Museum where it will probably eventually be put into "storage" like many of the other Neolithic finds in the area!

Keep your eyes peeled. YOU may find the next Neolithic object in the Rivington area!

Approaching the Rivington Reservoirs from the north

Pilkington Quarry, Georges Lane, Montcliffe from the air

No idea where this photo originated .... But it shows the abandoned tank that used to be just up the hill from Rivington Green by the side of the road .... or so I've been told!

Beautiful photo by Ray Platt ..... found on The "I belong to Winter Hill" Facebook Page

More about the Whimberry Hill tunnel.

Since I *(Dave Lane)* first became interested in Winter Hill I'd always heard of this slightly mysterious "tunnel" in the northern flanks of the Hill in the Whimberry Hill area. Folk lore told me "it was ancient"

It was once a tunnel with both an entrance and an exit - and seemed to be underneath a small mound or hill.

To be honest I first visited it long before my mine and tunnel exploration days and all I ever did was merely looked into the entrance of the tunnel. I never ever went into it!

Over the many decades since then, I've heard ever so many reasons for its existence, a drainage channel, an exploratory tunnel for mining purposes, a flu pipe from a furnace to a chimney …… and one theory which says it's some sort of prehistoric or ancient burial mound with a man-made tunnel underneath it.

Although I've never been into it, people tell me it was a straight through tunnel with a clearly visible entrance and that the top exit was at the bottom of a small dip or "well" not far below the ground surface.

Apparently nowadays there seems to be a roof collapse in the middle of the tunnel and the exit pit is now filled in (rumoured to be by a farmer who filled it to prevent his sheep getting trapped in it).

Its location is at grid **68530 13681** at around 345m above sea level. The tunnel sides are dry stone walls of local rough rock about 10 courses high. The ceiling stone slabs are 80mm thick, 0.5m long with approx 1 meter of earth above the roof to the surface. The tunnel is approx. 34m in length and is 1.4m wide and 0.8m in height. The floor appears to be rough or solid.

When currently looking inside the tunnel it appears to be either blocked or the tunnel turns right about 7.4m in. The tunnel is at the **top** of a hill and its construction must be by digging a trench or cutting, building the tunnel and refilling on the top. All the local watercourses in the area are much lower than this tunnel.

So what exactly is this tunnel, how old is it, what was its purpose? It just can't be a drainage tunnel …. It's on **top** of a hill! … nothing to drain!" So what is it?

The most convincing argument that I've heard about what it might be is that it's a "Souterrain" …… yeah I know…. What's a souterrain? Google it!

"Souterrain" is a name given by archaeologists to a type of underground structure associated mainly with the European Atlantic Iron Age. One of the official definitions of it is "An underground passageway, chamber, or series of chambers, sometimes having a roof of stone slabs, built as part of an ancient settlement or fort, especially in the British Isles".

There are many photographs on the internet of souterrains around Western Europe and many look awfully similar to what we find here on Winter Hill

So what is it? We'll probably never know the answer until a full archaeological investigation is done at some time in the future.

The entrance and what it looks like inside .... Both photos were sent to me many years ago by Munki_Boy

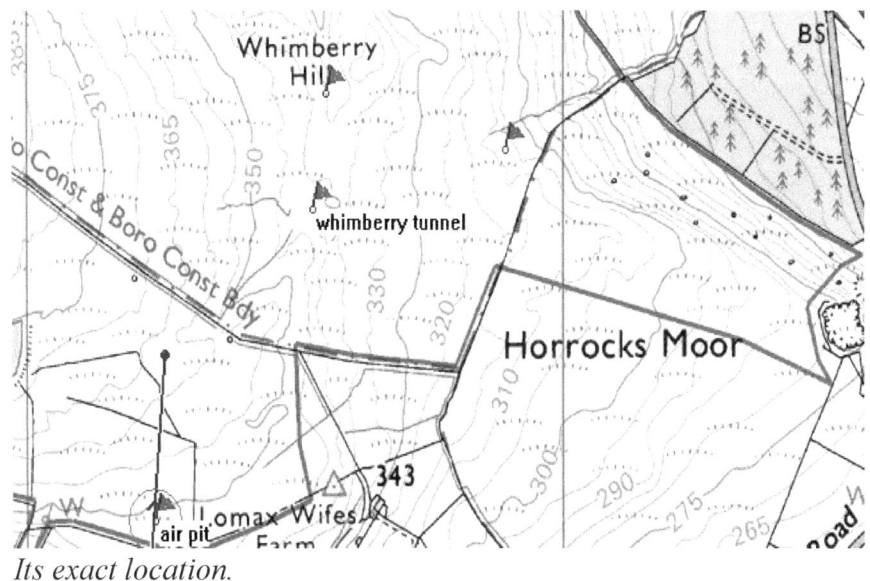

Its exact location.

Aerial view of Leicester Mill Quarry taken 20 years ago

The Winter Weather On the West Pennine Moors – Winters aren't what they once were…..

There are few more iconic winter scenes than this. We don't however have the long spells of cold wintery weather with snow on the ground lasting for weeks as we did just two generations ago

In general we have warm summers and cool winters. Our summers are cooler than those on the continent, but the winters are milder. The overall climate in England is called temperate maritime. This means that it is mild with temperatures not much lower than 0°C in winter and not much higher than 32°C in summer.

The global temperatures have warmed by around 1 degree Celsius since the Victorian era with the rate of increase apparently accelerating over the last 25 years (1993-2018) by 0.2 degree Celsius/decade.

Skiing in Rivington 1982 (Garry Rhodes MBE)

A frozen Dean Black Brook near White Coppice 1982 (Garry Rhodes MBE)

Digging out the Transmitter station, Winter Hill 1982 (Garry Rhodes MBE)

Rivington Pike from the Winter Hill Cairn, on one of the few days of snow January 2019

An avalanche 1982 near the Shore, below Noon Hill Stacks, Winter Hill (Garry Rhodes MBE)

More digging out at the transmitter station 1982 (Garry Rhodes MBE)

A wall of ice, Leicester/Lester Quarry, Anglezarke 1982 (Garry Rhodes MBE)

The average winter temperature for England is between 9 and 4 oC from October to March. Snow rarely falls in the English uplands if the temperature is more than 4C and will not sit for long on the ground when the temperature hits 4C.

Douglas Springs, Winter Hill January 2019

The mining track visible in the snow leading to the Wilderswood drift mine. January 2019

Frozen embankment over Dean Black Brook, White Coppice, Anglezarke 1982 (Garry Rhodes MBE)

A frozen river, Dean Black Brook White Coppice, Anglezarke 1982

Garry Rhodes and Derek Cartwright enjoying the sun and snow, January 2019.

Garry Rhodes and Ian Middleton, heading towards Noon Hill from the Winter Hill Cairn, January 2019.

Given this the minor climate changes set out above will have a significant effect on the longevity of ground snow. This might be one of the reasons we don't see the snow we did not that long ago.

Site of Brick, Tile and Stoneware manufacture on Winter Hill

As well as Hole Bottom Pipe/Tile kiln which can be easily seen from the mast road stoneware manufacturing took place in the middle of the moors.

Walking from the Pike to the mast across the moors a site of manufacturing can be seen on the left in the vicinity of Douglas Springs (the source of the river Douglas). SD 65616 14368

The photographs give some idea of the complex which appears to have one or two kilns and other structures. Clay was probably acquired on the same site by either mining or digging the clay out from near the surface open cast style.

The Douglas Spring Kiln, post moorland fires 2018.

The clay must have been dried, ground up and settled on site before use. Items seen around are tiles, flooring, bricks and sinks. The tiles below were seen exposed post the 2018 fires.

The site is quite remote with no recognisable track to it. Another possibly related structure exist 200/300 meters north which consists of stone building remains and a mound which could be a mine (SD 65861 14501).

The photographs clearly indicate the extent of the human activity with the vegetation changing from the surroundings to the area of industrial use.

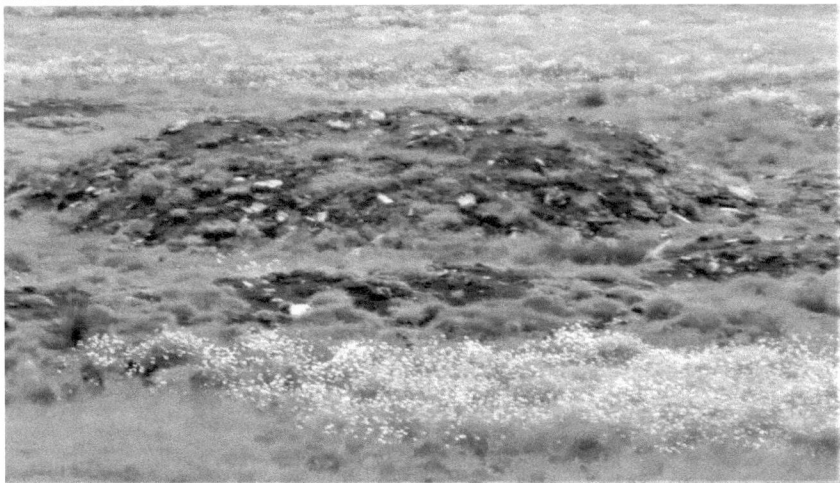

Douglas Spring kiln. The change in vegetation is striking signifying the extent of human activity

Up to the time of writing the site cannot be found in any listings or maps. Its possible that the complex had a short operational life span. On examination of the items found the working assumption is that the kiln was in use in the mid to late Victorian period and possibly into early twentieth century

Tile found after the fires (2018) near the Douglas Spring kiln

Sinks exposed post the moorland fires 2018 near the Douglas Spring Kiln

Lower Rivington Reservoir

I've been told that in this photo are of the two people who first discovered the Winter Hill Cairn .... But what and where is this stone - apparently on Will Nar - and is it still there?

World War II Bombing Decoy Site on Brinscall Moor

During the Second World War a secret department was formed at Britain's Air Ministry to develop a deception strategy to combat German bombing. This campaign was masterminded by Colonel John Fisher Turner, an engineer and retired Air Ministry officer.

Colonel Turner formed a team with the best film studio tradesmen, carpenters, and engineers who constructed a network of dummy airfields and hundreds of decoy sites around the country.

Decoy towns were built in remote areas which could be easily set alight. As soon as the first wave of enemy bombers attacked a target, emergency teams extinguished the resulting flames and then the decoy fires were lit. Due to the 'black out' across all towns and cities, the real target was then completely invisible. The aim was to fool the second wave of bombers that the decoy site was their target.

Tanks with the fuel released onto the burning coals

One decoy site was situated on Brinscall Moor at the top of Well Lane SD 633 202 (a second near Spitlers Edge/Hordern Stoops). At the top of Well Lane (Brinscall) an air raid shelter was built to protect the men who built the decoy fires which were designed to lead bomber attacks away from Preston, Blackburn and the Royal Ordnance Factory at Chorley.

The decoy site was built in 1941 as an 'SF' site and in 1942 a 'QL' decoy was incorporated into the site. 'SF' stands for Special Fires, but the name Starfish was more commonly used. Each Starfish site was a sophisticated set up, with fires differing in appearance, intensity and duration and the site itself had an infrastructure that included access roads, firebreak trenches and a means to control the fires remotely, usually from the air raid shelter.

An example of a "Starfish" site

The additional 'QL' decoy displayed simulated railway marshalling yard lights and factory lighting that would be present in the cities. SF and QL sites were frequently found together.

Tanks containing paraffin or diesel were placed on top of 7m towers, arranged to resemble rows of buildings or industrial complexes (see photos). A valve that operated like a toilet flush was opened to release the fuel on to burning coal, creating an instant blaze and engulfing the area in black smoke. Then the fire was flushed with water to send a column of steam into the night sky. This resulted in a convincing mock-up of a bombing raid that had hit its target.

By the end of the war there were approximately 630 decoy sites in the U.K consisting of 230 decoy airfields and 400 decoy towns including railway marshalling yards, steelworks, foundry and factory complexes.

It is believed that the decoy sites across the country drew some 5% of the bombs intended for real airfields and cities, saving an estimated 2,500 lives and prevented more than 3,000 injuries.

There are no records of any bombs being dropped on the Brinscall or Anglezarke Moors.

Little remains of the site today except a few pipes and outlines of buildings. At the top of Well Lane/Edge Gate Lane, turn left and the control bunker is on the right. Look to the right and you can see the earthenware pipes that were designed to prevent spilled diesel from the simulated fires from running down the brooks.

Behind the ruins of Solomon's Temple farm are some concrete bases with remains of the poles that held the decoy lights.

Part of the oil trap structures still visible today on Brinscall Moor, designed to prevent the oil used getting into the local watercourses

A second decoy site was constructed at Hordern Stoops just off the Rivington/Belmont Road

Thanks to Boyd Harris, the Chorley History and Archaeology Society and the Friends of Brinscall and Withnell villages

RAF Wellington Bomber Zulu 8799 Crash 1943, Anglezarke

Anglezarke Moor was the location of a tragic air crash on the 16th November, 1943. Wellington Bomber Zulu 8799 lost control over Hurst Hill on the moors, and all the crew were pronounced dead at the scene. A fitting tribute exists at Lead Mines Clough, lest we forget.

The plane had taken off from 28 Operational Training Unit at Wymeswold in Leicestershire on a night time training exercise, known as a Bullseye mission. Its pilot was Flight Sergeant Joseph B. Timperon, who came from Alice Springs in Australia and was attached from the Royal Australian Air Force approximately 8 months prior. Timperon was only 24 years old when he died, and precious little is known of the five young British crew members who died with him.

Nothing was heard from Flight No. Z8799 after take-off and at 0240 hours, the aircraft was officially recorded overdue. By this time, the crash had already happened.

The aircraft had got into difficulty whilst flying low over the moors. The pilot wrestled with the controls, trying to lift the plane above the closing summit below, but she would not rise.

The engines screeched as the aircraft crashed, and the wreckage was scattered over a large area.

The RAF investigation which followed decided that the tragedy had most likely been caused by a 'loss of control in cloud, possibly due to icing' which may have led to structural failure as it went into a high speed dive.

Rescuers had no modern equipment to locate the wreckage, and had to rely on the reports that had been given to them without particular note of grid reference. As dawn broke on Hurst Hill, five out of the six crew were found close to the main wreckage of the plane, but the tail gunner was found a good distance away.

The Crew RIP: RAAF; Flight Sgt Joseph B Timperon (Pilot)

RAF: Sgt Eric R Barnes (Airbomber)

RAF; Sgt Joseph B Hayton (Airgunner)

RAF: Sgt Robert S Jackson (Navigator)

RAF; Sgt George E Murray (Navigator)

RAF; Sgt Mathew Mouncey (Airgunner)

A Wellington Bomber of the type that crashed into Anglezarke Moor's Hurst Hill.

The interior of a Wellington Bomber.

A Fitting Memorial

The memorial at Lead Mines Clough – a fine tribute

In June 1955 a simple stone memorial was erected above Lead Mines Clough in memory of the six men who died in the Wellington Bomber crash. The idea of creating a permanent tribute to this tragic loss of life came from the Rotary Club of Horwich, as part of the club's special activities to mark the Golden Anniversary Year of the Rotary Movement.

Permission to erect the monument was sought from the landowners, the Liverpool Corporation, and full co-operation was received from the tenant farmers, who helped in every way. A local man, Mr. J. Dougill, voluntarily offered his services as a stonemason to dress a suitable piece of stone which he obtained from Brazley House in Horwich. A simple plate bearing the names of the crew was attached to the memorial pillar.

The unveiling ceremony was performed by Wing Commander B. I. Dias OBE, DFC of RAF Padgate, and the dedication by Rev. David Dick BD, President of Rotary International in Great Britain and

Ireland. Among those present at the service were relatives of all the crewmen including the aunt and uncle of the Australian pilot, whose parents were unable to visit the memorial until the following year.

Following the solemn words of the dedication, the silence was broken as three rifle volleys from the RAF firing party were fired across the valley.

As the last echo died away, two trumpets sounded the Last Post and Reveille, the traditional tribute of the Service to fallen comrades. Wreaths were laid at the base of the stone from relatives, the RAF, the RAAF and also the Rotary Club.

A service is still held at the memorial on Remembrance Sunday each year, and **long may it continue.**

The effects of War on our Moors

Tactics to frustrate Invading Armies
On the run up to war and during WWII the government embarked on various measures to frustrate the progress of any invading army. Some evidence of these tactics still exist.

Remembering that the road network during WWII was much different than it is today and of course SatNav devices hadn't been thought of.

First of all, signposts were either taken down or painted out to deny the invaders of vital directional information.

Secondly, any boundary stones had the information on them chipped away.

If you look hard enough some of these still can be seen (Georges Lane)

Thirdly, where stone walls existed on either side of a road, holes were made with a redundant telegraph pole hidden behind the wall which could quickly be slipped through the holes thus blocking the roads (see photos below)

Thanks to D. A. Owen

Boundary and direction marker with the words chipped away to frustrate any invading army (Georges Lane, Rivington/Horwich Boundary)

Hole in a dry stone walls to take telegraph poles to create road block to frustrate invading armies (top of Sheephouse Lane, Rivington)

Hole in a dry stone walls to take telegraph poles to create road block to frustrate invading armies (near Lester/Leicester Quarry, Anglezarke)

Live Firing Range and Targets

Large areas of Anglezarke moor appear to have been turned over to the military, British and later American for use as a firing range. A tank was positioned on the moors as a target. Post war this was pulled up to the side of the Rivington to Belmont road (see photo) and remained there for a number of years

Tank used as target practice at the side of the Rivington/Belmont Road

It is suggested that most of the vacant and abandoned farms around the area were targeted by weapons mounted on tanks, mortars and small arms fire, these include Drinkwaters near Great Hill, Higher and Lower Hemshaws, Old Rachels etc.

Higher Hempshaws farm, Anglezarke. Used for target practice in WWII and site where munitions were found in 1985

During the mid 1980's Liverpool Water Works Rangers came across munitions left around Higher Hemshaws. This resulted a many months of work by the Bomb Disposal units to clear the Anglezarke area, including Lester Quarries and all the then ruined farms

Munitions found on Anglezarke Moor piled up and waiting to be destroyed. Near Higher Hempshaws farm, Anglezarke, 1985/86

Munitions found by the military bomb disposal teams 1985/6

The Path and Paved Causeway, Hordern Stoops to Great Hill

A popular route for the walker is that from Hordern Stoops situated part way along the Rivington to Belmont Road across the moor and Spitlers Edge to Great Hill on Anglezarke Moor, or the other way around. Great Hill is access from other paths the most common being the route from White Coppice. Walkers often refer to the stroll as a "walk over Spitlers Edge". This is an interesting piece of moorland, the wall running along most of the paths length has a significance in history and the now paved causeway has its own story to tell.

Spitlers Edge is a ridge running along the eastern edge of Anglezarke Moor, from Standing Stones Hill to Hordern Stoops. The ridge, complete with a cairn (see below) and at 392 m is the high point of Anglezarke moor. Redmonds Edge links Spitlers Edge to Great Hill.

A section of the 1840's wall on Spitlers Edge

Along the length of the Spitlers Edge is a stone wall of some historical importance, this was built in 1841 as a relief measure to provide respite from the "Hungry Forties", this period in the 1840's was one of trade depression and repeated failed harvests resulting in the poor suffering terribly. Work was created for the unemployed, this wall being one of the schemes. The wall is the parliamentary division boundary between Chorley and Blackburn and continues across the Rivington/Belmont Road towards Winter Hill.

The name "Spitlers" is derived from the fact that in medieval times, the Knights Hospitallers of St John of Jerusalem used this route when travelling to their holdings in the area. The ridge provides the peaks that supply the source water to the Yarrow River and Limestone Brook.

The Cairn just off Spitlers Edge SD 64839 18545, 361 meters above sea.

The Modern Path and Paved Causeway

A significant portion of the path from Great Hill to Hordern Stoops is paved. Other sections are of hard core construction and at least one stretch of the path runs on the base of the 1840's wall. The stone paved causeway, a little over 3 Km running from Will Nar to Great Hill was constructed in stages commencing in the mid 1990's.

The first section (1995/96) was a 2 Km stretch spanning from Higher Anshaw along Spitlers Edge and Redmans to the boundary wall and fence which contains a style at the south east side of Great Hill.

Conservation volunteers had positioned some of the large stones that cross the small streams and gulley's along the path in preparation for the major work to commence.

A section of the paved causeway with a bridge crossing a gully

The flag stones came from various demolished mills from around the East Lancashire and possibly the West Yorkshire areas, many show signs of the fixtures and fitting positions from when they were on the floor of the mills. One wonders how many pairs of clogged feet have crossed these very flag stones while they were part of the Lancashire king cotton empires of days gone by.

One of the flagstones on Spitlers Edge with the tell-tale mill fixtures and fitting marks

They Flags were held in a reclamation yard in the Bacup area prior to being weighed and moved in batches ready for the transportation up onto the hills. The batches of flags could weigh no more than 900 Kg as they were to be lifted onto the moor via helicopter, e.g. two large stones and a small one would easily make up the 900 Kg maximum payload with some stones being more than 100 mm thick. Once dropped onto the moor the positioning didn't necessarily match the requirement on any particular stretch to be paved so the flags often needed to be moved again along Spitlers Edge via a dumper truck, not an easy task.

A stretch of the causeway, Spitlers Edge

The flagged causeway with the 1840's wall in the background

The next section to be paved was from the crest of Great Hill to the boundary wall and fence mentioned above, this stretch was completed in around 2002, with the last stretch from Higher Hempshaw's to the top of Will Nar completed as late as 2014. Will Narr is linked to the Hordern Stoops car park via a path of mixed hard core, stone paving slabs and the remains of a dry stone wall.

As well as the mills fixture markings the flagstones across the full present length have another interesting feature and worthy of study by the walker. Many show the fossilised ripples of the seashore of which they were once part all be it 300 million years ago.

Flag stone on Spitlers showing the fossilised bed of a river, estuary or sea

Fossilised ripples of a shore some 300 million years ago

This Hardcore stretch of the path diverts to run on the old wall base and continues for 2/300 meters

A stretch of the causeway snaking off across the moors towards Hordern Stoops

Walkers beware very marshy pools are dotted along the length of the pathway

Thanks to Andy Ryding for the history of the paved causeway. Andy with colleagues constructed the middle 2 Kilometre section in 1995/96 taking a little over two weeks.

A postcard of Rivington from Church Hill

Shooting Huts, Anglezarke

The area on the Ordnance Survey map in the vicinity of Limestone Brook known has "Shooting Huts" (SD 6361 1750) carries that title with good reason. A wooden structure, stood on that location for around 40 years (early 1940's until the early 1980's). This building was originally located for at least another 40-years about a kilometre to the south east on a level area near the well on the SE slope of Standing Stone Hill, Anglezarke (SD 6467 1730), broadly overlooking Sam's Pasture and Lower Hempshaws farm ruin.

The wooden building was placed at its initial location as a shooters rest when grouse was shot on these moors. The photo below is circa 1900 and the chap on the left is Andrew Crompton, his father sold the Rivington Estate to Lord Leverhulme around the time of this photo (Mark Fishwick). The chap to his left without coat is Cecil Winders, a Bolton Solicitor.

Shooting Hut at its original site near Standing Stones Hill, Anglezarke c1900. (Mark Fishwick)

The Hut is believed to have been moved soon after the outbreak of WWII. This would have been a difficult task and the suggestion is that pack horses were used to transport the dismantled structure. The building when positioned at the side of Limestone Brook doesn't appear to have any form of balcony as the original did and looks a much more simple structure. It is believed again that it might have been used as a shooters rest but little information exists to suggest the end date of the grouse shooting on these moors.

Rangers Service members maintaining a much run-down Shooting Hut, March 1981(Garry Rhodes MBE)

Drawing in pen of the Shooting Hut at the side of the Limestone Brook. Garry Rhodes MBE 1979.

The Rangers used the Shooting Hut as a shelter and a place to take their meals while on duty. At this time, log books/diaries were placed inside where local events and wildlife sightings could be recorded by anyone using the hut.

More repairs. Kevin Ellis on the right. Interesting walking attire of the day. March 1981, Garry Rhodes MBE

Kevin Ellis possibly studying one of the log books, March 1981. The flat stones were pulled from Limestone Brook to improve the entrance area or create a patio! (Garry Rhodes MBE)

The "last days" of the shooting hut. (photo Dave Lane)

The hut was demolished by the North West Water Authority in the early 1980's most likely due to the structure becoming unsafe. By all accounts the building was burnt on site soon after demolition. A sad end to a building which records show was at least 81 years old, having had different uses over its lifetime and moved location at least once.

RAF P51-C Mustang SR 411 Crash 1945, Darwin Moor

The mystery remains as to why the North American P51C Mustang, operated by the RAF, the world's finest long-range single-seat fighter, which crashed, killing the young Polish pilot **Warrant Officer Herbert Noga**.

The flight appears to be have been a simple ferrying job from the HQ of the legendary Polish 316 Warsaw Squadron at RAF Coltishall in Norfolk to either the Polish Air Force base at Blackpool or perhaps the vast US centre at Burtonwood.

The crash occurred just before 4 o'clock on Sunday afternoon, July 29th 1945, just a few weeks after the war in Europe had ended. Although it was a fine day, reports suggest it was misty from the industrial haze that hung over the area. It has been suggested that Noga was unaware of his height in the low cloud as his mustang hit the moor at cruising speed

Probably the first on the scene were the young Cartlidge brothers, Bill and Jim, and their pal John Knowle, who had been out playing. They heard the plane "coughing and spluttering" John recalled, they then heard the crash and immediately ran on to the moors. They discovered the Mustang splintered into pieces, embedded deep into the moorland peat and Herbert dead. They also found one of the plane's machine guns which they took for 'safe keeping'.

Of course, young lads playing with a heavy machine gun quickly attracted the attention of the local constabulary who took it away for even safer keeping.
Inquiries in Poland a number of years ago have resulted in little information emerging about the 24-year-old pilot.

Born in Raciborz, south of Warsaw, he was single and had escaped through Romania to reach England and there joined the Polish Air Force.

His squadron's last major involvement in the war involved shooting down German rockets and escorting hundreds of bombers in the attack on Hitler's mountain retreat at Berchtesgaden. On April 25th 1945, 240

Mustangs escorted 359 Lancaster Bombers on one of these raids. That mission could have been the last action seen by this aircraft.

Nearly 20,000 Polish airmen fought bravely throughout the war but they must have felt badly let down as it ended. With their home country now under the influence of Russia – hated more than Germany by most Poles – few planned to go back into political turmoil and uncertainty. The rest faced a life in exile with little encouragement from the British Government who didn't want to upset their Soviet allies. Warrant Officer Noga was buried with full military honours at Layton Cemetery, Blackpool.

The inscription on the memorial, surrounded by the graves of 24 Polish airmen, reads: ***"We Polish airmen gave our Souls to God, our Bodies to the British soil, and our Hearts to Poland."***

RIP; Warrant Officer Herbert Noga

The Polish communities from around the North West honour Warrant Officer Herbert Noga and remember him, laying wreaths and maintaining a photograph of the young Pilot at the scene.

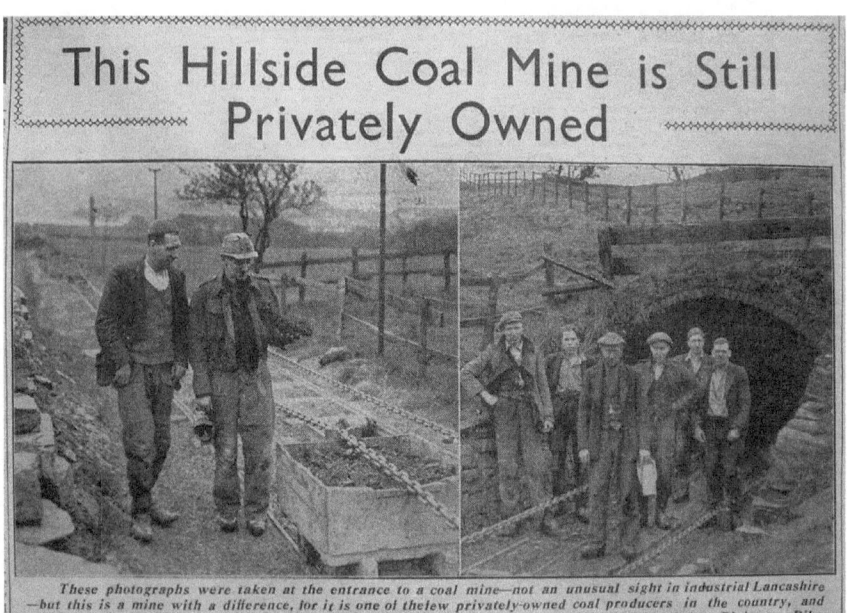

This Hillside Coal Mine is Still Privately Owned

These photographs were taken at the entrance to a coal mine—not an unusual sight in industrial Lancashire—but this is a mine with a difference, for it is one of the few privately-owned coal producers in the country, and certainly the only one in this district. Wildersmoor Mine, just a hole in the bleak hillside below Rivington Pike to local people, is almost a coal mine by accident. Owned by the Associated Clay Industries, Ltd., its chief function is the mining of first-quality fireclay, with an average yield of 300 tons weekly, but it also produces about 50 tons of good quality coal each week, and is licensed by the National Coal Board. There are two seams, with 50 miners employed, and the workings extend approximately one mile and run alongside Scotchman's Stump. The mine is of considerable age, but was first worked extensively upon the appointment of the present manager, Mr. R. Adamson, in 1915.

The photo shows a "disused mine" shown on the OS maps of Winter Hill. It lies on the track/path that goes from Ormstons Farm up to Georges Lane just near Pike Cottage. I'm assuming the circular concrete is a capped shaft. Leading uphill from there, was a tunnel heading under Georges Lane but the whole entrance area has collapsed in the apparent landslip. Water was built up inside the collapsed tunnel and now emerges from a small hole at the base of the landslip. I don't know if it's still there, but there used to be a piece of railway track in the bed of the stream

Mill Hill, Rivington

The Winter Hill Treasure Hunt. February 1983.

Some 36 years ago I (Dave Lane) buried 10 genuine Roman coins on or around the Winter Hill/Rivington area. It was intended to be just for West Pennine Moors Rangers but news travelled fast and others started searching as well. I've just found a copy of the original clues document: All the coins were in black 35mm film canisters

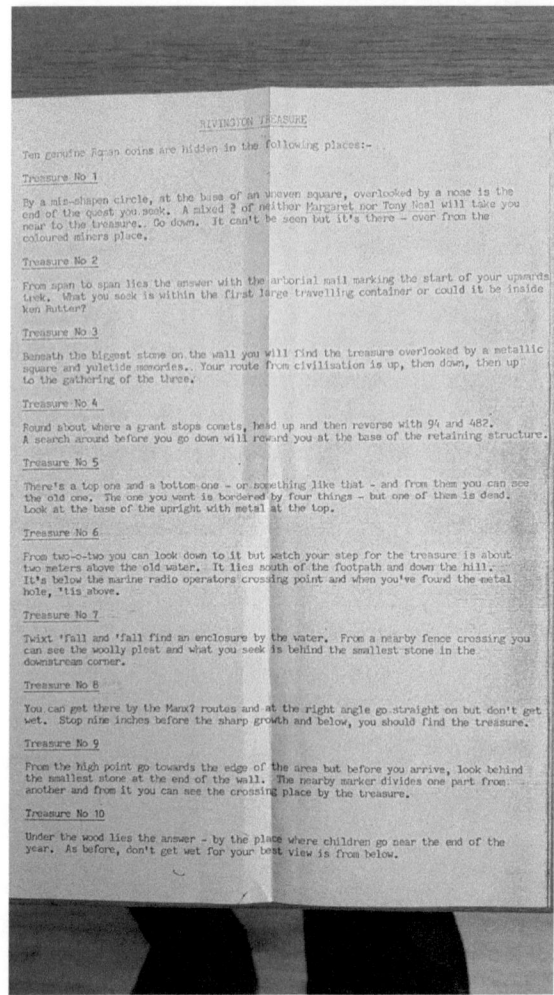

I'll put a more legible version of this on the next page ….. but why am I mentioning all this in this book? ….. There were 10 coins buried ….I was notified by the finders of six of these coins …. but nobody ever contacted me about the other four, numbered 1, 2, 3 and 4. **There just "may" still be 4 Roman coins still to be found!!!!!!!**

Treasure No 1
By a mis-shaped circle, at the base of an uneven square, overlooked by a nose is the end of the quest you seek. A mixed three quarters of neither Margaret nor Tony Neal will take you near to the treasure. Go down. It can't be found but it's there – over from the coloured miners place

Treasure No 2
From span to span lies the answer with the arborial mail marking the start of your upwards trek. What you seek is within the first large travelling container or could it be inside Ken Rutter.

Treasure No 3.
Beneath the biggest stone on the wall you will find the treasure overlooked by a metallic square and yuletide memories. Your route from civilisation is up, then down, then up to the gathering of the three

Treasure No 4.
Round about where a grant stops comets, head up then reverse with 94 and 482..A search around before you go down will reward you at the base of the retaining structure.

Treasure No 5
There's a top one and a bottom one – or something like that – and from them you can see the old one. The one you want is bordered by four things – but one of them is dead. Look at the base of the upright with metal at the top.

Treasure No 6.
From two-o-two you can look down to it but watch your step for the treasure is about two meters above the old water. It lies south of the footpath and down the hill. It's below the marine radio operators crossing point and when you've found the metal hole, 'tis above.

Treasure No 7
Twix fall and fall find an enclosure by the water. From a nearby fence crossing you can see the woolly pleat and what you seek is behind the smallest stone in the downstream corner.

Treasure No 8.
You can get there via the Manx (??) routes and at the right angle, go straight on but don't get wet. Stop nine inches before the sharp growth and below, you should find the treasure.

Treasure No 9
From the high point go towards the edge of the area but before you arrive, look behind the smallest stone in the wall. The nearby marker divides one part from another and from it you can see the crossing place by the treasure.

Treasure No 10
Under the wood lies the answer -by the place where children go near the end of the year. As before, don't get wet for your best view is from below

The Saturday morning mine exploration group!!!!!!

Jacob's Ladder. Where is it, what was it for and is it still there nowadays?

Much of this information and the photo's in this article were obtained from "Hidden History of Horwich and the surrounding area" Facebook pages and "www.Anglezarke.net"

(The original ladder)

High Bullough Reservoir was first constructed in 1850 and at that time it was known as Chorley Reservoir. The name High Bullough come from the name of a nearby house of that name – this is the house we now know as Manor House

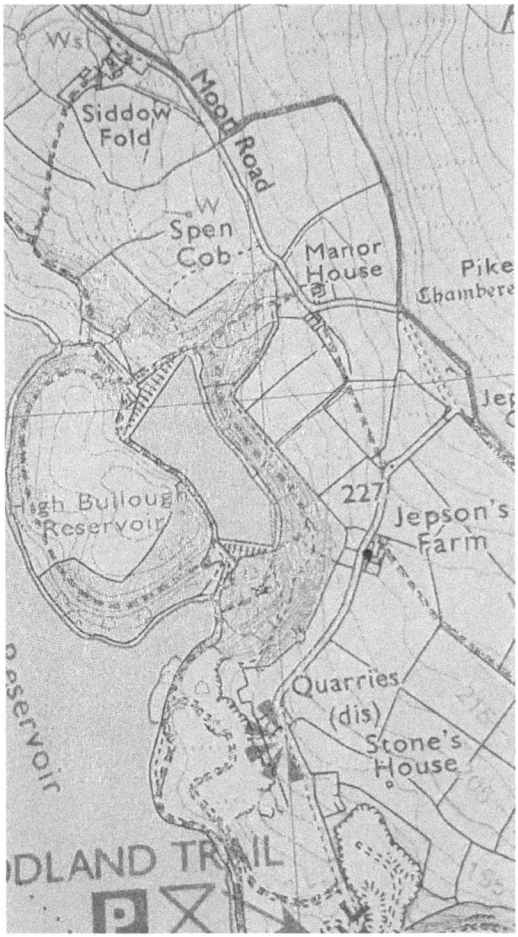

Due to the location of the reservoir, a ladder was built so that water company employees could quickly access the reservoir. Near Jepson's Farm, the company built a recess into the cliff face, stone lined it and then added three or four ladders. Then a series of stone steps lead down to the reservoir.

The ladder was apparently used by the warden of the reservoir in order to provide easy access for its maintenance. There was no real access from any road/path network at the time (like we have today) so whoever was responsible at the time used it as a 'shortcut' to get there.

Harry Partington's 1966 drawing

Today the whole area is overgrown, the steps slowly getting covered and the last short section to the ladder is treacherous when it is wet and muddy. It also appears that the bottom section has been filled in - but that may just be plant growth covering it.

As you can see from the picture below (2019), some of the original stone steps have survived!

The reservoir has a surface area of 6.9 acres with a perimeter of 0.6 miles. It has two embankments that are, in total, 330 yards long, one to the north and one at the southern end.

It can hold 48.3 million gallons of water and is approximately 40 feet deep.

Water outflowed from the northern end and was carried by a 12 inch pipe down to a holding reservoir near Crosse Hall Lane.

That pipeline goes below what is now Anglezarke reservoir.

The reservoir is now disconnected from the water supply but still contributes to Anglezarke Reservoirs supply in times of heavy rain.

High Bullough's only overflow, that being at the southern end, discharges into Anglezarke Reservoir, just north of Lister Mill Quarry.

Fires on Winter Hill through the years.

Writing this in September 2019, the large fires on the moors that burnt for 48 days in June/July 2018 are still very real in the memory with bare areas still not fully recovered still being visible

This was a big moorland fire which at its height involved crews from 30 fire engines battling a blaze stretching over an 18 sq km site. A number of volunteers were also involved. One has to say however that a tiny number of members of the public hardly covered themselves in glory insisting they had every right to access the burning moorland right up to the moment it was finally extinguished.

Volunteers helping to protect people from the Winter Hill fire were verbally abused. The four-mile no-go zone that was in place around the West Pennine Moors as firefighters continued to battle hotspots, but people were seen smashing through the locks to the footpaths and ripping down signs.

People were even bragging on Facebook that they were climbing over the fence and going on walks.

This was of course not the first big fire on the moors. There have been many occurring in different places on the moors over the years and this last one was the third or fourth large fire that I have experienced in the last few decades. The one previous to the 2018 fire was the one which destroyed parts of the southern flanks of the hill down to the Bolton/Belmont Road. There have been a number of others which have destroyed large areas of newly planted trees.

"Slightly before my time" in 1938 local newspapers contained details of a large moorland fire in 1938 which destroyed an area similar to the 2018 one and in many of the same places! The headline read "Worst Moor Fire since 1901.

"Since Easter there has been an epidemic of small fires on the moors around Bolton, particularly on the Belmont and Smithills side. Over the weekend a high wind fanned the smouldering peat into flames, and very quickly the whole of Smithills Moor was on fire Large volumes of smoke pouring from the moor, which could be seen from as far away as Lytham, gave the first indication.

Smithills Estate employees were called out by Mr R Lowther just before noon on Sunday, and on Monday they were still on the job of beating out the fire, having been at work for more than 24 hours. Practically the whole of the moors in the estate have been affected- something like 400 acres. The damage is inestimable for innumerable grouse nests have been destroyed. The beaters came across many nests where the hen had been suffocated sitting on the nest vainly seeking to protect the young birds.

Mr Lowther told our representative on Monday that it will probably be seven years before the moors are in good shooting condition again.

At that time, stretches of the moor were still smoking while here and there the wind was fanning the flames. Many of the shooting butts have been damaged.

Mrs Wood and Mr Walsh, occupants of Hole Bottom Bungalows, Winter Hill, whose homes were surrounded by Sunday's moorland fire

THE CAMERA ILLU

DESTRUCTIVE MOORLAND FIRE

Scenes on Smithills and Horwich moors, where a great fire, the most destructive for 37 years, has devastated 400 acres of moorland. Top: Shooting butt damaged by the blaze on the Bolton side of Smithills Moor. Below: Estate workers leaving Hole Bottom Bungalows in a lonely spot near Horwich, for a further spell of tackling the smouldering peat, after 24 hours' continuous duty. Behind is the blackened hillside.

On Saturday a fire which started at Easter was still smouldering and a trench, three quarters of a mile in circumference was cut round it to try to prevent spreading. Just before noon smoke was seen travelling across the Smithills Moor from the Belmont side and extra men were taken up.

Mr Lowther said that he was informed that the fire started on the other side of the pump at Belmont and came up "like wildfire" through the Smithills Estate wall.

The fire spread quickly. At one time Hole Bottom Bungalows, Winter Hill, were surrounded by burning heather and it seemed like the houses might catch fire. One of the occupants, Mrs Wood, told the "Journal and Guardian" she was afraid to stay in the house, so she packed up what clothing she could and went to a nearby farm. When it was realised that the house was not in danger she returned.

Mr Lowther went up to the bungalow to "evacuate" the occupants if necessary, for next door to Mrs Wood live Mr and Mrs Walsh and

their baby, and he was afraid they might be in danger. Fortunately they were away from the house at the time.

By Wednesday it could be felt the fire was under control. The peat was still smouldering in many places, and from Belmont to Rivington a careful watch was being kept lest the wind should fan it into flames again. Smithills Estate has suffered most , but a third of the moorland under the supervision of the Liverpool Corporation has been burned, as well as a small portion of the Bolton Corporation watershed on the Belmont side.

Fortunately for the Waterworks Dept. the wind has been east, and has swept the fire away from Belmont towards Rivington, where it has reached as far as Noon Hill. Liverpool Corporation Waterworks Dept and Smithills estate employees were beating out the fires and digging trenches until late on Tuesday night. So the biggest moorland fire Bolton has known for many years may be regarded – given normal good fortune – as ever.

Just 37 years earlier almost to the day, there was yet another large fire on Smithills Moor which did extensive damage towards the end of May 1901. Then the fire engines from Ainsworth's bleachworks turned out and more than 300 men helped to beat out the flames."

So what does all this tell us? Beware of fires on Winter Hill and Anglezarke moorlands. Some fires may start quite naturally without any human intervention.

Some may have been started deliberately but others have almost certainly been started just by human stupidity and ignorance.

This is being written in September 2019 and people are STILL taking "once only" barbeques onto the moors …. Gimme a break! These folk just don't deserve to have such wonderful places on their doorstep. Various areas in the UK are now beginning to draw up strict local laws to combat this kind of anti-social behaviour with heavy penalties.

The sooner this kind of legislation is enacted in this area the better.

Stones of the area

The area of land covered by this book is covered in soil and peat but the underlying rocks are exposed in many areas in quarries, rock outcrops, and in underground mines and tunnels. Earlier articles in this volume try to explain the basic geology of this area and give some idea of the types of rock which occur in this area.

Often, one comes across isolated rocks all over the area which makes you wonder "what is this rock"? "Is this a natural outcrop" or "is it sort of man made in some way". Some rocks are pretty obvious ….. it's a millstone or it's a Neolithic cup and ring marked boulder. Other rocks are not so easy to interpret.

Individual Stones
Interesting individual stones and stones with markings can be found across our moors, a selection are presented below

Two man-made slots in a stone. Potentially bronze age moulds with molten bronze poured in to form bronze tools. Rushy Brow, Anglezarke. SD 630174

Potential boundry marker in Winter Hill alonge Deane Ditch. The "A" possibly indictaing Colonel Ainsworts land.

Stone with writing near Holdens Farm, Burnt Edge spelling out "W.H. 1898"

Stone seen on the path between White Coppice and Great Hill, above the White Coppice quarry's. The groves possibly made by ropes used to pull up quarry or mining tubes.

Stone with markings possibly made by the sharpening or cleaning of metalic farm tools. Found to the west of Dean House, Dean Wood, Rivington.

Some "rock markings" are just part of local industries …. Such as quarrying.

Quarry Blast Holes
When quarrying for stones explosives were used. Holes were made with the explosives inserted and rammed in using other material to create an explosive package which when detonated would blow apart the quarry face creating large amounts of lose stone, which could then be moved away.

The hole were made using a large metal auger with one man holding the auger and a second striking it with a hammer.

After each strike the man holding the auger would rotate it slightly thus creating a bored hole.

Later drills were used mainly pneumatic powered. Blast holes can be seen at various locations across the moors in remaining quarry faces. A few examples below.

In a quarry face, Adams Delph, Belmont Moor

In the quarry face, Leicester/Lester Quarry, Anglezarke

In a quarry face, Adams Delph, Belmont Moor

In the quarry face, Leicester/Lester Quarry, Anglezarke

ROCKS! Go take a closer look at them.

I just love rocks! They're all around us. If you learn how to "interpret" the rocks, they can tell you the history of our area, the climate at the time they were formed, the manner of their formation.

It's not rocket science …. Anyone can learn to "read the rocks" …. especially with a little help from the Internet.

So how do you start? You go out collecting rocks ….. not just "stones" you find on the surface, but samples of the rocks that lie beneath our feet …. There are quarries everywhere, the moors are littered with rock outcrops.

When you see a "natural" rock it looks pretty dull!!!! It really does! But what you're really looking at, is a rock which has been weathered for perhaps hundreds or even thousands of years and which is stained and discoloured by years of grime and pollution. It's time to get down to basics and get inside that rock!

You need to break it open. This will display the grains within it as they were laid down millions of years ago. I use a small geological hammer and on occasions a much larger mallet to bash rocks open! No finesse at all, just grab a rock and bash it open.

Look at all the different colours, the different kinds of grains, the sizes of the grains …. are they all the same size, are the grains rounded or rough and angular, are they "frosted" or clear. All these clues can point us to how the rocks may have been formed all those millions of years ago.

Apart from in the Lead Mines Clough area, what you are going to find on Winter Hill and Anglezarke is sandstones (sometimes called gritstones), shales, conglomerates and even coal - all of which you can see with your eyes, no microscopes involved

You will be able to see individual grains of the basic minerals that comprise that particular piece of rock.

It will help if you had a small magnifier then you could look at the individual grains to try to work out whether they were carried by water or wind …. and how fast was the water or how strong the winds …. and what direction were they flowing/blowing from!
You can find out all this from pieces of raw rock – which you can collect totally free of charge from Winter Hill and Anglezarke. There are quarries and exposures all over the place. Google may help!

A really cheap hobby and interest - that people of all ages can learn about!

A sandstone is a sandstone ….. errr no …. they come in almost limitless varieties laid down in all sorts of different conditions over vast lengths of time. Most of the rocks laid down on Winter Hill and Anglezarke can be dated to around 358 million years ago to a time known as the Carboniferous Period.

Just go take a closer look at your local rocks! They're all different. They're free to collect …. And you might learn an awful lot from looking at them and studying both them and the location where you found them

Two of my favourite photo's of the whole area ..... 1. Watermans's Cottage, Upper Anglezarke Reservoir. Photo by Nigel Newton

2. Terraced Gardens in Winter. Photo by Darryll Hilton

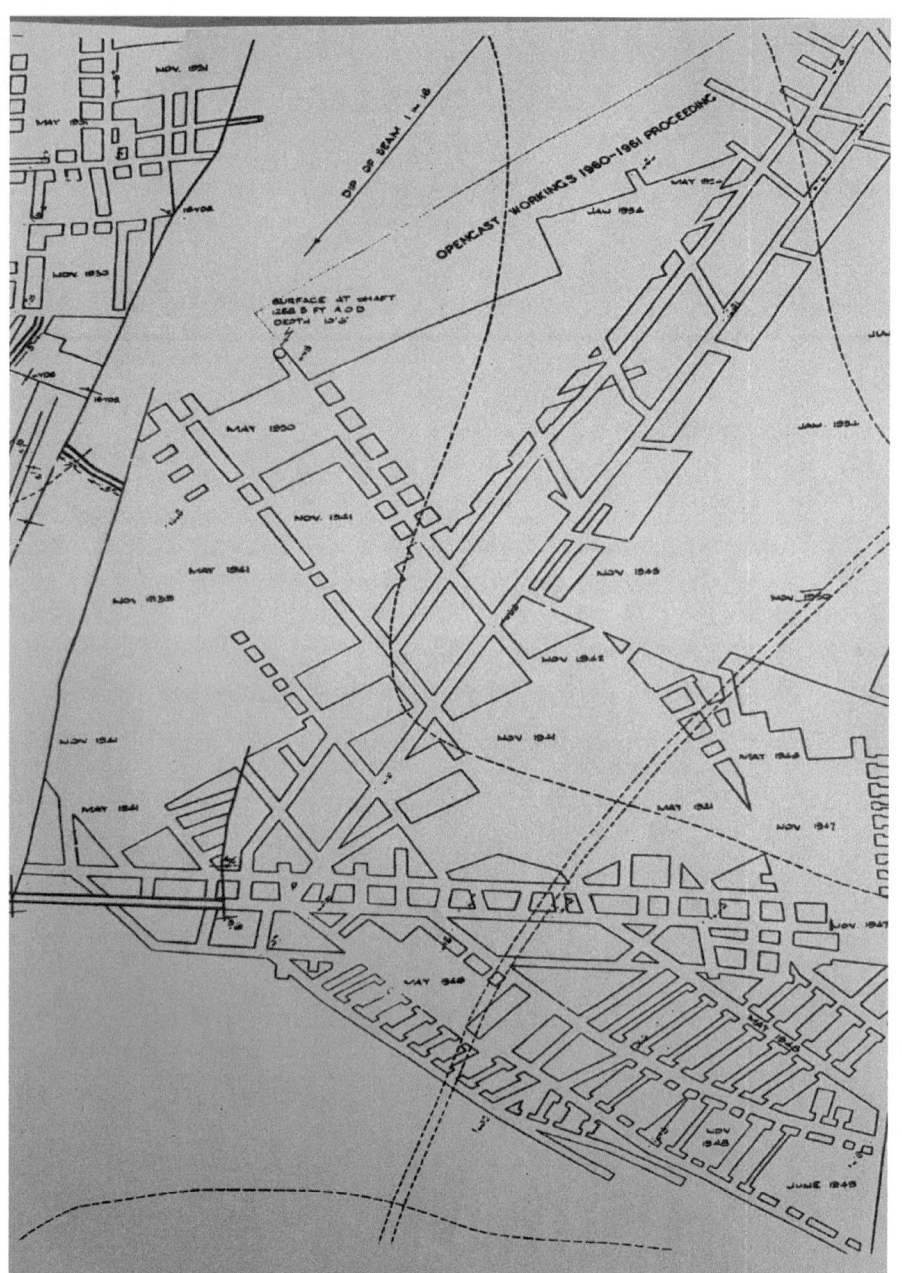

Another map of the underground tunnels of Winter Hill. The double dotted line running from the mid RH side to the bottom middle is the road up to the TV mast around the Five Houses area. Clearly marked at the top of the map is the overcast mining area which was dug in 1960-1961, If you are walking in this area knowing this map, you should have a real idea of what is underneath your feet

The Rivington Terraced Gardens today.

Time passes so quickly in a lifetime - and I have so many memories of all the changes that I have experienced as to how the terraced gardens have changed over the years. At one point in my life, I used to spend an awful lot of my spare time in and around this area.

I was one of the original North-West Water Rangers who patrolled the area every weekend (along with Gary Rhodes, one of the other contributors to this volume).

To us, the gardens were rather magic, a preserved history of the area, a place of beauty and a simply wonderful area to enjoy …. and quite an adventure at times – skiing down the tracks in winter, finding unknown "things" … the underground water tank, the rare trees and plants, the hidden springs, the unknown quarries, the tiny "hidden spots" in the gardens perfectly sculptured and designed.

I remember the lunchtimes spent getting warm in the top room of the Pigeon Tower eating butties and drinking hot coffee trying to get warm. I simply loved the whole place.

I have to admit, it was all rather overgrown, a bit derelict, and quite a few of the structures were just falling apart. Many of the pathways were so overgrown you would never even know they existed. The rhododendrons were so lovely to see in season, but they were totally overtaking the whole site …. as were many other types of rampant growing plants – and something just HAD to be done to try to sort things out!

Along came BTCV …. British Trust for Conservation Volunteers … who set up their base at Tan Pits Farm on the southern banks of the Lower Rivington Reservoir

Their team of volunteers started the almost impossible task of trying to halt the decades of neglect of the gardens. The whole place really was in a bit of a state! It was a real mess.

At that time I was a probation officer in a team trying to set up "Community Service" in the North West UK and one of the first tasks ever in the history of Community Service was to get criminals to clear out the pools of the waterfall cascades in the Gardens of decades of mud and rubbish. I have to admit, I felt quite sorry for some of them spending hours in the falls, wet through, totally knackered .... but somehow rather pleased with what they'd managed to achieve .... and I think most of those involved felt the same. The whole Community Service set-up was supervised entirely by BTCV

There were so many jobs for BTCV to do. Cutting down the rhododendrons, making the pathways more visible and useable, removing unwanted overgrowth etc. One hell of a big job! I think they did a superb job, they ran a vast range of courses to help people to become involved in conservation work, they produced a massive amount of printed manuals and leaflets about nature and conservation (one of their leaflets is reproduced earlier in this book)

Without large amounts of money being contributed or pumped into the conservation efforts, it was just an impossible task to halt the vegetative progress of time!

Things have now improved .... quite dramatically!

The following information is taken directly from the websites at **www.rivingtonterracedgardens.org.uk and also from the Groundwork website at** www.groundwork.org.uk/projects/rivington-terraced-gardens/

In 2016, Rivington Heritage Trust, as part of a partnership with Groundwork Cheshire Lancashire and Merseyside and United Utilities successfully secured £3.4 million in funding from the Heritage Lottery Fund as part of a three year £4.2 million restoration package to conserve and revitalise Rivington Terraced Gardens.

We won't be trying to restore the Gardens to their original plans – this would be far too costly both to create and maintain.

People have also grown to enjoy the Gardens in their current wooded state.

We want to make sure the structures can be safeguarded and carry out work to allow the spirit of Mawson's original design to remain.

Our Aims

Our focus is on stabilising and consolidating existing decaying structures within the Gardens, so that they can be enjoyed by generations to come:

- The Gardens contain 11 Grade II listed structures, including the Pigeon Tower, the Seven Arch Bridge and five summerhouses. Each will have a complete facelift during the capital work and will be opened for visits as part of events and open days.
- The Italian and Japanese Lakes are being drained, de-silted and re-lined before being refilled again, ensuring their long term future.
- We are undertaking a comprehensive programme of path and drainage work to improve access to and around the gardens and will be also be introducing a package of minor changes to improve accessibility.
- We are working with conservation volunteer groups to bring the woodlands on site into better management to encourage a greater number and variety of plants and animals.
- We are undertaking a wholesale review and improvement of the signage and interpretation of the site's landscape and heritage.

The improvements to the Gardens will enable them to be better managed in the future, safeguarding heritage for generations to come.

A programme of skills development and volunteering is underway and will capitalise on the park's unique and diverse features and establish it as a living and vibrant resource for local people to become involved, improve their skills and to help preserve our much loved Terraced Gardens.

Groundwork CLM currently acts as accountable body for the partnership, administering the grant monies, delivering events and volunteering with the growing support of the Friends of Rivington Terraced Gardens group.

The vast amount of work done so far has produced a fantastic 45 acres of hillside, a magical place of hidden paths, caves, structures and lakes

The Gardens were originally created for soap magnate Lord Leverhulme as a spectacular venue for him to relax in and entertain. Situated on the hillside below Rivington Pike, the Gardens were designed by noted landscape designer Thomas Mawson between 1905-1922.

Rivington Terraced Gardens are totally unique, with iconic structures like the Pigeon Tower, the Seven Arch Bridge, the Summer Houses and Loggia.

There's also the Pulham rock faces around the pathways and the lakes. The Italian Lake is where Leverhulme used to take his morning swim and the beautiful Japanese Lake was once looked upon from glamorous oriental pagoda-style tea houses.

There's always something happening at the Gardens, with lots to do and activities for people of all ages and abilities. You can attend one of the fun events, get involved in the conservation and repair project, join the garden and research team, or just come with the family for a great day out. (See things to see and do – below)

The History

Following Lord Leverhulme's death in 1925, the property was sold and the gardens began to fall into disrepair. The houses were demolished after World War II, and Rivington Terraced Gardens were left to the forces of nature. Sixty years later, United Utilities now own the land and a project to repair and conserve the Gardens is well underway

In 2016 £3.4Million in funding was secured from the Heritage Lottery Fund as part of a £4Million restoration package. The plans are being driven forward by a partnership of the Rivington Heritage Trust, Groundwork Cheshire Lancashire and Merseyside and United Utilities.

Conserving and protecting the gardens

Work is underway to stabilise and consolidate the decaying structures within the Gardens, so that they can be enjoyed by generations to come. Access to and around the Gardens is also being improved so that more people can visit.

As the project progresses and more of the shrubs, self-seeded trees and mud are cleared away, the original shape of Lord Leverhulme's garden is becoming more visible. New paths are being discovered, new stairways uncovered, and visitors to the gardens are beginning to see how it once might have been.

We don't plan to restore the Gardens to their original plans as this would be far too costly to create and maintain. People have also grown to enjoy the Gardens in their current wooded state. The improvements to the Gardens will also mean they are better managed in the future, safeguarding their heritage for generations to come.

A programme of skills development and volunteering have already helped to establish it as a living and vibrant resource for local people to become involved and improve their skills.

Some of the volunteers helping with the restoration of the Terraced Gardens

What on earth is Devils Ditch?

Much of the information below is taken from The Anglezarke Moor Survey of the 1980's by Lancaster University)

In the middle of Anglezarke Moor, there is a long shallow ditch about 200m to the south of Round Loaf. GR SD 6412518135 to 63601768.

The ditch shows clearly as it runs past Round Loaf some 200m to the north.

"This is a long, fairly straight ditch on the edge of the Anglezarke Moor plateau which shows up as light tufted grass with some heather on either side. In the main the ditch has a very regular width and a flat bottom. For much of its length there is a stream at the bottom of the ditch but at the South-west end it follows a course outside the line of the ditch.

There is little sign of a bank on either side of the ditch except at SD 63651770, where it can be partly explained by natural processes. At its North-east end the ditch goes over a slight rise and at its South-west end it disappears over a sharp break of slope and loses it's clearly defined edges.

From old RAF photo's there is a clearly defined continuation from SD 63381744 to 63011695 where it disappears into an area of enclosed land. The line between this section and the surveyed section is interupted by Lead Mines Clough. There is also a continuation to the North-east between SD 64241809 and 64581830. Overall the ditch is at least 2.1km in length.

The absence of raised banks favours a natural interpretation for the ditch. On the other hand it's continuance over a slight rise and across substantial drainage systems indicates that it is not formed by natural drainage.

Similarly the regularity of the ditch's alignment, width and profile also support a man made origin. It is similar in form to other sites in Yorkshire which are also devoid of outer banks, and there is a possibility that this site is a track.

So what is it? What is the ditch, why was it there, who built/dug it, if anyone , what purpose did it serve? Is it formed naturally or was it once just a track or something similar

I don't think anyone right now has the first clue about the answers to any of these questions! Sorry!!!!!

More about the ditch (including Lidar images of it) can be found at **https://chorleyarealocalhistory.weebly.com/devils-ditch.html** This whole website is a mine of information especially about all the archaeological remains in the Anglezarke area. A great site.

Overflow from the Yarrow Reservoir

The Fossils of Winter Hill and Anglezarke …. What can you find … and where?

Earlier in this book brief mention was made that it is possible to find fossils in this area. Over the years a number of people have asked for more information about these …. So here it is! The bulk of this has been lifted in its entirety from another of my publications!

Fossils of all shapes and sizes can be found on and around Winter Hill. That doesn't mean they're easy to find …. But they ARE there, if you either know where to look, or you use careful thought to determine the likeliest places to find them.

Fossils of both plants and animals can be found along with fossils of past world events (ripple marks left by a river or from the sea bed), "trace fossils" (the marks left on and in rocks showing where creatures had moved, burrowed or lived millions of years ago).

So where are the fossils? There are fossils underground in the old coal mining tunnels left underneath Winter Hill but this is the one place that I am NOT going to recommend anyone goes, it's far, far too dangerous. Much easier is to search on the surface to see what can be found. For example, Winter Hill used to be the site of many coal mines.

When the coal was brought to the surface, it was often "contaminated" with dirt, un-burnable materials etc and these rocks were discarded and became rubbish dumps or tips for the coal waste. You can often recognise these areas on Winter Hill as they form small "piles" and in almost every single case, the grass growing over them is of a totally different colour and type to the natural moorland vegetation. A hint …..either use your eyes when walking on the hill …. or try using high magnification in "Google Earth"!

Streams and rivers form valleys especially when flowing down the sides of hills. As these valleys are created, they cut deeper and deeper and often expose the rock strata in the banks and in the valley sides. Once you get used to which strata often contains the fossils, you'll find a number of places on Winter Hill where they can be found.

Some fossils can be found literally "lying around". The one illustrated is a complete section of the root belonging to a particular variety of tree from the *Lycopsid* family. It is around 300 million years old. It was lying amongst the rocks on the side of Hurst Hill on Anglezarke clearly visible to any walker who passed that way.

As well as plant remains, animal fossils can also be found, the bulk of which are water living creatures such as bivalves (*Dunbarella*), goniatites (*Gasrioceras*), and brachiapods (*Lingula*) etc.

Different types of fossils are often found in different layers or different strata of rocks. Each layer or strata of rock represents a particular environment that existed when the sediments forming that rock, were first deposited.

Each layer, however thick, took a particular period of time to be "laid down", and that period could have been just one day, one year, 100 years or even a few thousand years.

Don't forget, the rocks forming Winter Hill took tens of millions of years to form, and during that period great climatic and physical changes were taking place.

Sea levels rose and fell (or areas of land were raised up or fell). Whichever of these scenarios is correct, the outcome was that at different times the land was sometimes dry, at other periods it was covered in fresh water, at others by sea water.

The area was probably similar to this during some of the Carboniferous Period around 320 million years ago.

There were swamps abounding at some periods, flooding at others, sometimes with raging torrents or strong currents and sometimes in slow moving or stagnant water. Each rock layer formed tells its own story, and from careful examination of the rocks and the sediment grains within them, one can usually determine at least something about the environment that it was created in.

Any fossils which may be found, often make this interpretation easier and more accurate.

Geology is a fascinating subject, and when undertaken on a practical level, often involve some detective work, a great deal of interpretation, a hell of a lot of walking, and a certain amount of learning - but the results of ones investigations are very satisfying.

By looking at the rocks, by interpreting what one sees, measures and observes, it is possible to paint a picture of what this part of OUR world was once like. The fossils found come to life.

Go on, find out more about the area where we live. Go onto Winter Hill and to other neighbouring areas and see what you can discover. It's NOT easy to find the fossils but they DO exist – in MANY different locations ……. and they're free!

The Lycopsids.

By far the largest numbers of fossils found under and on Winter Hill belong to the *Lycopsid* family of Carboniferous plants and some of them are the largest plants that lived in those times, some growing to over 50 meters in height. The family is also known as club mosses or quillworts.

There are many different varieties of plant in the *Lycopsid* family and they include:

Lepidodendron (these are the commonest species found)
Bothrodendron
Syringodendron
Ulodendron
Lepidophloios
Sigillaria

These *Lycopsids* formed large forests in the lowland swampy or delta areas that abounded at certain periods in Carboniferous times.

The coal measures are full of fossilised remains of these plants and both their stems, leaves, seeds, cones, barks and roots can be found in differing states of preservation.

No flowers existed at these times.

Many varieties of *Lycopsids* were large "trees" but were unlike their modern day counterparts in that they probably grew very quickly and had very little "wood" parts, the bulk of the trunk or stems being "pithy" rather than "woody".

The roots (known as *Stigmaria*) were not deep rooting and in many varieties of *Lycopsid* they took the form of "rhizomes" or runners when growing in the very wet areas of the swamps.

It is very rare to find fossils of *Lycopsid* leaves still attached to the stems, but often the tips of the stems along with the terminal cones can be found - although even they are not too common.

When *Lycopsids* were growing, they put out a vertical pole, trunk or shoot with small leafs attached. This pole grew very quickly and it is thought that the crown of the plant (the equivalent of the upper branches and foliage of a modern tree) did not appear until the *Lycopsid* was almost fully grown.

Due to their manner of growth, it has been suggested that perhaps the forests may have been fairly light and airy places.

A number of genera and many species of *Lycopsids* are distinguished by the shape of their leaf cushions (the distinctive markings on the bark): *Lepidodendron* has diamond-shaped cushions that are taller than they are wide, with the leaf attached at the upper end of the cushion; *Lepidophloios* leaf cushions are also diamond-shaped, but they are wider than they are tall, with the leaf attached at the lower end of the cushion. *Paralycopodites* has leaf cushions that are intermediate in shape between *Lepidodendron* and *Lepidophloios*. *Sigillaria* has square or rectangular leaf cushions arranged in **vertical rows**, with hexagonal leaf scars. *Bothrodendron* leaf scars are faint or absent in external impressions.

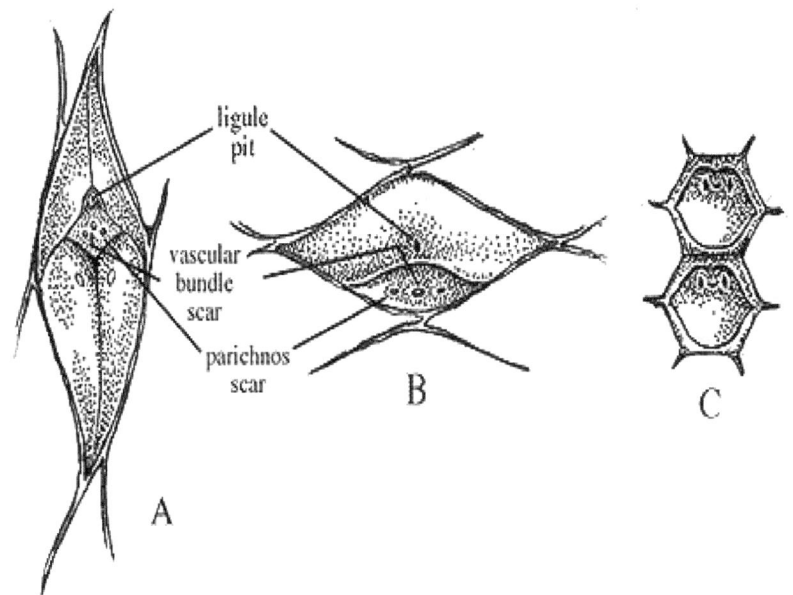

Leaf cushions in arborescent lycopsids. (A) Lepidodendron, (B) Lepidophloios, (C) Sigillaria.

A piece of Calamine trunk found by Alan Davies about 15 feet under the surface, 200 yards south of the TV mast.

Let's move on to describing some of the individual species of *Lycopsids* which provide us with many of the fossils found in this area.

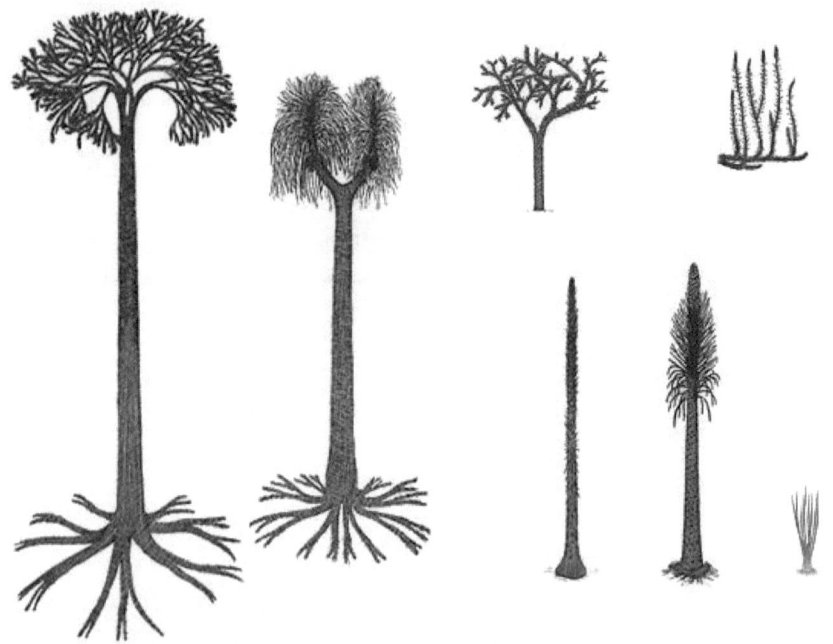

Far left Lepidodendron (up to 50m), left Sigillaria (around 40m), middle top Valmeyerodendron (0.6m) top right Protolepidodendron (0.2m), bottom middle Chaloneria (2m), bottom right Pleuromeia (2m), bottom far right Isoetes (30cm)

Lepidodendron – the tree sized "club moss".

The *lepidodendron* is probably one of the commonest fossils found in coal measures - along with others called *Calamites* & *Sigillaria*. The *Lepidodendron* is one of a family of plants known as "*Lycopsids*" which came in all shapes and sizes with the Lepidodendron being the biggest.

The *Lepidodendron* grew up to 50 meters in height, with trunks up to 1 meter in diameter. The trunks rarely branched and they produced very little, if any wood, with trunks consisting mainly of pith capped with a tough bark-like epidermis. The "bark" was solid, and unlike modern trees did not flake and it was covered in diamond shaped "leaf scars" or "leaf cushions" which increased in size as the tree grew. When the plant was juvenile, grass-like leaves (shown below) grew straight out of the sides of the tree from the leaf cushions but appeared to fall off as the tree grew larger.

The *lepidodrendons* are believed to have a life of only 10 to 15 years and grew to their full height very quickly. They were believed to be green in colour including the "trunk". The un-branched thick trunk was capped by a crown of bifurcating branches on which grew clusters of leaves which were long and narrow rather like grass and which were arranged in a spiral pattern. The branches ended in cigar shaped cones which contained spores and not seeds.

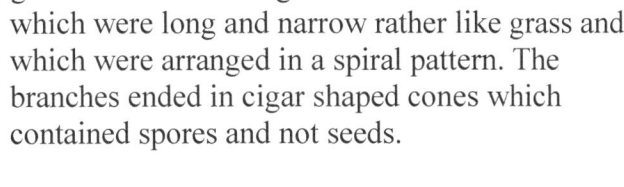

Left: Lepidodendron cone.

Fossil remains of *lepidodendron* are found all over Winter Hill both underground and in the surface spoil tips.

By far the common fossils found, are of the trunk part of the plant and are easily recognised by their alligator skin like patterns.

Although they must exist, I have yet to find any fossils of the cones or leaves. It is usual to find only small fossilised pieces of bark and full pieces of 3 dimensional trunk are rarities.

Lepidodendrons grew in the wettest part of the swamps in dense stands with densities of up to 2,000 plants per hectare.

It is no wonder we find so many fossilised parts of these plants although there are very few complete plant fossilised specimens anywhere in the world. Because only the separate parts of the tree are

found as fossils, different scientific names are given to the different parts of the plant:
Lepidodendron, the stem
Lepidophyllum, the leaves
Lepidostrobus, the cone
Lepidostrobophyllum, the cone scale
Lepidocarpon, the megaspore
Knorria, a layer of sub-bark

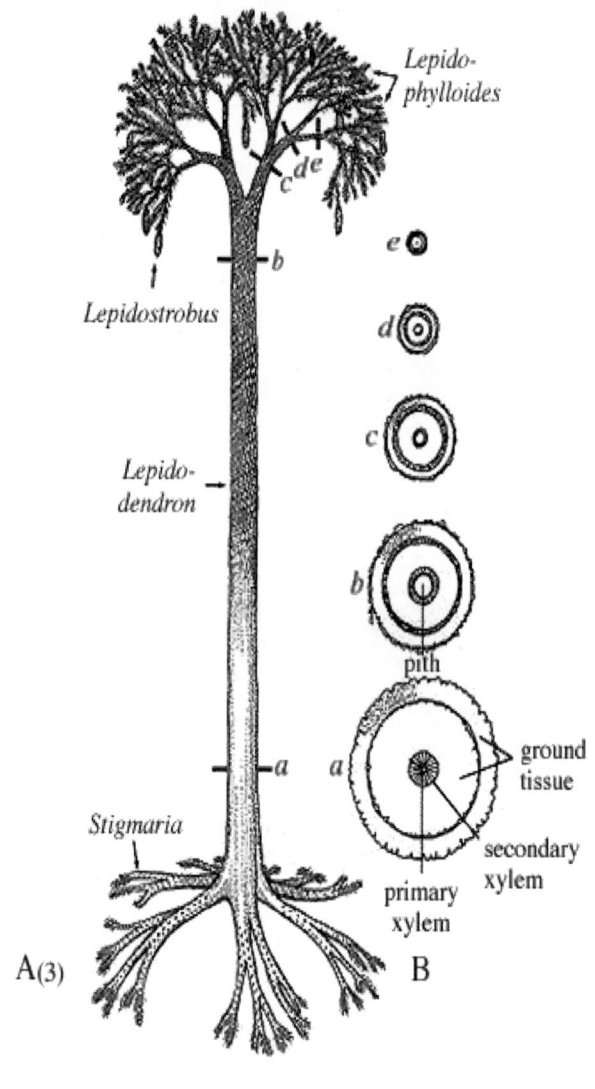

The plant was anchored at the base not by a deep root system (don't forget, the *lepidodendron* is not strictly speaking a "tree") but by several shallow running Y-shaped branches which are called *Stigmaria*. The *stigmaria* had had spirally arranged roots coming from them.

There are many different varieties of *lepidodendrons* and here in the North West UK at least six different types have been identified:- *L aculatum, L lanceolatum, L Lycopodioides, L ophiurus and L wortheni.*

The "bark" of Lepidodendron aculeatu.

The *Lepidodendrales* (the collective name for the whole *Lepido* plant family) were the most elaborate and diversified of all the *lycopods*, and dominated the Carboniferous, but with the drying of the climate during the later Carboniferous and early Permian periods, they went into a steep decline. By the middle Permian, they were all gone. Inefficient movement of water and nutrients through the stems of these tall plants, resulting from a lack of secondary xylem is cited as one of the reasons for their extinction.

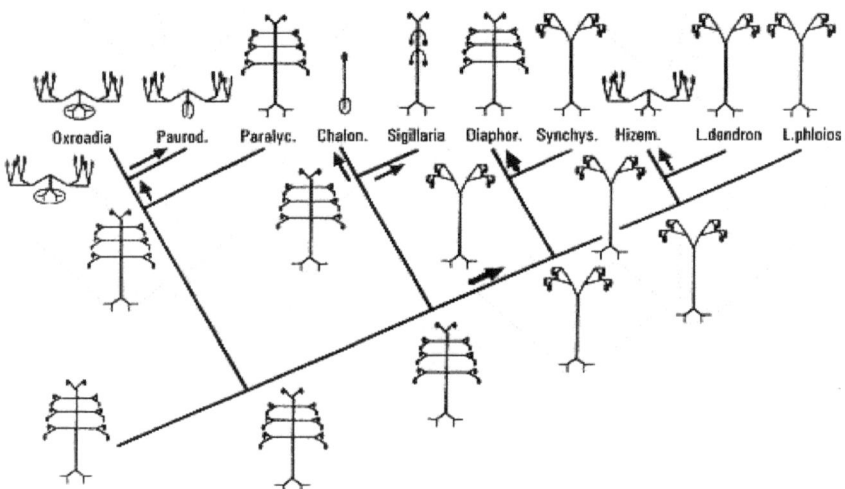

Cladogram (a diagram showing the evolution of one plant type to another) of late Carboniferous Lepidodendrales, showing generalized growth habit. Only the diminutive unbranched Chaloneria managed to continue the lineage into the Mesozoic period. As well as lepidodendron remains, we also find many fossils of the Sigillaria family in the NW UK coal seams.

Lepidodendron trees rooted horizontally, indicating humid environments.

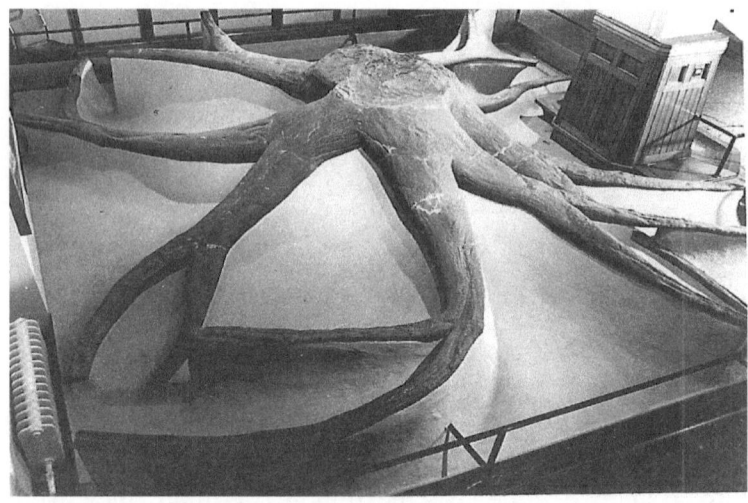

Stigmaria (root of lepidodendron) at Manchester Museum (photo J Watson). Although I didn't spot this exhibit on my last visit to the Museum, I'm reliably informed that it is still on show in the Stratigraphic Hall.

An example of lepidodendron bark found by Mark Wright on 3.3.2007 in the Wilderswood Mine near Horwich.

There are many different varieties of *Lepidodendron* trees. In the main, all are identified by the leaf scars on the trunk which come in all shapes and sizes. The bark fossil of the Wilderswood specimen shown on the previous page - leaves no room for doubt - it comes from the "***Lepidodendron lycopodioides***". The twigs with leaves on THIS variety of *lepidodendron* are shown below.

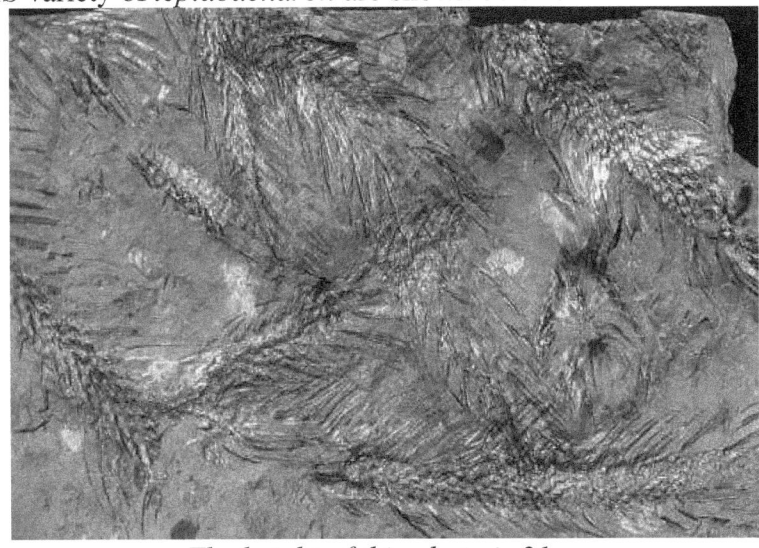

The height of this photo is 21cm

A similar – but totally different – type of twig and leaf from the same period. This comes from the "Bothrodendron minutifolium", another member of the Lycopsid family.

Examples of other different varieties of Lepidodendron tree barks.

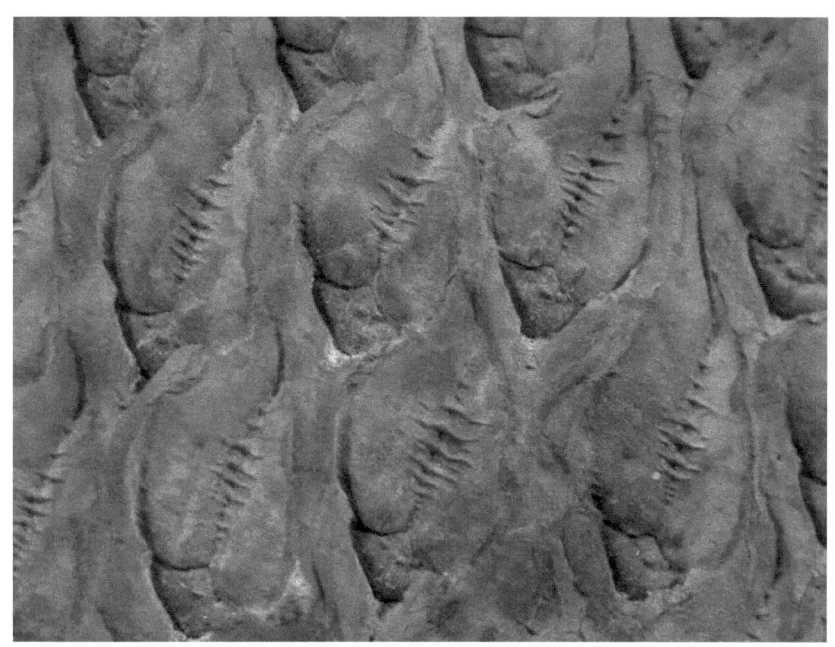

The bark of the Lepidodendron varies from the highly decorated patterns illustrated on the previous page which appear on the upper parts of the trunk, to the more "barky" trunk markings on the lower areas of the tree. The leaf cushion markings appear only at the upper part of the tree trunk. An example of the lower bark is shown below.

Outer surface of Lepidodendron lower trunk.

In Lepidodendron the leaf scars are diamond-shaped, and in Sigillaria they are arranged in vertical rows. The rhizomes, or root systems, of both genera, known as *stigmaria*, were thought to be distinct plants when their fossils were first discovered. Actually they served to support the trees and to produce new shoots. Lepidodendron and Sigillaria are classified in the division Lycopodiophyta order Lepidodendrales. *Lepidondendron* became almost completely extinct by the end of the Carboniferous period.

Stigmaria found on Smithills Moor by Ian Harper

Piece of Stigmaria root found by Alan Davies 15 feet below the surface, 200 yards south of the TV mast on Winter Hill.

Sigillaria

Sigillaria are another member of the lycopsid family and have been found on Winter Hill and in surrounding areas.

The clubmoss trees of the genus *Sigillaria* formed an important part of the coal swamps in the Late Carboniferous. They could reach a height up to 30 meters and bore grasslike leaves in the upper part of the unbranched or once divided trunk. The leaves were attached directly to the stem and they left scars when they were shed.

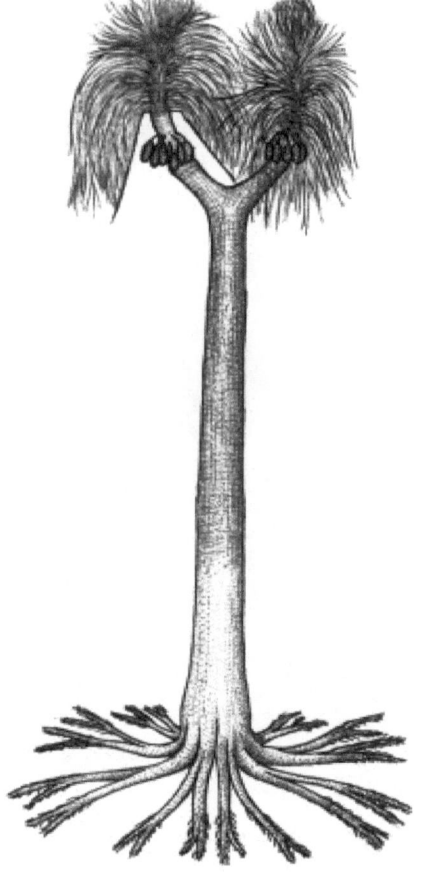

Characteristic of the genus of *Sigillaria* is the fact that the leaf scars were arranged in vertical rows. On the ground of these leaf scars many species have been described. The trunk was somewhat thickened at the base. The spore-cones were attached in or under the crown directly to the stem. They are called *Sigillariostrobus*.

The underground parts of the tree can hardly be distinguished from those of *Lepidodendron* and they are again called *Stigmaria*. In many ways the *Sigillaria* are very similar to *Lepidodendron* – but the bark patterns are totally different.

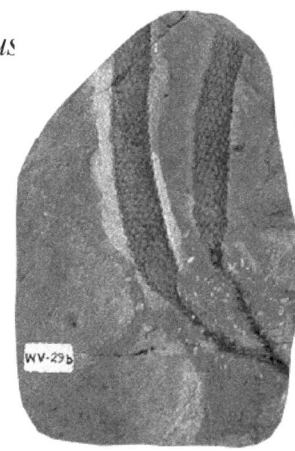

Sigillariostrobus the name assigned to the reproductive organs or cones of *sigillaria*. Unlike the cones of the *lepidodendron* tree, which grew individually at the very tips of the branches, the cones of *sigillaria* grew in clusters and were attached further back on the branches.

As a *Lycopod*, and although it is related to the giant *Lepidodendron*, it has several distinguishing features apart from just the bark patterns and the cone positions. It often had a tall branched trunk and possessed long, grass-like leaves. It is thought to have had a photosynthetic aspect to it trunk making it green instead of the usual brown colour.

Specimen of Sigillaria

And ... a Sigillaria specimen found in the Wilderswood Mine, Winter Hill on 3.3.2007

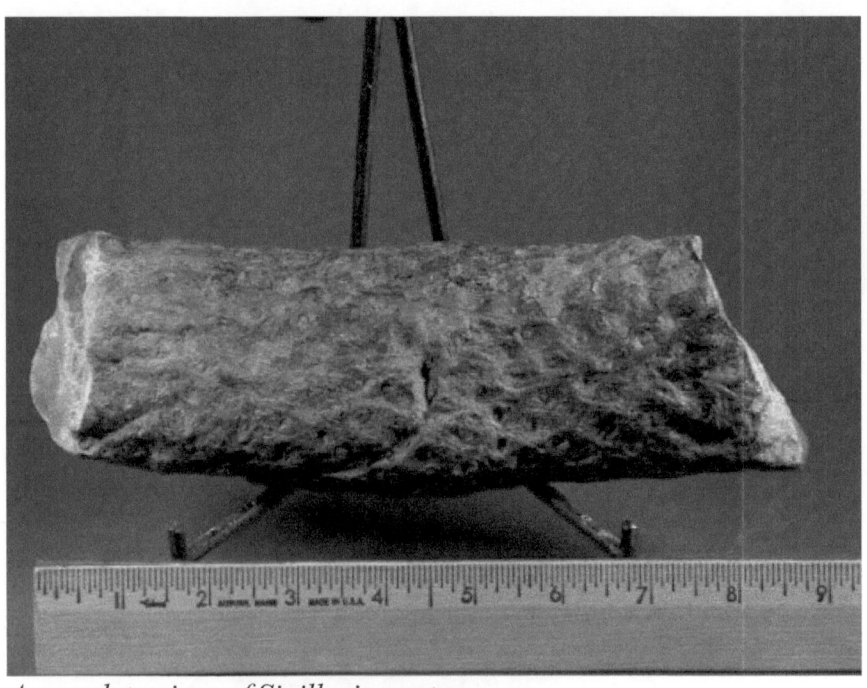

A complete piece of Sigillaria root

Sigillaria Identification table (Westfalian A and younger)

after Chaloner & Collinson:
An illustrated key to the commoner British Upper Carboniferous plant compression fossils (1975).
Adapted after Josten: Die Steinkohlen-Floren Nordwestdeutschlands (1991)

Only twelve (common) north-west European species are included!
So be careful in using the table.

1a. Leaf scars in vertical rows on clearly-defined ribs with straight or curved sides.	**1b**. Leaf scars not situated on such clearly-defined ribs.
2a. Leaf scars at least 1.25 times as high as broad.	**2b**. Leaf scars about as high as broad, or shorter.
3a. Leaf scars oblong, pear-shaped, sometimes with a small plumula (plume, fountain) on the top. The vertical distance of the leaf scars is relatively large: two to three times the height of a scar. Sigillaria rugosa	**3b**. Leaf scars rounded rhombic. The vertical distance of the leaf scars is less large: about the height of one scar. Sigillaria elongata
4a. The leaf scars show rounded lateral angles or no lateral angles at all.	**4b**. The leaf scars show clearly-defined lateral angles.
5a. The vertical distance of the leaf scars is very small. Often the leaf scars are almost in contact with those above and below.	**5b**. The distance of the leaf scars is larger: at least half the height of a scar and often larger. Leaf scars are much narrower than the ribs. They have an oval outline. Sigillaria ovata

6a. The leaf scars are in contact with those above and below. No transverse line above the leaf scar. There are longitudinal wrinkles in the furrow between the ribs. <u>Sigillaria cumulata</u>	**6b**. The vertical distance of the leaf scars is small: half the height of a scar or less. Clearly-defined transverse line above the scar. No other wrinkles. <u>Sigillaria tesselata</u>
7a. Vertical distance of the leaf scars less than 5 mm.	**7b**. Vertical distance of the leaf scars more than 5 mm.
8a. Vertical distance of the leaf scars mostly less than half the height of a scar. Leaf scars hexagonal with rather acute lateral angles. <u>Sigillaria boblayi</u>	**8b**. Vertical distance of the leaf scars from very small to a maximum of one height of a scar. Leaf scars more pear-shaped. <u>Sigillaria mamillaris</u>
9a. Plumulas (little plumes, fountains) above the leaf scars. <u>Sigillaria schlotheimiana</u>	**9b**. No plumulas of any significance.
10a. Clearly defined lines descending from the mid-points of the sides. Moreover a smooth surface or a surface with a very fine marking. <u>Sigillaria principis</u>	**10b**. No descending lines or very small ones. Clearly defined transverse lines between the leaf scars. <u>Sigillaria scutellata</u>
11a. No ribs present at all, though the leaf scars are arranged in vertical rows. <u>Sigillaria brardii</u> (older stem)	**11b**. Every leaf scar on its own "leaf cushen", which is clearly separated from the surrounding leaf cushens.

12a. Leaf cushens transversely lenticular with acute lateral angles. <u>Sigillaria brardii</u> (young branch or stem) 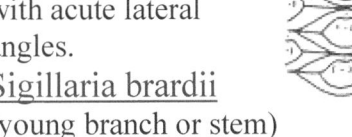	**12b**. Leaf cushens forming a honeycomb-like structure. <u>Sigillaria elegans</u> 

Sigillaria boblayi

Sigillaria cumulate

Sigillaria elegans (young)

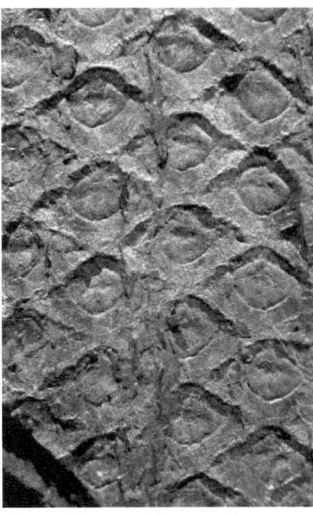

Sigillaria brardii

Sigillaria principis

Sigillaria scutellate

Sigillaria schlotheimiama

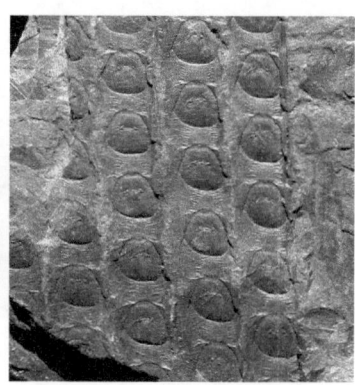
Sigillaria mamillaris

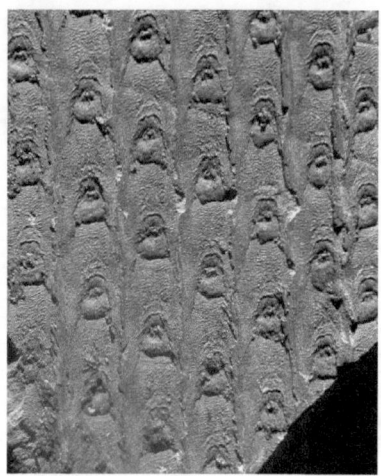
Sigillaria elongata

Sigillaria tessalata

Some varieties of *Sigillaria* have trunks which shed the outermost parts of the stem surface (this is known as "decertification" – the removal of the outer bark). This leaves a trunk surface that whilst distinctive, is different from the original surface, and the exact species cannot be identified. One of the commonest decorticated forms of *Sigillaria* is known as *Syringodendron* and an example is shown below.

Syrigodendron found by Alan Davies

Yet another locally found Sigillaria, again found by Alan Davis

So what's this?

A large fossil in the roof of a tunnel in the Wilderswood Mine at Horwich. Dave Turner is posing underneath it! A close up is shown below.

Now this one is interesting! Why? Because it could be either the trunk of a tree or a giant leaf from a different type of tree. The fossil has longitudinal lines most of which are of the same size. If these lines were interrupted with transverse lines (which would mark the place where the branches grew from) then it would be the trunk of a tree (a plant called a "*Calamite*"). This example however, does NOT have any transverse lines nor does it have any branch or leaf "scars" …. It might therefore be a leaf …. HOWEVER ….the ONLY leaves that display this type of marking (the leaves of the "*Cordaites*" plant or tree) ONLY grow up to a maximum of around 12cms in width – and this specimen is considerably wider than that!

In view of the above – and until more information is forthcoming – I can only assume that this is the trunk of a very large tree but the specimen is NOT long enough to show the transverse lines or any leaf (or branch) scars. If it IS part of a tree trunk, then the only Carboniferous period tree with texture and markings such as this is the "*Calamite*" tree, specifically a variety such as "*Calamites carinatus*".

Shown below is what a calamite bark "should" look like with the transverse lines clearly visible:

I'm going to assume that the Wilderswood fossil IS a calamite so let's move on to this type of plant next!

Calamites

These plants are very similar (but much larger) to the modern horsetail plant. They grew to around 30 feet in height and were topped by shoots with cones at the ends. They are NOT members of the *Lycopsid* family. They tend to be one of the commonest fossils found in this area.

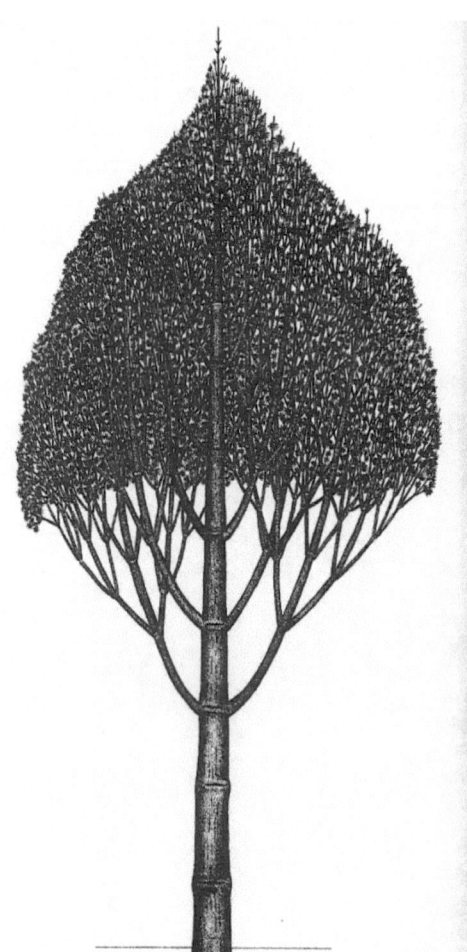

The stems branched, and the different branching patterns form the different varieties of the calamite plants. There are at least eight different varieties found in the UK. There are different shapes and sizes of cones on the different varieties, in some cases these being dependent on the exact position of the spore containers on the cones.

The different varieties of calamite found in the UK are:
C. brongniaratii
C. carinatus
C. cistii
C. goeppertii
C. multiamis
C. schuetzeiformis
C. suckowii
C. undulatus

Calamite remains are usually fragmentary, and such has usually been the case on Winter Hill. Plenty of small pieces of trunk (with the exception of the giant fossil illustrated earlier) - but none big enough to be able to determine the exact variety.

The writer has found many pieces of *Calamite* on the Winter Hill waste tips.

 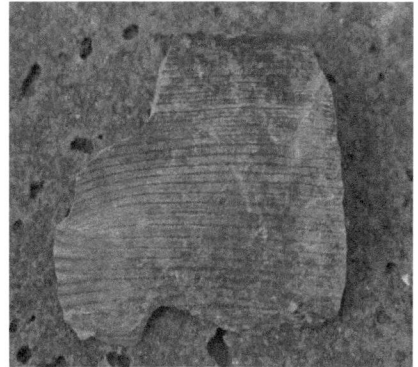

There are many different varieties of *Calamites*, most having different styles of bark markings but all display vertical ribbing, a "bamboo-like" appearance and are distinctly transversely segmented. The trunk and stems were hollow rather like drinking straws or hollow tubes.

When the trunk snapped or otherwise fell into the muddy swamps, the inside of the tube would be filled with sediments and this is why we often find "pith casts" of the insides of *Calamites* as fossils.

Calamites reproduce by means of spores, which were produced in small sacs organized into cones. They are also known to have possessed massive, underground rhizomes which allowed for the production of clones of one tree.

This is the only group of trees of their period known to have a clonal habit.

This type of asexual reproduction would allow them to spread quickly into new territory, in addition to aiding in anchoring them firmly in the unstable ground along rivers and in newly deposited delta sediments.

The rhizomes of *Calamites* look quite similar to the stems in most cases, but have nodes that get progressively closer together as they get out approach the growth tip that spreads outward through the soil).

Calamites formed dense thickets along the edges of rivers, streams, swamps and waterways. The *Calamite* stems branched regularly and

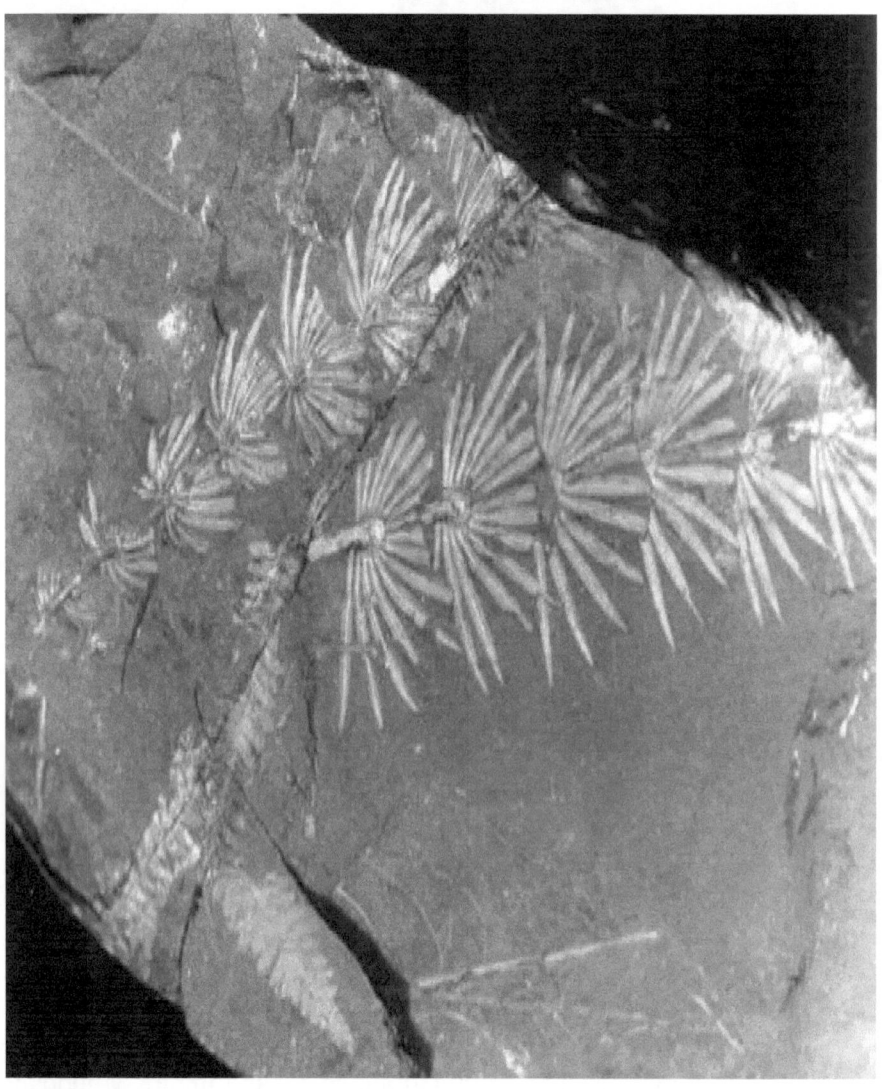

it is mainly the different patterns of the branching which differentiates one variety from another. The foliage was fairly sparce with leaves forming in whorl like patterns. The whorls are known as *Asterophyllites* or *Annularia. The* cone of a Calamite is called a *Calamocarpon.*

The illustrations below show the leaves of different varieties of calamites:

Annularia galioides

Annularia sphenophlloides

Annularia radiate

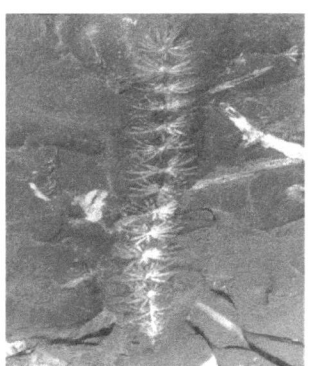
Asterophyllites equisetifomis

Annularia stellata with spore cones

The term *Calamites* is the name assigned to Carboniferous plants belonging to the order of *sphenopsids*, also known as "articulates" because of their jointed stems. We know there are different varieties of calamites because of the differing fossils that we find …. but in practice we really know little about their overall appearance and different geologists and illustrators have interpreted the fossil remains in different ways to produce drawings of what they may have looked like.

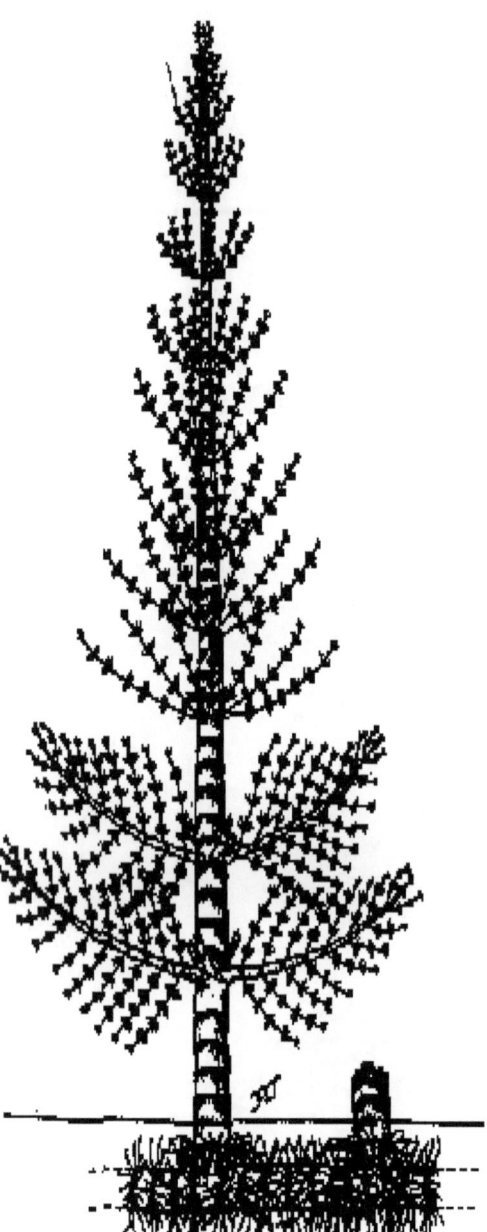

The drawing on the left is the third such illustration given in this book. Note the extremely thick rhizome and the similarity to the present day "horsetail" weeds. In most cases the stem of *Calamites* is flattened, but sometimes it is more or less three dimensional. In this case the fossil shows no internal structure: it is just petrified sediment. This is the reason that it is difficult to get an impression of the composition of the *Calamites* tree.

A large section of Calamite trunk clearly showing the transverse jointed stem.

f the fossils of *Calamites* are ts of the central cylinder of the trunk. After the tree had died, this cavity got full of sediment, after which the bark and the wood of the trunk decayed. So only a cast of the central cylinder remained. The longitudinal ribbing on it is the counterpart of the serrate pattern on the inside of the central cavity.

The transverse lines at the cast indicate where the diaphragms were placed in the central cylinder. These diaphragms or nodes are characteristic for horsetails. They gave rise to the whorls of leaves and branches. The photo shows calamite branches.

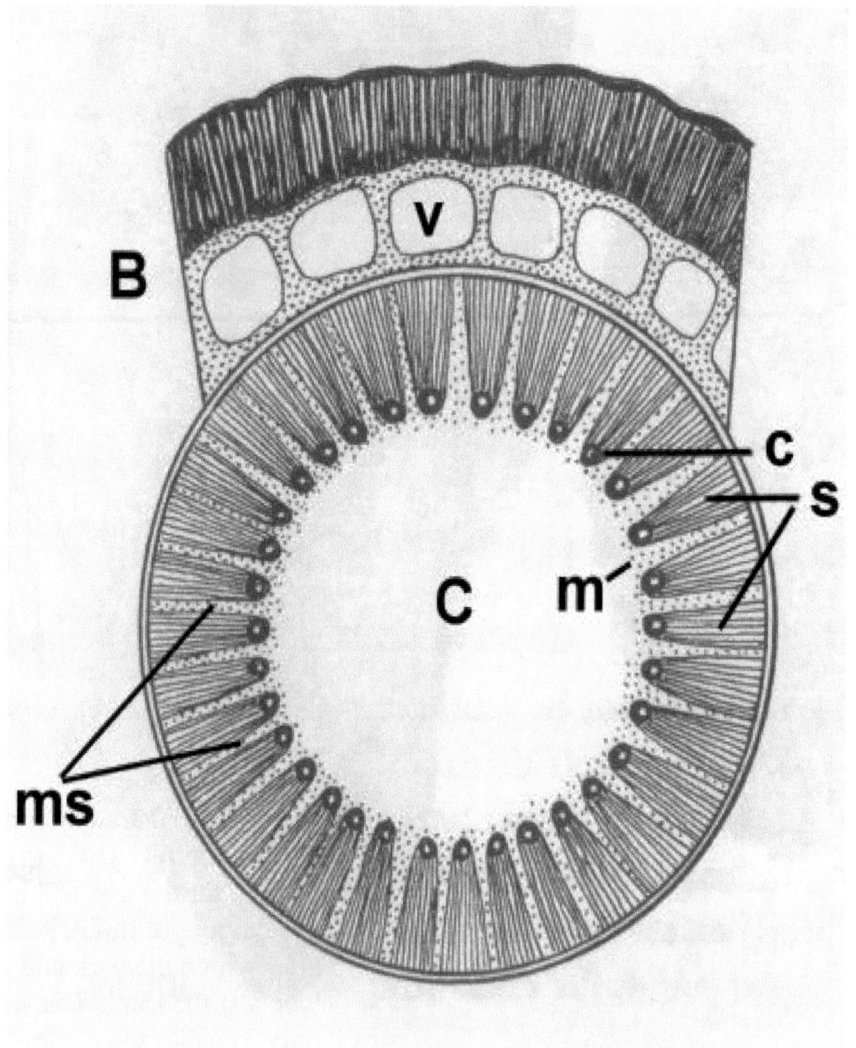

Section through calamite stem. B= Bark, C=central cavity, m= pith, ms=rays, s = secondary wood/xylem, c= carinal canal, v- valecular canal.
This description of the cross section is taken from the web page "Wood of the horsetail tree *Calamites*" at
<u>http://www.xs4all.nl/~steurh/engcalst/ecalstam.html</u>

"Look at the drawings above and below. In the transverse section the circle with the small round holes attracts attention. At the place of those holes the very first wood vessels (the **protoxylem**) of the young plant were located. These were of a very small diameter.

Around them the **metaxylem** developed, also with very narrow cells. Next the secundary growth started from the cambium, a one-cell-thick layer of tissue, forming secondary wood to the inner side and *no* phloem to the outer side. It was a unifacial cambium. In the course of this process canals arose at the place of the protoxylem and the metaxylem. These are called **carinal canals**. So the holes are transverse sections of these carinal canals.
Between the successsive xylem bundles protrusions of the pith were formed: the **rays**. These are, however, not always present. In the latter case the secondary wood forms a unbroken cylinder.

In the, rarely preserved, **bark** are air ducts at regular distances from each other. They are called **vallecular canals**. Because of these canals the outside of the living *Calamites* tree showed longitudinal grooves and ribs. This ribbing is seldom visible because the bark is hardly ever preserved."

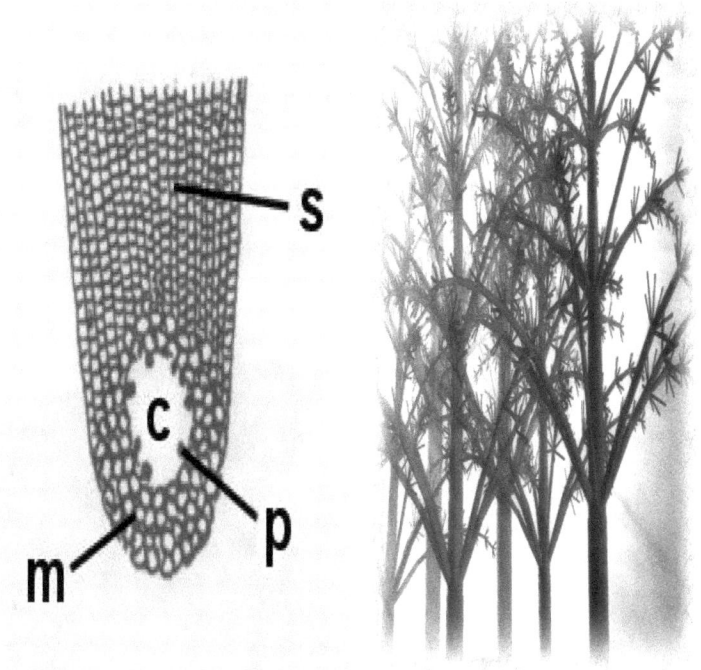

Bundle of wood vessels
c = carinal canal, p = protoxylem,
m = metaxylem, s = secundary wood/xylem
After Stewart & Rothwell, 1993

Calamite stems. Note the vertical lines on all pieces. On the larger specimen there is a horizontal line, and the indentations on this line indicate the points where the branches/leaves would have been attached.

A larger piece of rock filled with Calamite fossils.

A closer look at the last photo.

The tip of a Calamite shoot

Small piece of Calamite with the leaf scars clearly visible.

This photo shows the massive size of a fully grown Calamite trunk. You can tell it's a Calamite tree by the faint horizontal line which cuts across the vertical lines. This example was found in Wilderswood Mine underneath Winter Hill. Photo by Alan Davies.

A collection of different bark fossils found either on or under Winter Hill.

Piece of fossilised tree root found on a coal tip by Dave Lane within 200 yards of the Winter Hill mast

The result of 15 minutes fossil searching on top of Winter Hill. These specimens are exactly "as found" and are unsorted and unwashed. They are also extremely brittle and are easily damaged. Some pieces of Calamite tree bark are clearly visible.

The Ferns.

Ferns seem to pop up not all over Winter Hill but in Carboniferous rocks throughout the North West UK. Some of them are perfectly preserved, others are extremely poor. Most of those I have found on the top of Winter Hill are particularly brittle and need extreme care to carry them home. For this reason, many of the ferns illustrated will be from the Crock Hey opencast mine near Wigan (now closed and the land reclaimed).

There are two basic types of "ferns", the "small" ferns we all know and love that grows profusely here in the UK today …. then there are the "tree ferns", the ones found in other countries (and in some garden centres). The bulk of fossil ferns we find in this area originate from the tree fern variety of plant.

Identification of fern fossils is a minefield for the beginner, and there are multitudes of different varieties, species etc. In view of this, I make no attempt to write about the subject other than to present a few photographs of fern fossils in my collection and others found in this area by other collectors.

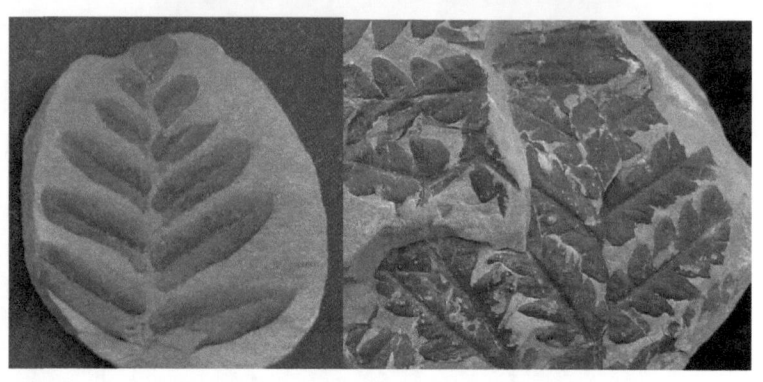

One of the finest fern specimens I've seen from this area, all the leaf veins are visible.

Marine Bands – what are they?

A Marine Band is a layer of sediment, noted for its marine fossils such as *goniatites* and *bivalves*, and is very useful for correlating rocks from different areas. The Carboniferous rock record on and around Winter Hill contains a large number of these marine bands and all have been given different names depending on either the richness of the band in a particular species or the name of the coal seam nearby. For example three bands found near Hempshaws, near White Coppice, are known as the "*Pygmaeoceras sigma*", "*Reticuloceras superbilingue*" and "*R. metabilingue*" bands respectively.

Specific Marine and Freshwater Band fossil locations.

1. The *G. cumbrience* Marine Band is exposed at 64521530 in Shore Brook where a nine inch black paper shale yields the following fauna: *Posidoniella sp, Anthracoceras sp, Homoceratoides aff divaricatus, Gastrioceras crenulatum and G. cumbriense*.

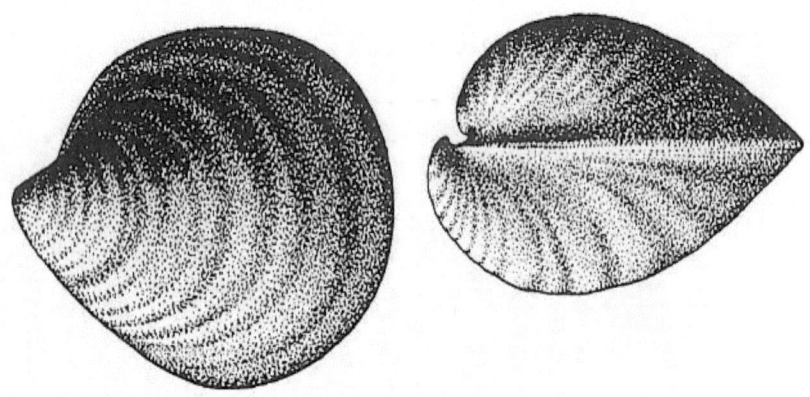

Posidoniella sp.

2. A similar fauna was obtained from an exposure at 63861458 where the Marine Band can be found 600 yards E, 10 degrees N of Rivington Hall.

3. Shales above the Helmshore Grit, along with the associated marine bands are well exposed in the stream at 650165 at the head of the Yarrow River N.E of Hempshaws. The total section is as follows

Shaly mudstone, blue-grey, with ironstone in lower part
>30 ft
Shale, dark platy with calcerous nodules – the "*Pygmaeoceras sigma*" marine band   9 in
Shale, dark   7 ft 6 in
Shale, slightly sandy, with "*Reticuloceras superbilingue*" band
2 ft 3 in
Shale, mudstone, blue grey   25ft
Shale, blue platy, with the "*R. metabilingue*" band   9 ft
Mudstone, sandy   4 ft
Flaggy sandstone, Helmshore Grit, coal "smut" on top
The *R. metabilingue* Band contains: *Crurithyris sp, Dunbarella sp, R. bilingue* and *R. metabilingue*.
The *Superbilingue* Band contains *Dunbarella sp, Posidonia sp, Homocereratoides divaricatus, Pygmaeoceras sigma* and *Reticuloceras superbilingue*.
The *sigma* Band is almost entirely *Pygmaeoceras sigma* with occasional *Lingula mytilloides* and fish fragments.

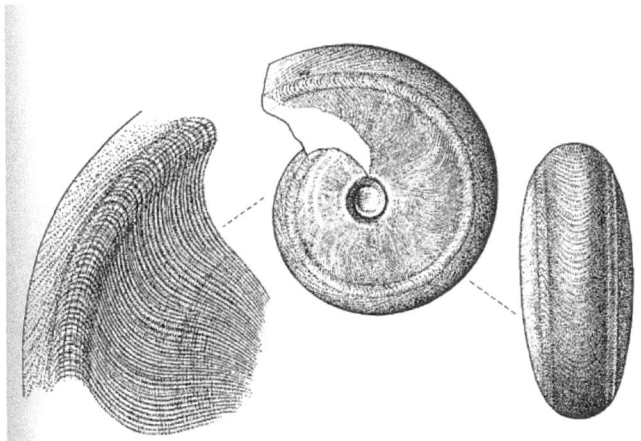

Reticuloceras bilingue

4. A *metabilingue* band can be found in Lead Mines Clough in the shales on the bank of the stream (62831636) below the first waterfall (where the fault with the Fletcher Bank Grit is also exposed).

The fauna extends throughout the bank of shale and includes: *Dunbarella sp, Posidonia insignis, Anthracoceras sp, Pygmaeoceras sigma, Reticuloceras metabilingue,* orthocone nautiloids and *Huanghoceras sp.*

This illustrates the identification difficulties in spotting some Marine Band Fossils. These flattened specimens of Goniatites were found at Lead Mines Clough. Each piece of rock contains one specimen which are vaguely recognisable by their circular shape. These specimens were found by Alan Diggles – thanks for giving them to me Alan!

5. The *sigma* band can be found at (622159) at the foot of the shale bluff beside the road, 350 yd N of the S.E corner of Anglezarke Reservoir where 9 inches of dark platy mudstone yields *Lingula mytilloides* (at the base), *Posidonia insignis, Posidonia sp* and the goniatites *Homocerattoides sp* and *Pygmaeoceras sigma.*

Posidonia sp.

6. The *Gastrioceras cancellatum* Marine Band is exposed in Dean Brook (64351538) 150 yds S of Higher House where 15 inches of grey black shaly mudstone produces: *Caneyella multirugata, Dunbarella sp, Gastrioceras cancellatum, G. crencellatum, Reticuloceras superbilingue* and fish debris

7. *Gastrioceras crencellatum* Band is exposed 60 yds W.NW of Hollinshead Hall (66231992) 3 m N of Belmont and shows: *caneyella sp, Agastrioceras carinatum, Anthracococeras sp* and *Gastrrioceras crencellatum.*

8. If you fancy a trip further afield, the Six Inch Mine Marine Band crops out 120 yd S E of the Old Hall, Feniscowles in the N bank of the River Darwen (63782572) where the following have been collected: *Caneyella multirugata, Dunbarella papyracea, Posidonia gibsoni, Gastrioceras subcrenatum, Homoceratoides divaricatus, Hindeodella sp* and fish remains.

9. In Stepback brook, west of Darwen Hill (67312065), 1300 yd S 42 degs E of the pub at Ryal Fold, the same band as above contains: *Caneyella multirugata, Dunbarella papyracea, Posidonia subcreatum and Hindeodella sp.*

There are a number of other Marine Band outcrops in the area but you'll have to look for them yourself …. Sorry!

Anything else to be found?

As well as the plant and marine fossils mentioned earlier, there are many examples on Winter Hill (especially in the valleys and ravines flanking the sides of the hill) of fossilised ripple marks on the sandstone and in the shales.

Just like the ripples you see in the sand on the seaside beaches, ripples also used to form in rivers and on beaches 300 million years ago and have been preserved as fossils.

Some good examples can be found in and around the stream bed in Tigers Clough and there are several specimens to be seen in the Shaly Dingle area.

The one illustrated below was found at the bottom of Shore Brook near to the Rivington to Belmont Road road just past Moses Cocker Farm (there's also several exposed coal seams in this area).

A number of flagstones in the steps of the many staircases in the Terraced Gardens have ripple fossils on the surfaces. There is also a massive piece of sandstone with ripple marks in a small quarry above

Curley's Fisheries (where you can also get fabulous and reasonable all day breakfasts!) at the bottom of Georges Lane, Horwich.

In many of the shales found in the area there are fossilised raindrops on the surface of some of the finer mud layers.

Next time you're out walking on Winter Hill or any surrounding areas, keep your eyes open for bits of rock that represent the really ancient history of Winter Hill and this part of North Western UK. None of this "it's almost 200 years old" rubbish .... Fossils represent the REALLY old stuff ..... over 300 million years old. This REAL history is there for collectors to find if they don't mind searching for it ....and unlike most things in life today, the fossils and rocks are free and won't cost you a penny. Get out there. Look and collect the real history of the area.

Have fun

PARTICULARS AND PLAN

OF THE VALUABLE

FREEHOLD ESTATES,

OF

"LEE HOUSE" AND "BROOK HOUSE,"

Together with that excellent and old-established Millstone Grit Quarry, known as the

ORIGINAL LEICESTER MILL QUARRY,

Situate in the Township of ANGLEZARK, near CHORLEY, in the County of Lancaster,

WHICH WILL BE

SOLD BY AUCTION,

BY MR. JABEZ B. JONES,

At the ROYAL OAK HOTEL, Chorley,

On MONDAY, the 14th day of SEPTEMBER, 1868,

AT THREE O'CLOCK IN THE AFTERNOON,

In the following Lots, subject to Conditions then to be produced.

The Estates are distant from Chorley about Four miles, and are pleasantly situate, contiguous to the extensive Reservoirs belonging to the Liverpool Corporation Waterworks. The Brook House Estate is well wooded, and from its picturesque character it affords a rare and most desirable site for the erection of a *Villa Residence.*

Mr. JOHN CATTERALL, Lee House, will show the Estates, and Particulars, with Plans, may be obtained from G. M. WILLIAMS, Esq., Hale Cliff, near Warrington; Mr. JAMES DERHAM, Surveyor, &c., Chorley; and Messrs. FARRER, OUVRY & Co., Solicitors, 66, Lincolns' Inn Fields, London.

L. SYERS, PRINTER, 14½, WATER STREET, LIVERPOOL.

Appendix 1

This book contains the research and information compiled by many people. Below is a list of those who have contributed to this publication. In every case where we are aware of the writer, we freely acknowledge use of their work and have mentioned them below. In those cases where we have been able to contact them, we give our thanks for their permission to use their work. In those cases where we have been unable to contact the writer (only a few), we apologise in advance for not consulting with them. If they would care to contact us we will either add their name and reference to this list - or even remove their contribution from the book if this is what they would prefer. As this publication is not "for sale" in any normal fashion, we hope people will not be too offended if their contribution is not acknowledged below or if we have not been able to obtain their prior permission.

Our thanks to **everyone** involved. The names are in no particular order!

It **IS** a scrapbook …. We just add things and stick them in whenever we feel like it …. and not always in any chronological order!

D A Owen   "Rivington and District before 1066 AD"
H M Ordnance Survey
L H Tonks   "Geology of Manchester and S E Lancashire Coalfield"
Paul Baxendale
Ian and Sue Harper
Alf Molyneux
Alan Davies
Mark Wright
Clive Weake
John Bell
Garry Rhodes
Rodney J Ireland   "Geological walk on River Douglas north of Horwich
Bolton Mountain Rescue Team. http://www.boltonmrt.org.uk
Bill Learmouth. TV mast construction photo's + cover photo
British Trust for Conservation Volunteers (North West)
Dave Healey

Christine Tudor. "Rivington Pike. Erosion Control & Management Plan"
Ian Trumble (Archaeologist, Bolton Museum)
Harry Houghton
T Morris   "Rivington Review"
Norman Hoyle. "Reservoirs from Rivington to Rossendale"
Gordon Readyhough
J Rawlinson
Munki-Boy
Steve Glover
Charlene Bessell
Judith Matthews
Paul Lacey.
Winter Hill Website: http://www.winterhill.org
A O'Rourke
Eric Hewis http://www.pbase.com/ezz/image/50313504
David Swain
Darryll Hilton
Ray Platt
Manchester Evening News
A O'Rourke
Robert Yates "Past Vegetation, future global warming"
Alan Foster
Ian Duff
Nigel Newton
Henry Lisowski
Andrew Mad Murdock Coward
Coralie Foster
Jonathan de Ferranti: http://www.viewfinderpanoramas.org or http://www.viewfinderpanoramas.org/panoramas/ENG/Winter.gif
Friends of Withnell and Brinscall villages
Boyd Harris
Harry Partington
William Kay
Rivington Visitor Centre
Chorley History and Archaeology Society
Andy Blundell
Andy Ryding
jakeofwinterhill.blogspot.com
http://winterhilllancashire.blogspot.com/

www.white-coppice.co.uk

Conybeare W D and Phillips W 1822. Outlines of the geology of England and Wales, Part 1. London pp 470. Only one part of this work was published, in this, reference was made to an account of the Anglezarke Mines to be given in a subsequent part. This has resulted in some confusion amongst later references to Anglezarke.

Dana J D et al 1951. The System of Mineralogy" Vol 2. New York. 7th ed pp1124

De Rance C E 1873 "On the occurrence of lead, zinc and iron ores in some rocks of Carboniferous age in the north-west of England" Geol mag 10, 64-74

Farrer K E 1903 "Wedgewoods letters to Bentley" Vol 1 London

Herr J 1875 "On lead mining in the districts of Stransfield, Holmes Chapel, Rossendale and Great Hambleton. NW Yorkshire and NE Lancashire" Trans Mc/r Geol Soc 13 2-15
Lancashire Record Office DX/931 – DX/987c

Leigh C 1700 "Natural History of Lancashire, Cheshire and the Peak in Derbyshire" Oxford

Loch C W 1946 "Forgotten Mines in Lancashire" The Mining Magazine 74 290-297

Maw J 1802 "The Mineralogy of Derbyshire", London 1st ed p 211

Meteyard E 1866 "The Life of Josiah Wedgewood", Vol 2 London p 643

Parkes S 1815 "Chemical Essays" Vol 2, London p 483

Public Record Office Hist MSS Comm "The Kenyon Papers" 49
Raistrick A 1934. "The London Lead Co", 1692-1905, Transactions Newcomen Society 14, 119-162

Shaw R C 1940 "The Records of a Lancashire Family" Preston 304

Watt J 1790A "Some Account of a Mine in which the Aerated Barytes is Found" Mem Lit & Phil Soc of Mc/r 3 pp 598-609

Watt J 1790B "On the Effects produced by different combinations of the Terra Ponderosa given to animals", Mem Lit & Phil soc Mc/r 3 609-618

Williamson I A 1977 "Geological routes around Wigan" (No 1 White Coppice & Anglezarke. Wigan & Dist. Geological Society

Williamson I A 1963 "The Anglezarke Lead Mines, Mining Magazine 108; 133-139

Withering W 1784 "Experiments and Observations on the Terra Poderosa" Phil Trans Royal Soc 74 293-311

Appendix 2

There are a number of books and web sites published which contain information about Winter Hill and its locality. Below is given a brief list of some of them. If anyone knows the titles and authors of any not listed please get in touch with us via *dave@daveweb.co.uk* and we'll add them.

M D Smith	Rivington, Lancashire
	Leverhulmes Rivington
	About Horwich
	More about Horwich
	About Anglezarke
P L Watson	Rivington Pike, History & Fell Race
Kenneth Fields	A visitors Guide to Rivington
Gladys Sellers	Walks on the West Pennine Moors
Dave Lane	Carboniferous Fossils of Winter Hill & surrounding areas
John Rawlinson	About Rivington

Norman Hoyle — Reservoirs from Rivington to Rossendale

George Birtill — The Enchanted Hills
Heather in my hat.

John Dixon & Jaana Jarvinen. — Walks around the West Pennine Moors

David Holding — Murder in the Heather (published in 1991 by The Friends of Smithills Hall)

Robin Smith — "Smithills Moor & Two Lads" (Halliwell Local History Society)
"Two Lads, My theory"

Paul Salveson "Will yo' come o' Sunday Morning"

E.K Isaac - "Anglezarke Moor, A geographical description and field guide". Published by the Ribblesdale Branch of the Geographical Association. N1 1 1972

Boyd Harris - Anglezarke.net

www.white-coppice.co.uk

Richard Skelton – List of Anglezarke farms

David Clayton – Lost Farms of Brinscall Moors

Daniel Calderbank – Underground Above Horwich

Lambert Sale – The Remains of the Mining Industry in the hills above Horwich

John Smith – A guided walk round Wilderswood

Chorley, Duxbury, Adlington Local History –
https://chorleyarealocalhistory.weebly.com/

www.groundwork.org.uk/projects/rivington-terraced-gardens/

www.rivingtonterracedgardens.org.uk

https://chorleyarealocalhistory.weebly.com

Please don't be offended if we've missed anyone or any organisation out! Just let us know (email address on page 2), and you'll be listed in the next edition ….. if there ever is one!